A REVOLUTIONARY FAITH

Cultural Memory
in
the
Present

Hent de Vries, Editor

A REVOLUTIONARY FAITH

Liberation Theology Between Public Religion and Public Reason

Raúl E. Zegarra

STANFORD UNIVERSITY PRESS

STANFORD, CALIFORNIA

Stanford University Press
Stanford, California

Printed in the United States of America on acid-free, archival-quality paper

Cataloging-in-Publication Data available upon request.
Library of Congress Control Number: 2022030506
ISBN: 9781503635371 (cloth), 9781503635586 (paperback),
9781503635593 (ebook)

Cover design: Lindy Kasler
Cover photo: Gustavo Gutiérrez speaking at a course on theology, 1980. Courtesy of the Instituto de Pastoral Andina Archive. Photo: Benno Frey.

To Gustavo Gutiérrez, David Tracy, and Hans Joas,
giants of a revolutionary tradition in which they always,
undeservedly, made me feel at home

In memory of abuelito *Raúl,*
another, very different, giant

Contents

Acknowledgments

I would like to express my profound gratitude to the institutions, mentors, friends, and family members who have nourished, encouraged, supported, and loved me through the process that led to the publication of this book.

Professors William Schweiker and Hans Joas, dear friends and mentors, deserve special mention. Bill's impressive talent for systematic thinking, his commitment to a humanism that does not give up faith, and his encouragement of rigorous scholarship pursued in community and collegiality, have been great influences in my work. Hans, as many pages of this book show, has been a decisive inspiration as well. His contributions to contemporary thought are multiple and profound, and I can only be grateful for the ongoing opportunity of learning from him. To Hans I owe many intellectual debts, but one of them is the encouragement to keep working on this project and to consider Stanford University Press as its home. For his kindness, generosity, and permanent support, I will be forever thankful.

I am grateful to the University of Chicago Divinity School for believing in my project from its inception and giving me the support needed to bring it to fruition over the years. My current position as a postdoctoral fellow has allowed me to remain actively engaged with the University of Chicago's community of inquiry, and has, without doubt, improved this book at every step. One last word of gratitude is in place for the Divinity School and Dean James Robinson for kindly providing support for the indexing of this book.

The friendship and support of Professors Gustavo Gutiérrez and David Tracy have been a true blessing over the years. I cannot find words adequate to express the importance of Gustavo's presence in my scholarship and personal life. I can only thank him, in the hope that he knows what words cannot say. Among other things, I owe to Gustavo the friendship of David Tracy. And to David, I owe several long and warm conversations over my years in Chicago, conversations marked by his unsurpassable kindness and erudition. Gustavo and David are without question the most important theological inspirations of my work. I really hope these pages do some justice to all they have taught me.

My gratitude goes also to my dear friends and colleagues in Perú, especially those connected to Instituto Bartolomé de Las Casas in Lima. The Las Casas Institute archive is without any doubt the best archive for the study of liberation theology in Perú. Having easy and frequent access to it over the years made this book richer and stronger. But more than anything, having a chance to discuss the history and development of liberation theology in Perú with some of its key protagonists, some of whom became protagonists of this book as well, was a true gift. Gracias.

I would like to express a word of thanks to the editorial team at Stanford University Press, especially to Erica Wetter and Caroline McKusick. Erica and Caroline have supported this project at every step, making it better and stronger with their guidance. My gratitude as well goes to Hent de Vries, the Cultural Memory in the Present series editor, for welcoming my book into this prestigious series.

Finally, I am especially grateful to my family. For over the years they have given me the space, love, and support needed for this strange craft that we academics have decided to pursue. Ilana Ventura's help, however, went beyond her love and support. Ilana read every single page of this book, and made it, without a doubt, a book that could not exist without her. For your support beyond measure, mi amor, I am most deeply grateful.

The memories of my last conversation with my grandfather Raúl warm my heart while writing these lines. The last time we talked, he learned about the beginnings of this project and was quite excited about what the future will bring. It saddens me that he is not here to share this part of the present, but his memory and infinite presence will forever inspire my life.

A REVOLUTIONARY FAITH

Introduction

Religion can be a powerful engine for progressive social change. Many religious communities and individuals want to make their societies more just. We frequently witness their involvement in organizing and activism related to matters of racial justice, gender equality, poverty eradication, animal rights, climate change, and so forth. Historians, sociologists, anthropologists, philosophers, and, occasionally, theologians have devoted a significant amount of attention to religious social activism and continue to do so.[1]

However, most of what we know—through either our anecdotal experience, the news, or the work of scholars—about religious organizing and activism relates to what religious communities and individuals *do*. Very rarely do we see any sustained focus on *how* these religious people come to the conclusion that their faith demands their intervention in the political sphere. Further, this gap—the missing focus on the *how*—explains why people unfamiliar with religious social activism take issue with the idea that religion can produce progressive social change. For example, religious activism is often dismissed by "conservatives" as the political instrumentalization of faith. Similarly, religious activists are often dismissed by "progressives" because they are perceived as odd and unreliable outliers. After all, religion is still considered by many as inherently against social progress.

A Revolutionary Faith attempts to fill this scholarly gap. I do so by paying attention to the process of articulation of religious beliefs and political concerns that takes place in religious organizing and activism—the *how*.[2] Moreover, attention to this process of articulation is of critical importance to address quite apparent deadlocks in current debates regarding social justice issues in democratic societies, especially in the United States. A brief characterization of these debates may make this point even clearer.[3]

"Progressives" tend to favor the consolidation of a safety net and the expansion of rights—social, economic, cultural, and so on—for all, but particularly of those groups historically oppressed and marginalized: women, people of color, the LGBTQ+ community, and so forth.[4] This advocacy is often pursued with suspicion about the role of religion and religious people, if not with open hostility toward both. Religion and religious people are construed as an obstacle to social progress. Of course, such a construal is explained by the fact that religious people have indeed opposed progressive causes, both in personal histories and in the long history of Western democracy. However, this construal is also the reflection of certain biases against religion—both individual and historical—that are often unwarranted. Karl Marx, one of the seminal figures of the multiple currents of the progressive movement, considered religion the first obstacle to and the primary target of the cause of social progress.[5] But, of course, one does not need to read Marx to know about and embrace this widespread conviction.

"Conservatives" see the expansion of the safety net and the correlative expansion of individual and communal entitlements as a threat. On the one hand, this expansion would represent a threat to people's liberty and commitment to free markets—the Reagan-era idea that government expansion equals liberty contraction. On the other, this expansion of rights would constitute a threat to a traditional way of life that struggles to accept gender, racial, and sexual diversity. Furthermore, the conservative perception of a menace is fueled by the correlative perception that social changes are demanded with hostility toward a traditional way of living in which religion—mostly, White Anglo-Saxon Protestantism—has often been paramount. Certainly, this opinion is not completely wrong, as noted earlier. However, the entanglement of religion and political conservatism can be questionable, if not openly dangerous. The theological justifications of the accumulation of wealth and the correlative dismissiveness toward the plight of the poor are well known.[6] Similarly, religious arguments—and, more critically, constitutional protections of religious freedom—have been, and are still, used to justify racial, gender, and sexual discrimination.[7]

Is there a way out of this conundrum? Can we think about social justice—that is, fair access to basic goods mediated by social institutions—in a way that both defends the expansion of rights *and* respects people's religious integrity? As the experience of many religious individuals and communities shows, the answer to these questions is "yes." *How* to arrive at this affirmative answer, *how* these religious people arrive at it, is much less obvious. This is the central topic of this book.

Now, to understand the process of articulation of religious faith and political action, we must take a step back. As noted, most of the literature devoted to faith-based progressive activism focuses on the fact that religious activism does exist, describes it, contextualizes it, and occasionally attempts to understand its motivations. However, little attention has been paid to the *theological* rationale developed by religious actors to explain their need to take an active political stance.[8] And yet these theological arguments are crucial to understand such an intervention because, until just a few decades ago, the assumption—both sociologically and normatively—was that, in functional liberal democracies, religion was and must be a private matter. The assumption was that religion should remain confined to the home and the temples.[9]

For this reason, even today, some people see religious activism as a betrayal of genuine religious faith. Religion is supposed to be about prayer, worship, sacraments, and so forth. Hence, the idea that religious people can be political actors as *religious* people appears contradictory or suspicious to many. Of course, these suspicions directly depend on the *kind* of political intervention. The religious sanctioning of the political and cultural establishment is a long-standing practice of most religious traditions. Therefore, the apparent contradictions and suspicions that I am describing really come to the fore when religious actors *challenge* the political and cultural establishment. The suspicions and fears emerge when faith becomes *revolutionary*, when faith seeks *progressive social change*.

In this book I focus on one of the key contemporary theological and social movements whose challenge and rearticulation of the relationship between religion and politics has left a global and lasting influence: liberation theology. In the following pages, I will systematically address definitional, methodological, and fundamental questions about how I understand liberation theology, what I take its main innovations to be, and why these innovations matter. As I discuss in this book, the key contribution of liberation theologians—particularly of Gustavo Gutiérrez—was to reach a new articulation, a new balance between faith and politics, the sacred and the profane, *without* reducing politics to faith or faith to politics.

Rather than conceiving Christian social justice solely in terms of inward moral goodness and kindness toward the neighbor, obedient acceptance of our location in a providentially given social order, and charitable assistance to the poor, liberation theologians propose a paradigm shift.[10] Liberation theologians advocate for an understanding of Christian discipleship that must also be expressed outwardly via a critical assessment of the present social order and its role in the very existence and perpetuation of social injustice, as well as through the commitment to reform or eradicate the social structures responsible for the unjust suffering of millions around the globe. In doing so, liberation theology radically transformed the Christian tradition.[11] Liberation theologians urged people to insert themselves in the political struggles for justice *as* Christians. Instead of seeing this as the politicization of faith, liberation theology provided the theological resources to reinterpret the political as the ineluctable arena for the expression of people's *Christian* commitment to justice, especially for the poor and marginalized.

As noted earlier, this was accomplished *without* reducing politics to faith or faith to politics. Such balance took immense theological, political, and ecclesiastical savviness, and is—so I will argue—the lasting mark of liberation theology. And that is precisely what this book studies: *why* this balance was necessary (Chapter 1), *what* were the theological moves required to achieve it (Chapter 2), and *how* that balance was embodied and persists in the faith-based activism of people shaped by liberation theology (Chapter 3).

The first task (the *why*) requires close attention to the social and ecclesial context—global and Latin American—in which liberation theology emerged. Building on these historical developments, Chapter 1 also draws contrasts between Gutiérrez's work and how others have sought to interpret the relationship between faith and politics. Close attention to these differences shows the strengths and radical nature of the innovations of liberation theology.

The second task (the *what*) demands that we step back to unpack Gutiérrez's nonexplicit hermeneutics of the Christian tradition. This is needed to further explain whether his new articulation of faith and politics works as a *genuine* Christian response to the problem of the political engagement of the Christian believer. Thus, Chapter 2 sketches a theory of interpretation of religious experience and religious innovation—in dialogue with Paul Ricœur and David Tracy—that explains the necessary conditions to produce change within a tradition and the conditions that make such innovations still recognizable as genuinely belonging to the tradition.

The third task (the *how*) requires that we move from the world of theological reflection to that of lived religion. Accordingly, Chapter 3 turns to ethnographic material—including interviews conducted with key members of the liberation theology movement in Perú—giving color and texture to the more theoretical sections of the book. Here we witness, in their own words and narratives, the impact of Gutiérrez's new articulation of faith and politics, and the lasting legacy of liberation theology in Perú.

But *A Revolutionary Faith* is not only a scholarly contribution to liberation theology studies. The book's constructive goal is to start elucidating the necessary conditions to develop a theory of social justice that incorporates, rather than brackets, the liberating intuitions of religion (Chapter 4). And for this task, the new articulation of faith and politics developed by liberation theologians offers crucial insights. However, these are *insights*, indeed. As several scholars have noted,[12] liberation theologians have not yet provided a systematic approach to the question of social justice, nor have they offered concrete criteria to adjudicate between conflicting political claims. When it comes to these questions, liberation theologians have mostly provided negative accounts or rhetorical and spiritually rich calls to action. Or, if their conception of justice was embodied in their political action, such embodiment of their understanding of social justice was rarely systematized in their scholarly work.

For this reason, I will draw instead from one of the most powerful—and, as I will show, congenial with liberation theology—contemporary theories of social justice: that of John Rawls. My goal is to show that a systematic approach to the problem of social justice is crucial both to pursue the cause of progressive social change and to clarify scholarly gaps in liberation theology. Conversely, the work of liberation theologians will allow me to expand Rawls's theory, producing a more inclusive account of social justice, an account this book sketches in its closing chapter.

The key step in the production of this inclusive account of social justice is to show that theological and political ideas can converge—find critical correlation, as Tracy argues. Such a convergence takes place when the guiding thread that connects theological and political ideas is the cause of social justice, especially when it focuses on the poor and marginalized. Indeed, faith and politics can come together to establish strategic and substantial alliances for the common good, particularly when it comes to the needs of the most vulnerable among our fellow humans, nonhuman animals, and the environment. When this happens, even if it is rather briefly and contingent on specific projects, we witness the radical transformation of a tradition, a tradition that has developed a whole new relationship with the world. The world, which was considered for so long a place of sin and temptation, has now become the place in which we all can find the path of redemption. The world, *this world*, is no longer a trap, but a place in which redemption starts taking place. Other religions are no longer antagonist paths of salvation but true sources of wisdom that can come together to take care of creation. The nonbeliever is no longer a foe but a potential ally in the effort to lessen want, protect the most vulnerable, and work for social justice. This is a true revolution. What follows is a study of how this happened.

1

Tradition in Revolution

LIBERATION THEOLOGY'S
NEW ARTICULATION OF FAITH AND POLITICS

In this first chapter I focus on Catholic Latin American liberation theology, particularly on the work of Peruvian theologian Gustavo Gutiérrez and the communities of faith influenced by his contributions. My main interest here, and in the chapters to follow, is to show and examine how Gutiérrez's work produced a theological account of the relationship between faith and politics that allowed several generations of religious activists to intervene in politics *as* religious actors, motivated by their faith. I argue that the best way to understand this new articulation is as a *radically* new interpretation of the Christian *tradition*, one that was able to keep the key tenets of the Christian faith but reading them in a revolutionary new way. One central element of this new reading is that the question of poverty is increasingly understood as a *structural* problem that cannot be solved only through charity. Hence, the moral responsibility of the Christian believer facing the problems of poverty and injustice cannot avoid structural solutions. It cannot avoid politics.

I divide this chapter as follows. First, I offer some preliminary remarks about what I mean by liberation theology. Second, I give some general context to understand both liberation theology's historical context and its place in the book. Third, I turn to the work of Jacques Maritain and his New Christendom model, as an example of a powerful but also problematic articulation of faith and politics. Fourth, I study Gutiérrez's critique of Maritain, placing it in the context of Gutiérrez's approach to the process of secularization. Fifth, I examine prior attempts of a new theological articulation through the notion of integral liberation in some key Vatican II documents. Lastly, I examine what I, and Gutiérrez himself more recently,[1] consider to be the foundational contribution of his work: the notion of "one history." I understand this to be the crux of his liberation theology. The new awareness of the way in which sacred and secular histories relate is what allows Gutiérrez to make the transition to the political a *Christian* transition, without perceiving it as a betrayal of religious commitments or a reduction of religion to politics.

What Is Liberation Theology?

I present here a very brief typology of liberation theology that is recognizable in all its forms.[2] Note that "liberation theology" stands for a multiplicity of movements that developed in connection with the major religious confessions. In this sense, the use of the singular "liberation theology" should not imply a totally uniform school of thought or movement. Rather, the multiple currents of liberation theology are related to one another by what philosopher Ludwig Wittgenstein called "family resemblances." Liberation theology, then, names a family of viewpoints that gather around certain basic principles, some of which are shared by nonreligious movements of liberation as well:[3]

The first principle is the radical opposition to all forms of oppression. Historically, in Latin America, this started with the problem of poverty, but over time it became a larger and international struggle that included issues like race, gender, sexual orientation, nonhuman animals, and the environment.[4] With time this became a struggle that exceeded the world of the Christian faith and extended to almost all religious confessions.[5]

The second principle is the formation of a movement of solidarity with and among the oppressed in the struggle for emancipation and social justice. Here it is important to stress the "social movement" dimension of liberation theology and its attentiveness to the agency of the poor and marginalized themselves. Even though many leaders of the movement were not poor and held advanced degrees, the majority of the movement comprised poor people who, through their own process of discernment and organizing, decided to fight collectively for a life with human dignity and access to basic social goods.[6]

The third principle is the identification of different forms of structural oppression or institutional violence, and the correlative call for structural and institutional change. Indeed, instead of advocating for solidarity in the form of charity and individual acts of generosity, liberation theology's most decisive contribution is its faith-based advocacy for systemic change. This, in turn, leads to the need to intervene in the political process in a variety of creative ways: through churches, elected officials, policy proposals, nonprofits, human rights advocacy, and so on.

The fourth and final principle is the theological or religious commitments of the movement. Put briefly, liberation theology argues that opting for the poor and marginalized, and against their oppression, are essential tenets of the Christian faith. For believers influenced by liberation theology, this option is a theological, faith-based commitment, grounded on the conviction that the liberation of the oppressed is not merely a political or moral obligation but rather one of the most fundamental forms of expression of divine love and justice. The distinctiveness of liberation theology vis-à-vis other movements of liberation lies in this. The religious faith of the adepts of the movement is their strongest source of motivation and becomes also a place of spiritual nurturing in the struggle for a better life. Of course, the degree to which their faith shapes their politics varies, but what is undeniable is that their religious values are central to their political commitments.

From this characterization, two relevant implications follow. First, despite my focus on Gutiérrez's work, I approach the movement constructively. My goal is not only to provide a study of Gutiérrez's theology but to understand how faith and politics relate to each other in an attempt to think about social justice in a liberationist key. Second, despite the importance of professional theologians, I try to give equal place in the argument to the theological reflection of people without formal theological training. This is especially important since priests, nuns, and bishops in the Catholic Latin American context are rarely visible or actively involved in politics. Hence, how laypeople articulate faith and politics is crucial given that they are the ones making political choices on the ground. However, as I will show, the laity draws significantly from the contributions of professional theologians, making evident the importance of the theological articulation provided by Gutiérrez and others.

Liberation Theology's Background

I introduce the case of liberation theology as a creative new interpretation of the relationship between the Christian faith and the political. Liberation theology draws from the core values of the Christian tradition to reinterpret an old problem in a drastically new way. The problem of poverty and marginalization has been a recurrent part of human history, and an issue that Christian leaders and theologians have repeatedly addressed since the inception of Christianity.[7] But their historical response has had a restricted scope. The limited information we have suggests that the Church generally supported the poor and even defended them against the powerful, despite notable and well-known hypocrisies and contradictions. Church leaders and those among the Christian elites saw in their service to the poor a path to salvation, construing poverty itself through the lenses of Jesus's promises to the poor and demands on the better-off. However, the Church rarely questioned the social systems that allowed for the existence of such poverty in the first place. Moreover, the evaluation of poverty changed radically after the Protestant Reformation, when criticism of the monastic lifestyle led progressively to an emphasis on labor and economic prosperity in those regions influenced by Protestantism. Such prosperity was then theologically construed as a spiritual vocation and as a way of praising God. Here we see a transition from the medieval understanding of poverty as a path to salvation for the poor and the wealthy to a more negative approach in which poverty is seen as a sign of lack of religious fervor and hard work.[8] But in neither case was the role of social institutions—like the economy, the systems of government, and the Church itself—considered central in the begetting of poverty. Poverty was simply a given whose effects could be ameliorated but not an effect itself whose causes could be eradicated. It would take a long time for churches to start questioning the organization of society and its unjust structures. Only the new historical developments of the eighteenth and nineteenth centuries enabled churches to see the problem from a radically different viewpoint.

Key among those developments were the revolutionary struggles of the eighteenth and nineteenth centuries: the American Revolution, the French Revolution, and the Wars of Independence in Latin America, among other social processes. The common thread across all revolutions was the emergence of an emancipatory thrust, a deep feeling of discomfort with the current state of affairs, and the conviction that things had to change. The emergence of this emancipatory thrust—not, of course, without its own contradictions, as the persistence of slavery in the former colonies shows so clearly—expanded in complex ways that decisively touched the Christian tradition during the turn from the nineteenth to the twentieth century.[9]

Freedom and democracy were key in this process of transformation, but the Marxian critique of the organization of modern societies was central as well. Sociopolitically, this Marxian critique coupled with the values of freedom and democracy gave birth to what we may call Democratic Socialism, a middle way between free market capitalism and orthodox Marxism that will prove to be deeply influential in the emergence of Christian Socialism in Europe.[10] Here—in the late nineteenth and first half of the twentieth century—we find the seeds that will grow into the political theologies of the second half of the twentieth century, among which liberation theology stands out.

The cry for freedom and equality slowly but compellingly permeated the minds of many lay believers, theologians, clergy, and bishops. In the theological arena, these convictions emerged very clearly in the so-called Catholic Modernist controversy of the late nineteenth and early twentieth century. The Modernist controversy—initially, simply an attempt to apply modern methods of scientific inquiry from the historical and social sciences to the study of the Bible and Catholic teachings—created a fruitful tension between a desire for free inquiry and democratization in the Church, and the attempt to assert papal power and hegemonic authority.[11] Despite the apparent papal victory, with the condemnation of Modernism and the excommunication of biblical scholar Alfred Loisy, events like the Modernist controversy left a deep mark. The promise of freedom and equality shaped the convictions of many thinkers and activists in the first half of the twentieth century, and it led to the formation of important schools of thought that wanted to retrieve the values of the Christian tradition facing new dilemmas and possibilities.

The opening created by the Modernist controversy gave birth, only a few decades later, to the nouvelle théologie, with the Dominican School of Le Saulchoir and the Jesuit School of Lyon-Fourvière as the standard-bearers of a new intellectual and pastoral revolution. Central to this revolution within the Catholic tradition was the commitment to a critical reading of the Bible and the tradition (rather than a repetition of old formulas), the conviction that theology must be in permanent dialogue with the experience of the faithful (rather than remaining a highly theoretical discipline or the mere repetition of dogmas), and a sense of obligation to creatively engage new currents of thought and social phenomena, including Marxism (rather than issuing condemnations or leading with disregard).[12]

It is no coincidence that the key figures of these two schools (Marie-Dominique Chenu and Yves Congar, and Jean Daniélou and Henri de Lubac, respectively), were among the great theological minds that shaped the Second Vatican Council (1962–1965), one of the most consequential gatherings of bishops in the history of the Catholic Church. In fact, Vatican II was for these theologians a moment of personal and intellectual validation after years of censure and hostility. Just for that, Vatican II should be considered a moment of theological opening and democratization in the Catholic Church. But its consequences were and are still far greater, for Vatican II became a moment of "voluntary disestablishment" in which the Catholic Church freely embraced the values of democracy, ecumenism, and honest and horizontal dialogue with society in ways it had never done before.[13]

Such a new attitude toward the world is obvious, for instance, in the opening lines of one of the most consequential documents of Vatican II, *Gaudium et spes*: "The joys and the hopes, the griefs and the anxieties of the men of this age, *especially those who are poor* or in any way afflicted, these are the joys and hopes, the griefs and anxieties of the followers of Christ."[14] Even though this new attitude toward the world is a crucial and new development, another issue related to that change of attitude is significantly less discussed. I am referring to the concern for the situation of the poor. The twentieth century, especially its second half, is the century of the most innovative social teachings of the Catholic Church. One central element of these innovations is that the question of poverty is increasingly understood as a *structural* problem that cannot be solved only through charity.

These innovations directly shaped the council and Pope John XXIII, its convener. Consider, for instance, the influential radio address of September 11, 1962, just a month before the opening session of the council. In it, Pope John XXIII called for a "Church for all, but especially a Church of the poor."[15] Indeed, the question of poverty became a central issue for many of the bishops in attendance, led by the Latin American bishops and some of their allies in the curia, like Cardinal Giacomo Lercaro.[16] These bishops formed the group that is often called the Church of the Poor, which famously committed to the Pact of the Catacombs: the forty bishops present in the Domitilla Catacombs outside Rome pledged to live a frugal life and to stand in solidarity with the poor.[17] Soon after, hundreds of bishops all over the world joined in signing the document released by the original forty.

We should not be surprised that some of the Latin American bishops in attendance, most importantly Hélder Câmara, were key players in the organization and execution of the Second General Conference of the Latin American Bishops in the city of Medellín, Colombia (1968). After Vatican II, Medellín was the most consequential gathering of bishops, a meeting conceived as a direct, autochthonous, and creative response to the council's calling to read the "signs of the times." In Medellín, responding to that call, the Latin American bishops directly addressed many issues such as structural injustice, the causes of poverty, economic systems of oppression, and land reform. In this new conception of the role of the Church, Christians were to be committed to the struggle for social transformation to bring justice to all, but especially to the poor. Later, in the Third General Conference of Latin American Bishops in the city of Puebla, México (1979), the bishops defined this commitment as the "preferential option for the poor," and this became one of the guiding principles of liberation theology. But Medellín was really the turning point. In sociologist Christian Smith's words:

Medellín documents marked a radical departure from the rhetoric and strategy of an institution which, for centuries, had justified the killing of native peoples, provided a religious legitimation for an authoritarian, hierarchical social system, and aligned itself with conservative power elites. . . . Medellín was made the official statement and position of the Latin American Church. Three months later, at the twelfth regular CELAM assembly, Medellín was reaffirmed as the norm for inspiration and action in the coming years.[18]

Gustavo Gutiérrez studied in Lyon, was close to Yves Congar and especially to Marie-Dominique Chenu, took classes with Henri de Lubac, and attended the Fourth Session of Vatican II as the theological adviser of Peruvian cardinal Juan Landázuri Rickets. Further, as Smith underscores, Gutiérrez was "the single most important person"[19] in the making of Medellín. He was indeed not only one of its greatest theological minds but also a true organizer and mobilizer of people. Most of the key documents of Medellín were decisively shaped by Gutiérrez, but so too was the consensus that led to the approval of the documents.

In light of these events, I ask, how did Gutiérrez produce his *Teología de la liberación* (1971), the first systematic account of this complex theological and sociopolitical journey? I am particularly interested in how Gutiérrez justified expanding the Christian commitment to the political realm, the distinctions he was able to make, and how he differs from other authors in ways that position him as the foremost liberation theologian in the process of creatively but faithfully retrieving the key values of the Christian tradition in dialogue with a new situation. In subsequent chapters I examine how these ideas shaped the everyday choices of the faith communities formed by the preferential option for the poor.

The New Christendom and the Crisis of the Distinction of Planes Model

We need some further contextualization to properly understand Gutiérrez's notion of the unity of history. The Latin American Wars of Independence of the nineteenth century and the geopolitical prominence of Britain and, later, of the United States, deeply affected the relationships of church, state, and society in the region. The Catholic Church, until then owner of the monopoly over religious belief, progressively started to lose its condition of state-church. In a perhaps desperate effort to recover its old prerogatives, the Catholic Church often sided with the remaining

Latin American royalist parties, opposing the independentist movement and pledging alliance to the Spanish crown. Such a response only elicited suspicion and animosity from the liberal elites that had already seized power. The result was the progressive erosion—and ultimate dissolution—of the Catholic monopoly.

But this led neither to the secularization of Latin America nor to a drastic reduction of the Catholic presence in the region. This is partly explained by the Catholic Church's ability to learn its lesson from the European experience of secularization. Initially, however, the learning curve was not so obvious, as shown by the alliance with the royalist parties. Yet the alliance was in practice a bad choice. It only allowed the Church to retain some symbolic power. As Smith maintains, the processes of modernization, urbanization, and migration started to show that

the Church had overestimated its popular influence. The Catholic Church increasingly found itself in the first decades of the twentieth century unsuccessfully competing for the allegiances of the people against secular unions, left-wing political groups, African-derived spiritualist cults, and newly arrived Protestant churches.[20]

The Catholic Church in Latin America confronted this problem and tried to recover the lost ground. Critical in that process was the New Christendom movement, which emerged in Europe in the 1930s and arrived in Latin America a few years after. Smith notes that "this was, essentially, a strategy to establish Catholicism as a major institutional and cultural influence in Latin America's modernizing society."[21] Progressive for its time, the New Christendom movement was partially able to reverse the Catholic Church's conservative alliances. In their place, the movement's adherents defended the ideals of progress, science, modernity, and democracy. Catholic Action—a laity-led movement that encouraged Catholic influence on society through a critical discernment of reality—was the concrete articulation of the New Christendom model. Catholic Action expanded rapidly in Latin America, with significant success in the training of laypeople, organizing them to participate actively as Catholics in the spheres of education, culture, and politics. Several Christian democratic parties emerged in the region fueled by this movement. The victory of Eduardo Frei in the Chilean presidential elections of 1964 was probably the high point of Catholic Action's influence in Latin American politics.[22]

Despite its initial success, the New Christendom movement came under pressure in the 1960s. In Cuba, Fidel Castro overthrew Fulgencio Batista's government in 1959, starting the first socialist revolutionary government of the region. Then, in 1964, a military coup d'état ended democracy in Brazil. Frei's government in Chile started to receive strong criticism from the public and his political rivals. John F. Kennedy's Alliance for Progress with Latin America began to show significant limitations. Many people started to believe that the promise of democratic capitalism, fundamentally embraced by and associated with New Christendom, was inadequate for Latin America.

The critics were not only among the masses. In Brazil, the outspoken Bishop Hélder Câmara led the progressive Episcopal Conference of Brazil in its critique of the economic system, and many other bishops and members of the clergy joined him. Interestingly, Câmara (among other critics of the New Christendom movement) was initially part of Catholic Action. Somewhat ironically, the critical discernment of reality that this movement encouraged in its members led to a critical assessment of its own limitations in dealing with the new Latin American situation. Vatican II and the way it shaped the leadership of the Catholic Church in Latin America, especially from the time of the Medellín conference on, had a decisive role in this new critical awareness.

It is in this context that Gutiérrez's notion of the unity of history is situated. He opens his reflection by asking: "What relation is there between salvation and the historical process of human liberation?"[23] Or, more generally: What is the relationship between faith and temporal or secular realities?[24] Yet, since the organization of temporal realities depends on "the construction of the 'polis' . . . which encompasses and severely conditions all human activity," this general question naturally becomes a question about the relationship between faith and politics, for politics is "the universal determinant and the collective arena for human fulfillment."[25] Thus, the real issue is not whether faith and politics, salvation and liberation, relate to each other: they always do. The real issue is how they *do* it and how they *should*.

By the 1960s, as Gutiérrez notes in *Teología de la liberación*, people have become active subjects of their own histories, rejecting the idea that a ruling elite is destined to decide their future. Further, this has become especially true in the context of massive poverty and social injustice. In this new context, Gutiérrez maintains, we see an increasing radicalization of social praxis. People appear to be tired of reformist attitudes and demand, instead, a radical change in the social order. In Latin America, "this conflict revolves around the *oppression-liberation axis*."[26] But Latin America is also a continent in which the majorities claim Christian identity. Further, many among these Christians are key actors in the struggles to end oppression and to achieve more just and human conditions of living. Therefore, our initial question starts taking a new form. Is the Christian faith compatible with the idea of radical social change? Can Gospel and social revolution go together?

In order to respond to these questions, Gutiérrez first examines some historical responses to the general question about the relationship between faith and politics. The primary and most pervasive one is what he calls the Christendom Mentality. According to this viewpoint, "participation in temporal tasks has a very precise meaning for the Christian: 'to work for the direct and immediate benefit of the Church . . . assisting the Church in its evangelizing mission and safeguarding the Church's interests.'"[27] But this approach was severely affected by the revolutionary wars of the eighteenth and nineteenth centuries. It depended heavily on the Catholic monopoly over religious belief and the role of Catholicism as state-church. Of course, this Christendom Mentality has not disappeared and remains alive among many conservative and integralist Catholics today.[28] However, it has lost its currency because of the progressive and voluntary disestablishment of the Catholic Church during the twentieth century and especially after Vatican II.[29]

The new social challenges of the twentieth century—key among them the emergence of new social movements fighting for the democratization of their societies—led to the development of an alternative approach within Catholic thought. The French Catholic philosopher Jacques Maritain made it well known, coining the term "New Christendom" to describe it. A detailed examination of this approach gives us a better understanding of its contrast with Gutiérrez's theological outlook.

Maritain's New Christendom perspective is a response to what he perceived as a moment of cultural decay that he attributed to the tragic separation of human affairs from God's plan for humanity. He calls it the "tragedy of God." In this sense, Maritain's relationship with the achievements of the modern era and the process of secularization is rather ambivalent. On the one hand, he praises humanism and the great regard for the rights of the person progressively achieved since the time of the great social revolutions. On the other, he sees in this anthropological turn severe errors and, in fact, the roots of the tragic separation just described; humanism, either in its "mitigated" version of the sixteenth and seventeenth centuries, in its "absolute" version of the eighteenth and nineteenth centuries, or in its "atheist" version of the twentieth century, has the same fundamental problem: the idea that human fulfillment can be achieved without God's grace.[30]

Maritain's New Christendom attempts to respond to this conundrum. He proposes a theocentric form of humanism that embraces the anthropological turn without its historical mistakes—atheism being one of the most paramount for Maritain.[31] To avoid such mistakes, Maritain clearly distinguishes between the temporal (profane) and spiritual (sacred) orders and between their correlative temporal or natural and spiritual or supernatural goods. Ultimately, this is a distinction between the human good and the good of salvation. What is key here is that for Maritain the temporal good is understood as the good of the community in which the fundamental rights of all are recognized and respected. But this is a *purely natural good.* For him, the supernatural good of salvation is so utterly different from any ordinary human good that these simply cannot be compared. In this sense, Maritain will speak of the "Kingdom of God" to refer to the good of the spiritual, supernatural order: a good that is "wholly eschatological" and, fundamentally, nothing other than the final beatific vision.[32] From this follows that the Kingdom of God cannot be realized in the temporal order; not even "partial" realizations are possible.[33]

Understandably enough, tensions emerge out of Maritain's own characterization of the relationship between the temporal and the spiritual order, because the Christian tradition maintains that "the Kingdom of God is at hand." Hence, Maritain must admit that the Kingdom of God has already begun in history. And, in fact, he does, arguing that this has happened in the Church. But the tradition also holds, especially after the Reformation, that the *institutional* Church itself should not be wholly identified with the Kingdom. From this follows the idea that non-Christians may well represent an "invisible Church" making present the "soul" of the Church without belonging to it. Given that Maritain embraces these ideas, he has trouble drawing a line between natural and supernatural orders.[34]

Maritain's way out of this problem depends on his understanding of virtue and the way in which virtue allows us to enter into communion with God in the beatific vision. Relying on the classic Thomistic distinction between natural or acquired virtue and supernatural or infused virtue,[35] Maritain maintains that the temporal good, in principle, only requires natural virtue. In this sense, the ultimate temporal good is by no means comparable to the supernatural good of salvation because the latter requires grace, that is, supernatural virtue. However, no real good can be accomplished in the temporal order without God's assistance. In this sense, the natural and supernatural order fundamentally relate to one another insofar as the latter infuses the former with grace so that it can accomplish its ultimate, although still temporal, good. Conversely, the natural order relates to the supernatural order (and, in this sense, the Kingdom "has begun") insofar as in the pursuit of the natural good of the former the "environmental conditions" for the latter are developed or prepared. They do so through the perfection of the virtues, which enrich and strengthen the inner life of the person, preparing them for the ultimate goal of salvation.[36]

This emphasis on virtue is of tremendous importance for my argument. For despite all the effort Maritain makes to underscore that the temporal order and the temporal good are not mere means and have value in themselves, their value ultimately lies in their capacity to prepare the soul for—to make it merit—salvation. As theologian Dean Brackley explains in his examination of Maritain's take on virtue in *Science and Wisdom*: "From the point of view of human agency, it is the intention of the will and not the external action that is decisive as to whether a given action is meritorious or not."[37] From this follows why (as we will see shortly through Gutiérrez's critique) Maritain had difficulties explaining the role of the Church and the Christian in the world.

If what principally matters is our spiritual orientation and not so much our external actions, then the "construction of the world" becomes, strictly speaking, a temporal task. The Christian qua Christian must concern themself with spiritually "vivifying" or "inspiring" the temporal domain.[38] The transformation and liberation of the world from oppression and injustice is a temporal good not a spiritual one; it is, at best, preparation—insofar as spiritual disposition—for the supernatural good. So, at the level of Maritain's *theological* articulation of the problem, such transformation is not a *spiritual* priority. Rather, it is a political, temporal responsibility in order to create the conditions for spiritual growth and salvation.

This by no means diminishes the great achievements of Maritain and his decisive support of democracy and human rights, which had enormous influence in Vatican II and beyond.[39] Yet his distinction between spiritual and temporal orders has important limitations. Most of them are related to the historical context and problems to which Maritain is responding. Indeed, he saw his Distinction of Planes model as a necessary development in order to preserve *both* the sacredness of the Kingdom of God (against atheist historizations of the concept) *and* the sacredness of human conscience and human freedom (against attempts to return to some form of the respublica Christiana). However, what Maritain did not fully contemplate was the possibility of preserving the sacredness of both without a sharp distinction of planes. Moreover, he did not consider the possibility of a more expansive Christian self-understanding in which "temporal" and "spiritual" tasks could be more fully integrated *within* the political process.

Why? He writes: "It is impossible that a vitally Christian transformation of the temporal order can take place in the same way and by the same means as other temporal transformations and revolutions. If this is to be it will be the fruit of Christian heroism."[40] Indeed, Maritain's immediate context is the kind of political transformation promoted by Soviet Communism and German National Socialism. Maritain's project for the political role of Christians, naturally, is radically different from these two options. Christian political participation must avoid "the danger of seeking sanctity only in the desert, and the danger of forgetting the need of the desert for sanctity."[41]

How can the Christian, the Church, do that? His response is the noted "vivifying influence": assisting the state and the body politic, radiating, "[stimulating] the inner forces and energies of other agents . . . whose

place is less high in the scale of being."[42] In this way, the Church neither becomes one with the state (the model of the respublica Christiana)
nor gives up its responsibilities in the political realm. Yet, avoiding these
extremes, the Church and Christians also avoid the mistake of thinking
that *Christian* social transformation can happen through the same means
that other forms of social transformation pursue. Of course, this does not
mean that laypeople cannot participate in politics, run for office, and the
like. It means that in doing so and in their political activity they will be
operating, at best, inspired by Christian ideals ("as a Christian"). In Maritain's view, Christian action proper ("as a Christian as such") is spiritual
action related to Christ's Church.[43]

But what if the temporal task of constructing a more just society
could also be a *spiritual* task? Can political participation—not only vivifi-
cation—be a manifestation of one's faith, of one's spiritual calling? Maritain's model has trouble accounting for these alternatives because he is
worried about the assimilation of the Christian intervention in the temporal order into any form of temporal intervention, especially those of the
totalitarian politics of his time. Yet, keeping his caution, we do not have to
be limited by his context. Instead, inspired by his democratic convictions,
we could consider other possibilities.

Secularization and the Affirmation
of Ordinary Life: Gutiérrez's Critique

As Gutiérrez notes, Maritain maintained that the "task of constructing the human city would consist above all in the search for a society based
upon justice, respect for the rights of others, and human fellowship."[44]
Gutiérrez believes that this approach helped to develop a position in which
the terms of the church-world relationship were better defined. Indeed, by
the 1950s and 1960s, the mission of the Church had become the "evangelization and inspiration of the temporal sphere" and not anymore one
of isolation or total monopoly. This shift owed a great deal to Maritain's
efforts. However, as noted earlier, Maritain believed that "the Church is
not responsible for constructing the world."[45] Maritain's New Christendom approach held that the Church should only evangelize and inspire
the temporal order, not intervene directly in political action. The laity, in

contrast, is called to the construction of the world, a process in which they can establish alliances with other Christians and non-Christians as well.

Tellingly, of course, here the laity is construed—even if only for analytical purposes—as not being the Church proper. The obvious implication is that the Church, strictu sensu, is represented by its hierarchy, ordained ministers, and members of religious orders. Precisely for this reason, tensions emerge in the case of laypeople who act as members of apostolic movements such as Catholic Action. When that is the case, they should not go beyond the mission of the Church and the clergy. Thus, for the laity an important distinction emerges: action "as a Christian as such" and only "as a Christian." Gutierrez clarifies: "In the first case, Christians act as members of the Church, and their actions represent the ecclesial community. . . . In the second case, Christians act under the inspiration of Christian principles, but assume exclusive personal responsibility for their actions."[46]

This model quickly started showing weaknesses. One can easily perceive a certain arbitrariness and even rigidity in the distinction of the planes of action and the role of the actors allowed to participate in each plane. Further, there seems to be a division of spiritual labor between the clergy and the laity that implicitly suggests that the only true Christian action is the one realized either by the clergy or by the laity acting like the clergy. As I have observed, these tensions ultimately emerge from Maritain's own difficulties in distinguishing the temporal and spiritual orders, and from the kind of value he attributed to social-political action vis-à-vis the supernatural good of salvation.

Indeed, the model became contested in the second half of the twentieth century because of its pastoral and theological limitations. From a pastoral point of view, the problem had to do with the relationship between lay apostolic movements and the institutional Church, a relationship that could not be mediated any longer by the Distinction of Planes model. Simply put, "the life of these movements overflowed this narrow and aseptic conceptual model."[47]

Initially, it was a question of pedagogy: the political moment appeared to make evident that no religious formation could take place without there also being some form of political conscientization. Some form of *religious* consciousness raising vis-à-vis the political upheaval of the region appeared to be unavoidable. Questions about the role of the Christian faith in the midst of poverty and oppression became inescapable; a critical response coming from the sources of the tradition in dialogue with the moment became a must for many catechists and pastoral agents.

However, this was only a sign of a larger problem. The moment of political radicalization that Latin America (and the globe) was experiencing—with the hopes created by the Cuban Revolution, the civil rights movement, and the decolonization movement—demanded that the laity take a stand. The laity felt the gravity of the demand but also felt more empowered and capable of responding with autonomy. The control of ecclesial hierarchy weakened; friction and division emerged.[48] In addition, this moment of political conscientization made evident "that a large part of the Church is in one way or another linked to those who wield economic and political power in today's world." Gutiérrez, of course, noted the irony: "Can it honestly be said that the Church does not interfere in the 'temporal sphere'?"[49] Thus, Gutiérrez maintained that the Distinction of Planes model was an excuse "to dispense the ecclesiastical institution from effectively defending the oppressed and exploited and to enable it to preach a lyrical spiritual unity of all Christians."[50]

From a theological point of view, other problems arose. Gutiérrez deemed the Distinction of Planes model untenable because of the decisive influence of the process of secularization. Gutiérrez mainly understood as secularization the process of differentiation of the secular sphere from religious institutions and norms.[51] In this sense, soundly, Gutiérrez did not embrace the other elements of the so-called secularization thesis, namely, that secularization must also lead to the privatization and/or decline of religion. His nuanced assessment of the process allowed him to maintain a critical but positive relationship with the process of secularization, without assuming that it inherently means an attack on religious faith that will lead to a godless world. The key difference with Maritain here is that, overall, Gutiérrez sees the process of secularization as a positive development that has given due autonomy to the temporal order.

Here we should briefly digress and discuss secularization itself in order to have a better grasp of the importance of Gutiérrez's position. This appears particularly relevant since the most comprehensive intellectual history of liberation theology to date—Lilian Calles Barger's *The World Come of Age* (2018)—argues that liberation theologians proposed a "full secularization of religion."[52] I believe this misconstrues the approach of most liberation theologians, but it certainly does so when it comes to Gutiérrez's work. Clarifying this matter will further cast light on how faith and politics relate in his theology.

Let us start first by unpacking the meaning of "secularization" following the contributions of sociologist José Casanova to the secularization debate. Casanova's main achievement is his powerful and well documented critique of the so-called secularization thesis, namely, that modernization leads to the progressive privatization or even extinction of religion. Now, this does not mean that Casanova believes that secularization is a myth.[53] As he explains:

> The core of the theory of secularization, the thesis of the differentiation and emancipation of the secular sphere from religious institutions and norms, remains valid. But the term "deprivatization" is also meant to signify the emergence of new historical developments which, at least qualitatively, amount to a certain reversal of what appeared to be secular trends.[54]

The deprivatization to which Casanova refers is the emergence of massive and more than a handful of religious movements in the 1980s that put into question the thesis of the privatization of religion. These movements—liberation theology is a paradigmatic example—entered the public sphere *as religious movements*. They did so, however, not only to defend their traditional turf but to "participate in the very struggles to define and set the modern boundaries between the private and public spheres, between system and life-world, between legality and morality. . . ."[55] As we will see shortly, liberation theologians and the faithful who directly participate in liberationist political activism do so motivated by their religious faith, not to defend the old prerogatives of the Catholic Church. Rather, they do so to produce an innovative critical balance between the newly differentiated spheres of faith, politics, the economy, and so forth. Guided by their faith—but with implications that go beyond the traditional religious realm—liberation theologians and the communities shaped by their theology demand a new social arrangement in which politics and the economy are put at the service of the people, especially the most vulnerable. Hence, liberation theologians take advantage of the autonomy of the temporal order, gained through the process of secularization-as-differentiation, to push—on religious grounds—for a more just here and now. What we see here is a multi-layered and complex process that deserves careful consideration.

Thus, Casanova maintains that the secularization thesis must be reformulated. He claims that it should be understood as covering three different dimensions: (a) secularization as religious decline, (b) secularization as differentiation, and (c) secularization as privatization.[56] Casanova's five case studies (Chapters 3 to 7 of his book) compellingly prove that (a) and (c) are empirically and theoretically indefensible: decline is not real beyond some parts of Europe, and privatization—in the sense of reclusion of faith in the sole privacy of the home and temples—is not a modern structural trend.[57] What we must do is distinguish different *patterns* of secularization with different historical and regional trajectories, noting at the same time that the European pattern is neither normative nor the most widespread.[58] Furthermore, if we push the issue beyond active affiliation to religious denominations and think more generally about the multiple forms in which people acknowledge and revere what they consider sacred, the sub-theses of decline and privatization simply do not hold.[59] The main reason these two propositions are still defended in some circles seems to be some degree of theoretical bias regarding the process of modernization that can be traced back to, at least, the Enlightenment.[60]

Casanova maintains, however, that institutional differentiation remains "the valid core of the theory of secularization," at least in the societies marked by the influence of Latin Christianity.[61] Interestingly, his critique of (a) and (c) does not represent a rejection of the values of modernity, but a more creative and historically grounded retrieval of them. Therefore, religions can be a fundamental part of critically rethinking the modern project. But this, in turn, requires that religious thinkers and activists reflexively incorporate the positive aspects of the Enlightenment's critique of religion, namely:

The cognitive critique of traditional religious worldviews, the moral-practical critique of religious ideologies of legitimation, and the subjective-expressive critique of religious asceticism and alienation—while publicly upholding the *sacred* values of modernity, that is, human life and freedom.[62]

Casanova's book concludes: "It would be profoundly ironic if, after all the beatings it has received from modernity, religion could somehow unintentionally help modernity save itself."[63] In my view, this is exactly what liberation theologians do. They acknowledge the sacred values of modernity but do so *without* getting rid of the sacred. Liberation theologians critically embrace modern values like liberty, autonomy, and the enhancement of ordinary life *without* embracing the view that the power of the sacred must be confined to the temples or the privacy of our homes. Rather, liberation theologians argue that the power of the sacred may be essential in the defense of these modern values. Hence, Gutiérrez and his colleagues produced an imaginative articulation of secular and religious values through a new understanding of the way in which salvation and liberation relate to each other.[64] Of course, this new articulation does not represent a naïve embracement of values like liberty and autonomy, as if liberation theologians were not aware of the risks of the erosion of community, individualism, and the colonialist instrumentalization of the defense of liberty. Rather, Gutiérrez and his colleagues supported these modern values insofar as liberty, autonomy, and the enhancement of ordinary life serve the cause of liberation and the fight against oppression.

We can now draw a few conclusions from Casanova's argument, which will help us to better understand Gutiérrez's contribution. The process of secularization is indeed a reality, but not a uniform one. It varies in its range and depth depending on historical developments, location, and, certainly, theoretical assumptions. What seems to be undeniable is that *some* process of differentiation has occurred in most Western societies, a process that has challenged the conditions of belief, a key thesis of the work of philosopher Charles Taylor.[65] Decline and privatization of religion, in contrast, do not seem to be massive trends beyond the European context. Interestingly, however, the process of secularization has reshaped some religions in a way that allows them to critically refashion the nature of the process of differentiation. What matters at this juncture is that Gutiérrez's theology does not embrace the sub-theses of privatization and decline of religion. In fact, as Casanova shows, liberation theology embodies the very untenability of those sub-theses.

How shall we understand, then, Barger's idea that liberation theologians pursued a full secularization of religion? Unfortunately, Barger does not provide a clear sense of how she understands the process of secularization. However, we can provide an informed inference based on the trajectory of her argument. I believe it is fair to say that by "secularization" Barger means "turn to the saeculum," that is, a focus on our world, our age, that implies an inversion of emphasis switching from an emphasis on religion to one on secular matters. Not in vain Barger uses this idea of full secularization to introduce liberation theology's understanding of why Christians should become politically active in the struggle for social justice. Further, Barger's book is titled *The World Come of Age*, drawing from Dietrich Bonhoeffer's idea that the modern, "come of age" person should pursue a worldly, religionless Christianity.[66]

However, as Casanova explains, this understanding of secularization "only makes sense if we accept that, 'once upon a time,' much of reality in medieval Europe was actually structured through a system of classification which divided 'this world' into two heterogeneous realms or spheres, 'the religious' and 'the secular.'"[67] We must underscore that this system of classification is different from the acknowledgment of the existence of two worlds: the spiritual and the temporal. The religious/secular pair only belongs to *this world*, the temporal world. In this dualistic, mostly medieval system, the religious and the secular were deeply entangled but were also distinguishable realms: there was the Church and the secular institutions, there was the liturgical time and the secular time, and so forth. However, it was unquestionable that the religious realm—mediated by the Catholic Church as the sacramental presence of God's reign on earth—was superior to the secular, and that it permeated all secular institutions and activities.

In this sense, as Casanova argues, the most fundamental element of the process of secularization consists in the breakdown of this dualistic system of classification and the Church's role as sacramental mediator:

The wall separating the religious and the secular realms within "this world" breaks down. The separation between "this world" and "the other world," for the time being at least, remains. But from now on, there will be only one single "this world," the secular one, within which religion will have to find its own place. If before, it was the religious realm which appeared to be the all-encompassing reality within which the secular realm found its proper place, now the secular sphere will be the all-encompassing reality, to which the religious sphere will have to adapt.[68]

The problem with Barger's argument is that she does not seem to recognize the different levels of secularization noted earlier. Thus, she seems to assume a dualistic understanding of the organization of society, an understanding that has been gone for a long time, precisely due to the process of institutional differentiation. In this sense, it is mistaken—or at least misleading—to suggest that liberation theologians moved in the direction of completely secularizing religion. *Religion was already secularized.* Liberation theologians always operated in a social and religious system in which the religious realm did not have the dominion it had in the medieval system of classification. Religious faith and church belonging were already optional matters. Even if in Latin America the Catholic Church remained a powerful institution, it did not have the prerogatives it once had. It could not shape reality the way it used to do in the medieval and early modern periods.

Hence, this turn to the saeculum, to worldly matters, should not be understood as a form of secularization but as a *new articulation* of the balance between secular and religious matters, and between the spiritual and the temporal order. For Barger, full secularization ultimately means the *reduction* of the religious to the secular, of faith to politics. Therefore, it is not surprising that she maintains that liberation theologians locate "salvation *in* the political."[69] Similarly, she claims that for liberation theologians "the political *is* the total." Barger sees liberation theologians as completing the project of "'disenchantment of the world,' moving toward a rationalized religion purged of its belief in magic and the immanent forces of the supernatural." Lastly, it is not surprising that she maintains that liberation theology as a "theology *free of otherworldly transcendence* did not abolish God but asserted a holism ascribing religious meaning to the political sphere."[70]

All these assertions represent a misunderstanding of liberation theology as a whole, and of Gutiérrez's theology in particular.[71] As I will show, the key contribution of Gutierrez was to provide a *new articulation* of the relationship between faith and politics, the religious realm and the secular, by construing *history as one*. However, this does not amount to "making no distinction between the sacred and the profane"[72] or to a theology free of otherworldly transcendence, as Barger claims. Quite the opposite. Gutierrez's critique of Maritain shows the unwillingness to fall prey of any reductionism. To this critique we shall return now to further clarify the nature of Gutiérrez's innovation.

For the reasons just explained, Gutiérrez's evaluation of secularization and its "anthropological turn" is less ambiguous than Maritain's. In fact, Gutiérrez takes the process of secularization as an opportunity for Christian theology and the Christian faith. For this emphasis on the temporal order—what Charles Taylor calls the "affirmation of ordinary life"—has made the concern for human dignity and the enhancement of life absolutely central for the understanding of both the temporal good *and* the supernatural good. Thus, for Gutiérrez, any conception of the supernatural good that overemphasizes its spiritual dimensions without considering its temporal manifestations appears to be flawed. Put differently, any understanding of salvation that promises spiritual bliss in heaven without caring about the enhancement of life in earth seems indefensible from a Christian point of view given the anthropological and historical turns of the last few centuries.[73]

This is especially true in the case of the poor and marginalized. The Christian tradition has often interpreted the promises of Jesus to the poor in terms of future, heavenly consolation, assuming that the condition of poverty is an unavoidable fact of human existence. Thus, the Christian tradition has always cared about the poor in some form or another but has not very often considered—until the emergence of the movements of liberation in the past century—the possibility of radically transforming their situation. Ultimately, this reluctance had a theological basis, even present in Maritain: believing that the supernatural good would supersede any pains in this world.[74] Of course, this is a central Christian belief, but overemphasizing it leads to quietism and the passive acceptance of unjust suffering in the world.

It is not surprising that Karl Marx would call religion the "opium of the people." In this sense, we should see liberation theology as a direct response to Marx's charge, embracing the value of his ideological critique without siding with him in his atheist conclusions. Indeed, Gutiérrez is not ambiguous about this: through their struggle for liberation, Latin Americans "are freeing themselves in one way or another from the tutelage of an alienating religion which tends to support the status quo."[75] Perhaps, *with* Marx, liberation theologians could say that the critique of religion is "the premise of all criticism."[76] Yet, *against* Marx, criticism of religion is not the same as its destruction or ultimate overcoming. Rather, liberation theologians see in religion—in a faith oriented toward the liberation of the oppressed—the potential for emancipation that Marx thought was impossible without getting rid of religion.

For all these reasons, Gutiérrez maintains that the process of secularization, far from becoming a threat to the Christian faith, favors a more complete fulfillment of Christianity's values. It allows, in his words, "the possibility of effectively concretizing the potentialities of the Gospel and the Churches in order to contribute to the liberation of Latin American persons."[77] Charles Taylor, as if he were in direct conversation with Gutiérrez, puts it this way:

In modern, secularist culture there are mingled together both authentic developments of the Gospel, of an incarnational mode of life, and also a closing off to God that negates the Gospel. The notion is that modern culture, in breaking with the structures and beliefs of Christendom, also carried certain facets of Christian life further than ever were taken or could have been taken within Christendom. In relation to the earlier forms of Christian culture, we have to face the humbling realization that the breakout was a necessary condition of the development.[78]

Indeed, for Gutiérrez the break with "the structures and beliefs of Christendom" was a necessary condition for the development of anything like a theology of liberation. Of course, that break also implied the "closing off to God" that we see in what Taylor calls "exclusive humanism," a form of humanism that orthodox Marxism represents so well. But this risk, that Maritain saw as a tragic development, is not the only possibility; neither is it its most likely outcome. The disestablishment of the Christian churches allowed the emergence of new forms of *theological* humanism in which the enhancement of life and the openness to transcendence can coexist, enriching each other.[79] This is what social theorist Hans Joas calls "new forms of sacralization," an issue to which I will turn in subsequent chapters. I turn now to Gutiérrez's theological articulation of this new possibilities.

Between Tradition and Innovation:
The Roots of Integral Liberation

As we have seen, prior to the emergence of liberation theology and its fundamental theological contributions, two models for the relationship between salvation and the political prevailed. The first, the Christendom Mentality, was the most predominant, lasting roughly from the fourth century until the times of the revolutionary wars of the eighteenth and nineteenth centuries. It advocated a monopolistic model in which human and political activity was construed in terms of the interests of the institutional Church. The second, New Christendom, developed well into the twentieth century. It advocated for democracy and human rights, finding in Jacques Maritain its utmost representative.

However, this kind of approach, although better than the prior one, remained too metaphysical and abstract. Further, it had several inconsistencies both at the abstract and practical levels. Yet this perspective opened the door to a new understanding of the relationship between natural and supernatural orders, and the correlative political and spiritual orders. Such new understanding gives priority to a historical and existential point of view that maintains that "there is no pure nature and never has been; there is no one who is not invited to communion with the Lord, no one who is not affected by grace."[80] For Gutiérrez, this points to an indisputable element of the Christian faith, namely that "all persons are in Christ efficaciously called to communion with God. To accept the historical viewpoint of the meaning of human existence is to rediscover the Pauline theme of the universal lordship of Christ, in whom all things exist and have been saved."[81]

Such conviction permeated mainstream theological reflection in the Catholic tradition from the second half of the twentieth century onward. Most importantly, it shaped and dominated the theology and key documents of the Second Vatican Council. Vatican II embraced the use of the term "integral" to refer to the relationship between natural and supernatural orders. Thus, it rejected prior dichotomies,[82] expressing its commitment to a unified perspective in which the history of salvation and human history are part of one single and complex process.[83] *Gaudium et spes* clearly expresses this idea:

This council exhorts Christians, as citizens of two cities, to strive to discharge their earthly duties conscientiously and in response to the Gospel spirit. They are mistaken who, knowing that we have here no abiding city but seek one which is to come, think that they may therefore shirk their earthly responsibilities. For they are forgetting that by the faith itself they are more obliged than ever to measure up to these duties, each according to his proper vocation. Nor, on the contrary, are they any less wide of the mark who think that religion consists in acts of worship alone and in the discharge of certain moral obligations, and who imagine they can plunge themselves into earthly affairs in such a way as to imply that these are altogether divorced from the religious life. This split between the faith which many profess and their daily lives deserves to be counted among the more serious errors of our age.[84]

In this sense, the council speaks of the "integral vocation" of all Christians, attempting to overcome prior dichotomies, thus unifying sacred and profane histories.[85] Similarly, Pope Paul VI stresses that the Christian vision of human development must be one of "integral development" in which "the good of every man and of the whole man" is promoted. Hence, although the integral development of the human being is only completed in the ultimate communion with God, it must include "economic, social, cultural, and spiritual aspects" as well.[86]

Again, Vatican II sheds light on how this process of integration takes place both theologically and practically: through the defense of the dignity of the human person, which is the "foundation for the relationship between the Church and the world, and provides the basis for dialogue between them."[87]

The impact of these theological innovations and doctrinal statements of the 1960s cannot be overstated. Their most immediate consequence was the development of a more fluid relation between Church and world. Yet Gutiérrez highlights another consequence: the *religious* revalorization of human action in history. Thus "the building of a just society has worth in terms of the Kingdom, or in more current phraseology, to participate in the process of liberation is already, in a certain sense, a salvific work."[88] As I noted before, the Latin American Church took these developments with tremendous seriousness and creatively translated the insights of Vatican II into the social and political fabric of its region. Bishops, clergy, and religious and lay leaders understood that the situation of Latin America was one of severe poverty and inequality and assumed responsibility both for reflecting on the duty of Christians in such context and for acting on it. Recognizing the pervasive situation of "institutionalized violence" in Latin America,[89] these actors decided to stand in solidarity with the cry and struggles of the poor.[90] Such was the context of the emergence of the theology of liberation and the social movement it was able to expand and deepen.

But as happened with Black liberation theology in the United States, despite the social, political, cultural, and ecclesial developments just noted, further theological systematization was still required.[91] These were indeed "signs of the times" but still lacked a theological argument that would elaborate and specify *how* to fight for human dignity *as a Christian*, beyond the somewhat vague declarations of the bishops or the insights and praxis of the laity. In this sense, Gutiérrez's great achievement—parallel to James Cone's—was both giving expression to an already existing experience and giving orientation to it. This contribution was critical at the time, since many saw the political activism of Christians as incompatible with their faith, especially when they aligned with socialist parties. Thus, Gutiérrez writes:

This book is an attempt at reflection, based on the gospel and the experiences of men and women committed to the process of liberation in the oppressed and exploited land of Latin America. It is a theological reflection born of the experience of shared efforts to abolish the current unjust situation and to build a different society, freer and more human. Many in Latin America have started along the path of a commitment to liberation, and among them is a growing number of Christians; whatever the validity of these pages, it is due to their experiences and reflections. My greatest desire is not to betray their experiences and efforts to elucidate the meaning of their solidarity with the oppressed.[92]

How does Gutiérrez take these experiences to the level of reflection and argue for the *Christian* need for a political commitment to the liberation of the oppressed? Gutiérrez takes his cue from the aforementioned Vatican II documents. He claims that the answer must lie in an integrated vision of history in which the process of political liberation and the goal of eschatological salvation meet. But this, in turn, requires a transformation in our understanding of salvation, a transformation that the Vatican II documents already imply. The point lies in the transition from what Gutiérrez calls a quantitative view of salvation to a qualitative approach.

The quantitative viewpoint, which overlaps with the Christendom Mentality, focuses on the number of people saved. Its main concern is the question of *who* will be saved, struggling with the problem of the salvation of those who do not know Christ (so-called pagans, other religions, etc.). This is the Church of the "extra ecclesiam nulla salus." In twentieth-century Catholic theology, Gutiérrez notes, this problem has been basically settled. All people are called to communion with God, regardless of their religious affiliation, because God's grace is present in all things and moves all creatures, sometimes secretly. Hence, religious belonging cannot be the determining factor.[93] Instead, salvation becomes a qualitative issue; the question is about the *how* of salvation.

Yet this requires revisiting what constitutes sin, since salvation is ultimately the redemption of the creature from sin in order to attain full communion with its creator. The Christian tradition has always held that sin is, at its most fundamental level, breaking with God *and* neighbor. It follows that returning to communion with God implies reconstituting *both* relationships. But this cannot be accomplished trans-historically or, at least, not *only* in that way. The tradition is also clear in this regard. No sacrifice to God is legitimate if there is hatred among brothers and sisters. Reconciliation must take place first (Matthew 5:23–24). Further, the attention given to our brothers and sisters, especially to the least among us, is essential for our salvation; significantly more essential than our religious beliefs (Matthew 25:31–46). Salvation, then, understood as redemption from sin is not an otherworldly pursuit: "Salvation—the communion of human beings with God and among themselves— is something which embraces all human reality, transforms it, and leads it to its fullness in Christ."[94]

This approach decisively affects the religious significance of human action in history. As Gutiérrez stresses: "The absolute value of salvation— far from devaluating this world—gives it its authentic meaning and its own autonomy, because salvation is already latently there."[95] Salvation, therefore, becomes an "intrahistorical reality . . . [that] orients, transforms, and guides history to its fulfillment." Or, put differently: "The salvific action of God underlies all human existence. The historical destiny of humanity must be placed definitively in the salvific horizon."[96]

Gutiérrez's approach to the sociopolitical history of Latin America is decidedly *theocentric*, or perhaps more specifically, *Christocentric*. Gutiérrez reaches his conclusions about the role of the Christian believer in the struggles of liberation not solely from his political analysis but fundamentally from his "critical reflection on praxis *in light of the Gospel*."[97] Social and political analysis are crucial, but ultimately they are subsumed in the theological analysis that gives priority to the authority of the Christian scriptures and their interpretation by the tradition:

The ultimate reason for commitment to the poor and oppressed is not to be found in the social analysis we use, or in human compassion, or in any direct experience we may have of poverty. These are all doubtless valid motives that play an important part in our commitment. As Christians, however, our commitment is grounded, in the final analysis, in the God of our faith. It is a theocentric, prophetic option that has its roots in the unmerited love of God and is demanded by this love.[98]

The novelty of Gutiérrez is that he creatively reinterprets the Christian tradition's construal of key biblical themes and their theological developments in order to create an opening for a radically different, indeed revolutionary, construal of the relationship between Christian faith and social justice. However, crucial innovations must take place *within* the recognizable parameters of a tradition in order to be effective agents of change. The reason why I believe Gutiérrez's liberation theology has been such a crucial agent of change is that it was able to remain within the boundaries of still recognizable mainstream Christian theological reflection. Yet it took the Christian tradition to a qualitatively different moment of reflection by making the question of poverty and social injustice a fundamentally systemic and structural issue. In this sense, liberation theology has been crucial in a still-in-the-making transformation of Christianity, in which the response to the systemic problem of social inequality is no longer solely charity and almsgiving but a correlative systemic critique and proposal of new social structures.

The Unity of History: Creation, Re-creation, and Integral Liberation

I turn now to the last steps of Gutiérrez's justification of the political role of the Christian believer. The key issue is a new reading of the relationship between profane and sacred histories. Instead of embracing that dichotomy, Gutiérrez builds on and expands the insights provided by some of the key documents of Vatican II. Thus, he advances an integrated approach in which history is unified. In order to do so, Gutiérrez must justify his argument, appealing to the tradition itself in order to transform it. Gutiérrez's innovation consists of drawing conclusions that were implicit in the tradition yet never fully embraced. His accomplishment was to maintain that true salvation requires historical liberation, and that historical liberation cannot happen through charity alone. Rather, it requires the undoing of all forms of institutionalized oppression: economic, political, racial, sexual, and so forth.

This new creative interpretation was decisively prompted by a new awareness of the traumatic experiences caused by the massive poverty and marginalization of millions in Latin America. In this sense, what we see here is the transformation of institutionalized forms of violence into positive value commitments through the development of a new narrative, a new Christian narrative. Accordingly, liberation theology stands between the creation of something new and the re-creation of already existing values, becoming a prophetic voice that sets in motion a major process of moral reorientation.[99] In an analogous context, social theorist Hans Joas writes:

[This] underlines the fact that there are impulses at work within processes of cultural innovation that change publicly established situational interpretations. This may involve attempts to articulate experiences that the subject feels are not adequately expressed by public interpretations. But it may also be that the potential of an already available interpretative system is mobilized afresh; this often entails taking more seriously perceptions that were already possible, and indeed existed previously, but whose explosive force was suppressed by prevailing interpretations.[100]

Gutiérrez was able to produce this new prophetic narrative through his reinterpretation of the Christian understanding of salvation history.[101]

According to his proposal, we should understand the act of creation as the first salvific act. Creation is the beginning of human history. More importantly, the tradition teaches that this is not an isolated act that lacks intentionality or continuity in time. Rather, creation is an invitation to ultimate communion with God at the end of time, an invitation that is assisted by God throughout history. God intervenes in history, though historical acts that we should understand as permanent moments of re-creation in which the divine gives the creature sustenance to fulfill its goal.[102]

But the ultimate goal of salvation and communion with God is undermined by sin. Sin disrupts our relationship with God and the neighbor, as we noted earlier. Therefore, salvation requires liberation from sin; from our personal sin and from all captivities that the sins of others may produce as well.[103] In the Christian scriptures, this liberation takes several forms. However, its most paradigmatic moment in the Old Testament (and *the* most fundamental moment for the Jewish faith) is the liberation of the people of Israel from their Egyptian captivity. Gutiérrez highlights two key aspects of this. First, it is a historical event: the divine intervenes *in* history to liberate God's people from concrete situations of oppression. Second, this is not merely an act of inward, spiritual liberation, but the liberation from Egypt is a *political* act: "It is the breaking away from a situation of despoliation and misery and the beginning of the construction of a just and fraternal society. It is the suppression of disorder and the creation of a new order."[104]

Indeed, the Book of Exodus makes this plain. God is keenly aware of the situation of oppression of the people of Israel and knows that this oppression is caused by the abuses of Pharaoh and his system of slavery. So, God gives to Israel a liberator: Moses. It is through the leadership of Moses and the permanent sustenance of God that the people of Israel will be ultimately liberated. Not, of course, without pain and hesitation; even with Israel's attempts of returning to slavery instead of believing in the promises of God. As Gutiérrez notes, the liberation from Egypt is not an immediate and difficulty-free process:

A gradual pedagogy of successes and failures would be necessary for the Jewish people to become aware of the roots of their oppression, to struggle against it, and to perceive the profound sense of the liberation to which they were called. The Creator of the world is the Creator and Liberator of Israel, to whom is entrusted the mission of establishing justice.[105]

Gutiérrez sees this as a process of re-creation in history: "The God who makes the cosmos from chaos is the same God who leads Israel from alienation to liberation."[106] Hence the importance of this event, celebrated in the Jewish Passover. Indeed, the centrality of this liberating narrative permeates the memory and biblical texts of the Jewish tradition, but it is also present in the New Testament through new readings and retrievals. The writings of Saint Paul are clear in this regard. In them (Colossians 1:15–20, 1 Corinthians 8:6, Hebrews 1:2, and Ephesians 1:1–22, for instance), we see Paul inserting the work of Christ in this trajectory of creation and re-creation starting from the beginning of time by God the Father. Ultimately, it is in the redemptive action of Christ that the act of re-creation-through-liberation finds its complete fulfillment.[107]

For Gutiérrez, the theme of creation-liberation-re-creation is fundamentally connected to another major theme in the interpretation of the biblical tradition. He writes: "The Bible is the book of the Promise, the Promise made by God to human beings, the efficacious revelation of God's love and self-communication; simultaneously it reveals humankind to itself."[108] In the Christian tradition, the belief in a God who promises good news (eu-angelion) has a central role. Yet, since there is sin and injustice in the world, these loving promises can only take place through a process of liberation-re-creation through which each person and the human family as a whole will truly be able to enter into communion with each other. Further, since in a world of great injustices some suffer more than others, this love and these liberating promises have a preferential addressee: the poor and marginalized. However, these are *eschatological* promises:

> The Promise is revealed, appeals to humankind, and is fulfilled throughout history. The Promise orients all history towards the future and thus puts revelation in an eschatological perspective. Human history is in truth nothing but the history of the slow, uncertain, and surprising fulfillment of the Promise.[109]

We should draw two important points from this citation. The first is that "the Promise is a gift accepted in faith."[110] In this sense, the belief in God's promises of ultimate liberation, communion, and love is based on deep commitment to realities that people of faith have not seen yet fulfilled but that they expect in hope. However, faith in ideals beyond the real has great impact in human affairs. Ideals give us orientation and motivation to enact them in practice, even if they cannot ever be fully achieved. I will return to this topic in subsequent chapters.

On the other hand, precisely because of these reasons, we should keep in mind that the political engagement advocated by liberation theologians was always very aware of the incomplete nature of any human attempt to achieve liberation. Liberation can only find its fullest form eschatologically, in Christ. However, this does not mean that Christians should remain passive vis-à-vis the many forms of captivity and oppression people experience in the world. It only means that all works of liberation will always be inherently limited, awaiting their complete fulfillment in the end times.

In this sense, Gutiérrez attempts to find balance between those who believe that the Christian faith is exclusively spiritual and inward and those who maintain that sociopolitical change is enough for true liberation. Gutiérrez interprets both the Old and New Testament traditions as rejecting this dichotomy, arguing instead for the progressive fulfillment of God's promises throughout history. Progression here should be identified neither with a naïve conception of progress nor with theological supersessionism.[111] Great moments of disruption like the Holocaust and the steady presence of injustice are permanent reminders of our human brokenness and of the devastatingly tragic aspects of history.[112] Nevertheless, the point here is that a faith-based interpretation of history may still find hope in a God of Life and in the eventual fulfillment of the divine promises—some, always partially, in human history, and some only in the final encounter between creator and creature.

This is further explained if we pay attention to Gutiérrez's threefold definition of the process of liberation. For Gutiérrez, first:

> *liberation* expresses the aspirations of oppressed people and social classes, emphasizing the conflictual aspect of the economic, social, and political process which puts them at odds with wealthy nations and oppressive classes.[113]

Gutiérrez makes central to the process of liberation the struggle of the oppressed themselves. They are the main agents of the process; the theoretical work of theologians and intellectuals only attempts to articulate *that* foundational experience. For this reason, Gutiérrez's liberation theology understands theological reflection as a "second act." The "first act" is constituted by a contemplative attitude toward the experiences of faith, solidarity, and commitment of the believer, especially the poor.[114] He has called these experiences the "irruption of the poor,"[115] referring to the new recognition of the active presence of the marginalized in history and the growing awareness among them about their rights. Such awareness, however, makes explicit the latent conflict that exists in all societies, but especially those marked by massive systemic injustices. In this sense "liberation" means the end of a life lived in alienation, poverty, and disenfranchisement. Liberation here stands for the eradication of poverty understood as an evil that ultimately means anticipated and unjust death.[116]

Second, Gutiérrez continues:

> At a deeper level, *liberation* can be applied to an understanding of history. Humankind assuming conscious responsibility for its own destiny. . . . The gradual conquest of true freedom leads to the creation of a new humankind and a qualitatively different society.[117]

Here liberation focuses on the agency of individual and community, understood as the expansion of freedoms or capabilities to determine people's own destiny. We return here to the issue of a new creation. Yet this is a new creation that Gutiérrez does not understand in solely spiritual, inward, or individual terms. We find ourselves anew in the historical process. Gaining new awareness of our dignity and the sacredness of all human life, we decide to build a new society in which broken relations can be reestablished and justice can reign.

In this context we should situate what Gutiérrez and several others call "the preferential option for the poor." For this option, made by the poor themselves but also by all those who stand in solidarity with them, implies a moment of decision making in which individual and community become true agents of their own destiny. In doing so, people establish links of solidarity and decide to struggle together to make society more just, paying special (preferential) attention to those who suffer the most (the poor, broadly understood).[118] One may say that this is the moment for the creation of the conditions for the fulfillment of our freedom. Since the conditions do not fully exist and in many places are largely lacking, the process requires struggle. The goal is to have the possibility to choose the path that will bring to each of us fulfillment and happiness.

Finally, Gutiérrez concludes:

> the word *development* to a certain extent limits and obscures the theological problems implied in the process designated by this term. On the contrary, the word *liberation* allows for another approach leading to the Biblical sources which inspire

the presence and action of humankind in history. In the Bible, Christ is presented as the one who brings us liberation. Christ the Savior liberates from sin, which is the ultimate root of all disruption of friendship and of all injustice and oppression. . . . This is not a matter of three parallel or chronological successive processes, however. There are three levels of meaning of a single, complex process, which finds its deepest sense and its full realization in the saving work of Christ."[119]

Gutiérrez returns to some of my earlier observations, but the contrast with the second level of liberation is worth noting. Liberation in its second meaning points to freedom or the expansion of capabilities—that is, the expansion of our opportunities to choose and to act based on the "combination of personal abilities and the political, social, and economic environment."[120] That alone makes liberation a worthy goal. The same should be said about the struggle against oppressive structures, the first level. However, in Gutiérrez's view that is not enough—at least not from a theological viewpoint. In Christian theological terms, true liberation is salvation in Christ, in whom all history is recapitulated. Therefore, the process of historical liberation, of the struggles for emancipation and freedom, should be inserted within the larger single but complex process of divine creation and re-creation.

I take this point to be of great importance in two respects. First, it stands as a cautionary remark: no effort to bring liberation to our historical realities should ever be understood as final. This is an especially powerful word of caution against ideological coaptations of the message of Christian liberation that attempt to identify this process with the agenda of some political project. Instead, the eschatological horizon makes the believer more contingency-conscious and perhaps humbler in regard to the depth of the transformations that can be produced.

Second, this is also an invitation to remain hopeful. No human action can produce the kind of transformation we would like to see realized. Yet the believer may indeed have faith that for God nothing is impossible. Such belief can become a source of nurturing and strength, especially in the context of repression and death that often accompanies the struggle for liberation.[121] As we will see in subsequent chapters, such faith has been a key component in the activism of liberation theologians and laypeople who have remained committed to the preferential option for the poor, even under the most dangerous, pressing, and disheartening circumstances.

2

In Permanent Revolution

THE HERMENEUTICS OF THE
CHRISTIAN TRADITION

The preceding chapter not only offers an initial response to some of the pressing questions that this book attempts to answer, but it also opens new paths of inquiry. New questions are now before us. Indeed, conceiving liberation *and* salvation as part of a single, complex process—following and expanding the intuitions of Vatican II—allows Gutiérrez to find an answer that, without ever reducing faith to politics, frees the religious believer to become active in politics *as a believer*, based on the deep conviction that God deeply cares for creation and opposes all forms of oppression. However, we must now ask if his new articulation of the relationship between faith and politics, the religious and the secular, works.[1]

This powerful articulation depends on a variety of not-always-stated assumptions: certain conception of God and the sacred, an account of God's revelation and the human experience of such event, a correlative stance on biblical revelation and its interpretation, a conception of theology as praxis-oriented, and so much more. More important than anything, it depends on a particular understanding of how traditions work and, hence, of how they can be transformed. Therefore, we need to step back and unpack Gutiérrez's nonexplicit hermeneutics of the Christian tradition to further explain if his new articulation of faith and politics works as a relatively adequate *Christian* response to the problem of the political engagement of the Christian believer.

At the core of this contention, of course, is the fundamental fact that the meaning of being a Christian is "essentially contested," allowing multiple and not seldom antagonistic interpretations.[2] But not all interpretations are perceived as equally valid; in fact, not all can be valid. Some of Gutiérrez's critics, for instance, argued that his interpretation of faith and politics was an illegitimate blend of Christianity and Marxism. As I have shown in the preceding chapter and will further demonstrate in the following one, this is a misguided criticism. Nevertheless, the fact that this criticism emerged and still has some credit in certain circles suggests that it is crucial to provide further clarification about how secular and religious ideas relate. This chapter is devoted to all these issues. Then, in the next chapter, having gained some conceptual clarity, I return to liberation theology, this time examining the actual implications of Gutiérrez's new articulation in the life of many Christians committed to the struggle for liberation.

One of the central claims of this chapter—and of the book as a whole—is that religious traditions are always-already self-interpreting traditions, that they are always searching for definition, and that this fluidity is not the mere result of exogenous influences but part of the nature of what religious traditions are. Hence, religious traditions are in constant dialogue with their surroundings, permanently negotiating their loyalties and trying to respond creatively to internal and external demands. Indeed, as H. Richard Niebuhr maintains (referring to the Christian tradition), religious traditions are in "permanent revolution."[3]

My argument proceeds as follows: First, I provide a sketch of how religious experience takes place and is articulated, in dialogue with the work of Paul Ricœur. Second, I draw from this basic blueprint to focus on the articulation of religious experience in religious *traditions*, particularly in the Christian tradition. To that end, I present a sociological account of how traditions work in order to understand the Christian articulation of the religious experience of encountering Jesus of Nazareth both as a person and as a tradition himself. Third, I turn to the development of criteria to determine the fundamental elements of the Christian tradition. Here, the contributions of theologian David Tracy are of great importance. My goal is to highlight that the "Christian classic"—the self-manifestation of God in the person and the event of Jesus Christ—is characterized by its permanence and excess of meaning, and to show that this leads to plurality and ambiguity in its interpretation. Hence, what is needed is the development of criteria for relatively adequate interpretations.[4] Lastly, I go beyond the criteria for relatively adequate interpretations, stressing the necessary conditions for a constructive Christian theological language. Here Tracy's concept of the "analogical imagination" is crucial.

Manifestation-Proclamation-Institutionalization

Paul Ricœur's seminal essay "Manifestation and Proclamation" is a good starting point to address the articulation of what we may call "self-transcending experiences." By this term, following Hans Joas, I refer to experiences that take the self out of the realm of its ordinary self-centeredness and confront it with what is beyond its boundaries, often leaving some kind of mark, strong memory, or affective attachment. These experiences do not have to be positive or moral in quality: self-transcending experiences can emerge out of profound suffering and can also lead to the infliction of suffering on others, to violence, and so on.[5]

Hence, experiences of self-transcendence constitute special cases of distortions of ordinary meaning that demand interpretation. In fact, in their deeper forms they demand what theologian William Schweiker calls moments of "radical interpretation," meaning "reflective, critical inquiry aimed at the question of what has constituted our lives in terms of what we care about and what ought to guide our lives."[6] What matters for now is that in the process of articulating these experiences, *religious* interpretations emerge. However, religious interpretations are not the only ones produced. Political, aesthetic, psychological, and moral interpretations of the *same events* may develop as well. It is precisely this common ground that enables translation and communication using our analogical imagination, our capacity to see similarity-in-difference, a key idea in the work of David Tracy that will allow me to further warrant Gutiérrez's new articulation.[7] It is in this context that we should locate Ricœur's pivotal essay, whose decisive influence in Tracy's *The Analogical Imagination* will help me to tighten the argument of this chapter and of the book as a whole.[8]

Even though Ricœur, perhaps too quickly, identifies his object of study as "the sacred" instead of using a more encompassing category like "self-transcendence," he still offers a helpful blueprint for my own argument. In his essay, Ricœur distinguishes two dimensions in the interpretation of the sacred: *manifestation* and *proclamation*. He also maintains that they can be associated with the disciplines of phenomenology and hermeneutics, respectively.[9]

For Ricœur, "manifestation" has four basic traits that emphasize its almost exclusive phenomenological side.[10] First, the manifestation of the sacred is "experienced as awesome, as powerful, as overwhelming."[11] Here hermeneutics does not have a role because what we have is pure manifestation, a pure excess of givenness. Ricœur here is developing an analytical category accentuating difference, but he might have hardened the distinctions too much; the intense manifestation of something that gives itself to us cannot be identified with the sacred if, for one, language and conceptual categories for the sacred are not already in place.

It is probably wiser to speak of highly intense experiences of self-transcendence, perhaps experiences of effervescence as Émile Durkheim called them.[12] In addition, it is probably more accurate to insert "manifestation" in the level of what philosopher Johann Michel calls "proto-interpretations," that is, *pre-reflexive* operations by which we select among the signs that constitute the world that surrounds us.[13] In this way we can preserve Ricœur's intention correcting his overemphasis on the antihermeneutical dimensions of manifestation. Thus, we can certainly assert that here we have no hermeneutics if we defend a restricted meaning of the task of interpretation, in which *reflexive* procedures are developed to *consciously* attempt to solve a problem. Nevertheless, there is a proto-interpretative moment since the "pure givenness" Ricœur stresses is always interpreted-givenness, although in ways that are not thematized and may well be the product of cultural schemes.[14]

Noting this, Ricœur is right to identify experiences of especially great affective intensity as one of the fundamental elements of what we tend to call *religious* experiences. Another key aspect implied in the notion of givenness is that, at least in principle, those who have these intense experiences do not see themselves as causing them. The experience comes from elsewhere; the spatial metaphor "from above" is commonly used to describe these experiences.[15]

Second, Ricœur describes this manifestation of the sacred or numinous as a *hierophany*. By this Ricœur means that the sacred cannot be accessed directly by us, but that it can reveal itself to us through certain forms, structures, articulations. Rocks, trees, natural phenomena, but also certain cultural forms of behavior may become vehicles, "saturated with efficacy,"[16] by which the sacred manifests itself. Remaining in the world of the ordinary, the sacred becomes, at the same time, surreal (super-real). Here again linguistic articulations are largely absent. The emphasis is on manifestation, on the intense experience of being seized by a powerful disruptive experience that pushes us to transcend the ordinary boundaries of the self.[17] Furthermore, these experiences can also transcend the *selves*. As Ricœur here suggests and Durkheim's work demonstrates, certain forms of ritual become efficacious vehicles for the kind of "collective effervescence" that takes people out of themselves and puts them in contact with a reality that seems greater and higher.

Third, Ricœur highlights the importance of symbolism and ritual for the manifestation of the sacred. Some of these expressions (sacred spaces, liturgies, festivals) are forms of saturation through which the sacred is revealed. It is true, Ricœur acknowledges, that here discourse, and myth especially, may have greater participation than in prior stages of manifestation. Yet he also claims that the linguistic dimension is not autonomous and that therefore the analysis of these forms of manifestation remains a phenomenological and not a hermeneutical task: "The function of the myth is to fix the paradigms of the ritual that sacralize action. Today we read myths, transforming them into literature, but we have previously uprooted them from the act of recitation that had bound them to ritual action."[18]

Lastly, Ricœur considers the role of the natural elements. Ricœur admits again that the elements manifest insofar as they are interpreted symbolically. Thus, we have some "minimal hermeneutics." However, this is a *bound symbolism*, that is, a kind of interpretation that emerges *only* as a consequence of "the sacred valences of the elements themselves." Put differently, if symbolic interpretations are possible, it is because of the saturation of the phenomena themselves: "the showing founds the saying, not vice versa."[19] Perhaps we should say that the minimal hermeneutics is present in all four stages of manifestation in the form of proto-interpretations of varying degree. However, Ricœur's overall point stands: at the phenomenological level, one of the most salient elements of what we often call religious experiences is the experience of being seized by a powerful encounter in which we are not primarily or actively using our cognitive interpretative functions.

This fundamentally phenomenological account of manifestation corrects Ricœur's own tendency to overstress the importance of the "model of text." As Michel notes, this is a limitation of Ricœur's approach. But this limitation has negative implications for the regional hermeneutics of the sacred in decisive, although perhaps less obvious, ways. Joas perceptively notes that Ricœur tends to favor the hermeneutics of sacred *texts* in his writings about religion. Of course, such an approach is perfectly valid, especially for religious traditions for which a sacred text is an essential part of their formation and self-interpretation. Nevertheless, this preference for the "model of the text" tends to leave aside another crucial component of religious traditions: religious *experiences*. Moreover, many forms of religious articulation emerge from experiences of self-transcendence in which there is no presence of a sacred text at all.[20] Hence, the importance of the preceding account of "the logic of manifestation" as an attempt to strike a balance between protohermeneutical and strictly hermeneutical approaches to religious experience.[21]

To return to Ricœur's essay: The key issue here is that experiences of manifestation naturally lead to the need to stabilize and communicate them. Experiences that create distortions of meaning demand interpretation *precisely* to restore understanding, to return to a point where things make sense again. But this often requires new articulations. In the context of religious experiences, Ricœur calls this process the "logic of proclamation."

Here is where the hermeneutical stage proper emerges. Ricœur uses Judaism and Christianity as his main examples. In the Hebraic faith, Ricœur argues, we see a major transition from the logic of correspondences and numinous ritual manifestations to the linguistic articulation of the experience of the sacred. As he notes, in Judaism "the word outweighs the numinous."[22] Moreover, following Gerhard von Rad, he claims that the whole faith of Israel is organized around certain fundamental *discourses*. But this idea applies to the Bible in general. What we see there is a variety of discursive modes that, in Ricœur's view, are "diametrically opposed to the logic of correspondences. This new logic is the logic of limit-expressions."[23] Furthermore, this discursive articulation has a fundamental *ethical* substratum with concrete implications in history. The logic of proclamation implies a radical attempt to desacralize all sense of assurance, certitude, participation, or identity produced by the logic of manifestation. Instead, proclamation, paradigmatically expressed in the cry of the prophets, reminds all believers of the wrath of the Lord against those who adore idols and do not do justice.[24]

Against the sense of certainty and full participation in the sacred produced by the logic of manifestation, these discursive modes—parables, proverbs, and eschatological sayings—attempt to collapse our horizon of signification, to destabilize our religious assurance. Their goal is to interrupt the continuous sequence of life by dislocating our imagination, inviting us to pause and transcend the ordinary world of the self. This is accomplished through different rhetorical techniques where the appeal to paradox and to the "intensification" of proverbial formulas, for instance, is key.[25]

Take an example crucial for liberation theology, but also a formative text in the history of the Christian tradition: Matthew 25:31–46. This text, known in many translations as the parable of the final judgment, deserves particular attention given its location in the Gospel of Matthew, its focus on the poor, and its presentation of the ultimate limit-situation, namely, an eschatological judgment. The first thing we see in the passage is the Son of Man (huios tou anthropou) coming in his glory, something dramatically expressed by the presence of the angels and the throne (v. 31). Before him, all the nations (panta ta ethne, v. 31) will be gathered and the people will be divided much as when a shepherd separates sheep from goats (vv. 32–33).

A second sequence starts after the "then" (tote) at the very beginning of verse 34. The Son of Man is no longer mentioned and now "the king" becomes the center of the narrative. The king, however, is in continuity with the actions of the Son of Man given that he addresses those separated by him in verses 32–33. Now moral judgment is explicit: those at the right of the king, "the righteous" (hoi dikaioi, v. 37), will inherit the kingdom (v. 34), the eternal life (v. 46); those at his left will inherit eternal fire (v. 41). What is the reason for this radical separation? The answer is provided by the two almost identical speeches of the king (vv. 34–40 and vv. 41–45).

In order to inherit the kingdom, it is necessary to be merciful to the least of the king's brothers.[26] This mercy, however, is not an interested and instrumental one: the righteous did not help the hungry, the thirsty, the stranger, the naked, the sick, and the imprisoned because they were expecting any reward. Indeed, they did not know in advance that by helping the needy they were helping the king himself. This is proved by their surprise in verses 37–39. Their righteousness lies *precisely* in their lack of explicit knowledge: they were gratuitously merciful. In contrast, the ones at the king's left, without previous knowledge of reward or punishment, were uncompassionate with the suffering of the least of the king's brothers and sisters, and therefore they will perish.[27]

I use this example because it shows quite radically what Ricœur has in mind with his idea that the limit-expressions of the sacred text can produce destabilizing limit-experiences. He writes:

Religious language—at least *this* religious language—uses limit-expressions only to open up our very experience, to make it explode in the direction of experiences that themselves are limit-experiences. The parable, we said, redescribes experience. But it does not redescribe it in the fashion of one more poetic language among others, but according to its intending of the *extreme*.[28]

Ricœur's point is that the biblical text presents to us a surplus of meaning that attempts to bring the reader or hearer of the word to a limit-situation. The text itself qua text, qua linguistic product, is saturated with meaning, but in its saturation it stops being *just* a text and becomes a limit-experience itself, which saturates *our horizon* as readers and hearers of the word.

Let us return to Matthew 25 to flesh out this idea. The text is inherently paradoxical because it makes possible what is impossible. How is it possible to know what is unknowable? More clearly: How can we know *in the present* what is reserved for the *eschatological times*? We cannot. And yet the text tells us that we can. If we love the poor, the sick, the imprisoned, we will enjoy eternal bliss. If we do not, we will suffer eternal damnation. God's will reveals itself clearly in the text, it seems. Yet the text also introduces a destabilizing element: *not* knowing God's will but acting *as if* they did is what brought the gift of salvation to its recipients. We witness here a complex dynamic of veiling and unveiling of meaning, precisely due to the excess of signification presented through the text.

Yet Ricœur maintains that this excess of meaning and destabilizing power of the logic of proclamation allows it to fuse in several ways with the logic of manifestation:

All the antinomies upon which our mediation has been based now need to be reconsidered. The word, we said, breaks away from the numinous. And this is true. But it is not so to the extent that the word takes over for itself the functions of the numinous? There would be no hermeneutic if there were no proclamation. But there would be no proclamation if the word, too, were not powerful; that is, if it did not have the power to set forth the new being it proclaims. A word that is addressed to us rather than our speaking it, a word that constitutes us rather than our articulating it—a word that speaks—does not such a word reaffirm the sacred just as much as abolish it? It does so if hearing this word is impossible without a transvaluation of the values *tremendum* and *fascinosum* into obedience and fervor. For my part, I cannot conceive of a religious attitude that did not proceed from "a feeling of absolute dependence." And is this not the essential relation of humankind to the sacred, transmuted into speech and, in this way, reaffirmed at the same time it is surpassed?[29]

Based on this citation and my prior remarks in this section, we can draw some important conclusions. Religious experiences appear to be founded on intense, affective—both subjective and collective—experiences of self-transcendence. Moreover, these experiences seize us and are not understood as produced by our own power. In theistic traditions, this leads to the notion of the divine and even to the unification of divine power in the idea of one God—in monotheism. Lastly, they leave a mark on us, transforming—often radically—the way we see ourselves and our surroundings. Hence the presence of notions like "being born again," "new beginning," "conversion," and the like as ways to describe religious experiences.[30]

These experiences are then further socialized and articulated. At some point, in some places, these experiences are recorded in writing. Now they do not depend solely on memory or the experience of the first witnesses. Now they can be shared beyond the originating context. However, the process of recording these experiences in writing implies distancing oneself from the moment of original manifestation. Naturally, this destabilizes the original sense of full participation in the sacred. Self-doubt and criticism emerge in some of these writings. An ethic of suspicion develops, warning us of any attempt to identify human projects and actions with the divine will, undermining any self-assurance or self-righteousness.[31] Yet this ethic has positive content as well, as was evident in the example of Matthew 25. Further, the telling and retelling of some of these intense experiences may elicit new ones through intensification devices inserted in the texts themselves. The process can potentially be endless, depending on the intensity of the originating experience and its creative reception by future generations.

What matters at this point is that the dialectic of manifestation and proclamation gives us a sense of the general pattern taking place in the articulation of religious experiences. Since religious experiences are characterized for their self-transcending, intense, transformative character, it is natural that we will not be able to articulate and communicate them *fully*.[32] Rather, their surplus of meaning elicits a dialectic of disclosure and concealment that both undermines and allows the production of meaning. Indeed, the assurance of unity with the sacred elicited by the logic of manifestation is almost simultaneously undermined by the logic of proclamation. This reminds us of the radical distance between the human and the divine.[33] Further, this dialectic is also a cautionary reminder that prevents any easy identification of our human projects with the divine will. Lastly, this dialectic is an ethical invitation to always care for the oppressed and most vulnerable, especially if their suffering is caused by religiously justified forms of violence that attempt to erase the dialectic of disclosure and concealment.

Now, these observations should make us consider whether a third element could be added to this dialectic. Although not radically different from the other two, I believe that there is room to consider what I would like to call the *institutionalization* of meaning. By this I mean a moment of distanciation from the original disclosure that retains some of the commanding force of the originating event, as it happens with the logic of proclamation. However, the institutionalization of meaning operates at the level of *explication* and *justification*. This is precisely the role of the doctrinal genre in the Christian tradition, as we will see shortly: the doctrinal genre depends on manifestation and is essential for proclamation, but it operates mostly at the level of rational justification. In this sense, the process of institutionalization of meaning has a central role in the development of religious *traditions,* but not so much in the emergence of religious *experiences.*[34] In conversation with Cornelius Castoriadis, Joas further explains:

This does not imply that such rationalized discourse should not play any role at all. It is—in my eyes—the right instance for the justification and adjudication of cognitive and normative validity claims and thus crucial for parts of epistemology and moral philosophy. But Castoriadis's philosophy of creativity, novelty, and articulation points out—like pragmatism—that there is a wider framework—a framework in which the emergence of new hypotheses, new values . . . is taken into account and in which thus justification plays the role of critique, but cannot be considered to be constitutive itself.[35]

Therefore, what we see here is a pattern in the articulation of religious experience marked by the triad of manifestation-proclamation-institutionalization, in which each moment illuminates the other and becomes the precondition of any further articulations. Importantly, though, the same idea stated before still stands: deeply affective and transformative self-transcending experiences, among which religious experiences have a key role, cannot be *fully* articulated. This creates plurality and ambiguity in the narrative we produce about ourselves, our societies, and our traditions, but it also allows for their creative renewal. As Joas notes: "We might constantly strive for attunement between these levels, but we will only rarely and never permanently attain it. But in this very process—in the attempts to achieve this attunement—new values are produced."[36] To that effort to find attunement in the context of the Christian tradition I now turn.

Between Continuity and Innovation: Understanding the Christian Tradition

My argument so far has produced a sketch of a theory of interpretation of religious experience that allows us to understand the complexity of the process of articulating religious experiences. This process incorporates several layers of meaning-making, some so pre-reflective that we often do not notice them. Making sense of our experiences, of course, is particularly relevant when we face self-transcending experiences. These experiences are of very different kinds and depths, ranging from the disorientation produced by not following cues in a foreign culture and language to radical limit-experiences in which the power of what we may call the sacred seems to disrupt all prior understanding of the meaning of our lives. The latter are often described as religious experiences. However, as noted before, even though many of these experiences happen to the individual subject, as in the famous cases of the "religious geniuses" described by William James,[37] none of these experiences happen in true isolation. At the very least, they depend on certain evolutionary cognitive and linguistic developments, to which we must add prior cultural and social proto-interpretations. They also depend on the influence of some key meta-interpretations without which many of us could not have these experiences. Another way to express these ideas is to say that our efforts to articulate all our experiences, but especially those that we call "religious," take place within the framework of a *tradition*.

At its most basic level, a tradition is anything that is "transmitted or handed down from the past to the present."[38] A tradition may imply material objects, beliefs, practices, and institutions, and, very often, comprises all of them. Traditions must also have some recognizable elements, some basic patterns that establish continuity between past and present.[39] Yet these recognizable elements cannot be determined in *fully* adequate ways. Traditions, if they are *living* traditions and not only objects of study belonging to a long-dead past, have active participants in them. Traditions, therefore, are constantly subject to interpretation and re-creation. From this follows that only *relatively* adequate interpretations can be reached. These interpretations will identify the key elements of the tradition in a way that can be publicly acknowledged by the great majority of its adherents, always leaving room for creativity within certain general constraints and room for disagreement. This is the sociological side of what we already examined in the case of the articulation of religious experience at a more phenomenological level.

The very nature of these experiences renders the task of their articulation always incomplete. Introducing the complexities of the transmission of these experiences through history, from generation to generation, further aggravates the problem of which historical developments truly belong to a tradition and which do not. However, this problem is simultaneously an opportunity—and truly, the only path—for creative developments and innovation within a tradition. Given the inevitable plurality of articulations of the same foundational religious experience of a tradition (for instance, faith in Jesus Christ in the context of the Christian tradition), it is more accurate to speak of traditions *within* a larger tradition. In turn, acknowledging this plurality within allows the identification of "family resemblances" among shared ideals and practices without assuming absolute uniformity. This is especially true in the case of traditions like Christianity that have extended greatly over space and time.

In this regard, my approach to tradition is *pragmatic-hermeneutic* instead of normative or dogmatic. I focus on the actual historical trajectory of the tradition, investigating whether the ideals developed by the tradition have been embodied over time in the concrete *practices* that reflect them.[40] Consequently, I do not approach tradition (or the Christian tradition, more specifically) based on assumptions about what the tradition is or must be. In this sense, I embrace the relatively recent "turn" in the study of tradition, stressing the process of traditioning (tradere) over the content (traditum) that is supposed to be transmitted.[41]

Of course, practices embody ideals and, in this sense, tradere and traditum cannot be completely separated. Nonetheless, the analytical distinction is important because it allows one to see if certain ideals have really been embodied, if they have been given up, or if any of the many alternatives between these two options applies.[42] Sometimes ideals are *stated* as central tenets of the tradition but are not materialized in practices.[43] The focus on practices, then, not only makes the study of tradition more historically accurate; it also gives the critical edge that the "hermeneutics of suspicion" encourages.[44] As we already know, the emergence of liberation theology depends on this practical orientation ("orthopraxis," as liberation theologians call it) in the context of theological interpretation. Such a practice-oriented approach was crucial for the immanent critique of Christianity that liberation theologians pursued, underscoring, precisely, that many Christians have not truly committed to the stated ideals of the Christian tradition.

Jesus Christ: A Tradition

I turn now to the concrete case of the Christian tradition in order to expand on my previous observations. The point is not to produce a historically neutral account of the formation of Christianity. The goal is to highlight some of the experiences that led to the formation of the key ideals of the Christian tradition, in order to understand how the formation of new values can take place and, subsequently, properly situate the emergence of liberation theology.[45] In addition, despite my use of the singular noun "tradition," it is more accurate to speak of a plurality of Jesus-traditions and Christian traditions. This is true from the inception of the Jesus movement and more so when the movement developed over the centuries into a now millennia-old religion. However, despite this plurality, some unifying aspects bring together these different emphases or traditions within the tradition, creating an identifiable whole. To those unifying tenets I turn now.

What appears to be undeniable is that Jesus of Nazareth left a powerful mark among his followers. Getting to know this man, listening to him, and sometimes even just touching him, appears to have transformed many people's world in terms that very much resemble the overwhelming revelatory power that Ricoeur describes as inherent to the logic of manifestation. Indeed, the event of encountering Jesus appears to have seized its witnesses and to have left them with a deep sense of affective and subjective certainty. Something true and powerful happened to them. Clearly, more than a few people thought this man was no ordinary man. Some thought that he might be a prophet, perhaps God's chosen one; some even started to consider that he might be the very incarnation of the divine. People found in Jesus's preaching something transformative. There was something about his understanding of our relationship with the divine and the neighbor that stuck with people—something about his idea of merciful justice; something about the absolute value of human life; something about the special care for the poor, the sick, and all those who were left behind.[46]

In less than two generations, if we take Paul of Tarsus's letters as our referent, the self-transcending encounter with the person of Jesus became kerygma; proclaiming the good news became the standard way of sharing the Jesus-story. Theological constructions about the meaning of his life and death started to become more common too. Paul and many others started to see him as savior and justifier, forgiver of sins and giver of new life. This proclamation gave meaning to people's spiritual journeys and became a matrix by which to understand their place in the world, especially in a context where scarcity, foreign dominion, persecution, and death were part of their ordinary experience. But it did much more than that since the Jesus-movement soon expanded beyond its narrow originating context, that of the Jewish people in the Galilean region. In just a few generations, the followers of "The Way" became a massive movement that incorporated many people of non-Jewish origin, many of whom were wealthy and powerful.[47] Moreover, the movement kept growing as a tradition that has lasted until today and has spread all over the world.

But all this should point to a crucial issue, namely that the Jesus we know is the *Jesus-of-the-tradition*.[48] We know him through the witness and narrations of others. In a different piece of writing, perhaps one devoted to historical accuracy, that could be a liability. In our case, however, that very mediation reinforces the argument: the existence of such mediation and the presence of several accounts about the life and deeds of Jesus proves, from the value-formation point of view, that a powerful event indeed occurred. So powerful was it that it had to be shared. Using Ricœur's language, the logic of manifestation naturally led to the logic of proclamation. The self-transcending experience of witnessing Jesus's deeds and listening to his words invited his followers to share what they saw.

A crucial element in this process of transmission of the Jesus-story is that it soon became *written* transmission. The written proclamation of the belief in the manifestation of God in Jesus, what is often called the Christ-event, became a *normative* element of the tradition.[49] Of course, the weight of the written word has varied over the centuries and varies still now depending on the different theological and idiosyncratic orientations of the multiple Christian denominations. What matters, however, is that, despite these differences, the written proclamation of the Christ-event, especially in the New Testament, is a sine qua non of the Christian tradition. The explanation of this is twofold. First, the tradition only exists as we know it *because* it has been mediated through the biblical text. Second, the tradition has always deemed the biblical text to be a sacred word, indeed God's word. Consider the central role that the Prologue to the Gospel of John has in the Christian tradition, and how there "Logos" (word) is both identified with God (John 1:1: "the Word was God") and with the principle without which creation could not take place (John 1:3: "All things came into being through him, and without him not one thing came into being."). Hence, as noted before with reference to Ricœur, the written proclamation has also become a place of manifestation. The text itself is deemed locus revelationis; the Logos, Godself.

But the sacred text itself is a tradition,[50] or, more accurately, the product of multiple traditions within the canonical tradition. Here we face a complex and multilayered phenomenon that confirms the pattern of *manifestation-proclamation-institutionalization* that I identified earlier. For the sacred text is always-already the product of an interpretation (in our case, the proclamation of the Christ-event) and yet also the object that the subsequent tradition interprets. Hence, the text is *the product* of certain historical, cultural, social, and personal contexts, and the text is also *the producer* of new correlative historical, cultural, social, and personal contexts. It is precisely in the adequate correlation between originating events and the values they create, and subsequent new values that proceed from or give continuity to the original ones, that we find the substance and permanence of a tradition.

Traditions: Fundamental Tenets

My preliminary remarks on the Jesus-of-the-tradition should help us to identify some of the fundamental tenets of traditions. To start, we should find in the recognizable *continuity* between past and present a distinct feature of any tradition. Further, continuity is crucial for the sense of belonging of the adherents of a tradition, since tradition and identity formation are closely linked. This continuity between past and present is one crucial element in discerning between better or worse interpretations of the tradition. But, as noted before, the determination of such continuity can only be *relatively* adequate, first and foremost because of the inherent surplus of meaning of the originating event. The meaning cannot be easily contained and naturally unfolds in a plurality of interpretations. But there is a more practical side of this relative adequacy in the context of Christianity and all major, long-standing traditions. No interpreter can possess the totality of the tradition because its content has grown beyond the cognitive capacities of all human beings. Selection is inevitable. In fact, *selectivity* is another key component of any tradition.[51]

However, not all selections are equally adequate. The process of selection must be guided by some general norms and should develop some correctives as well.

This point is especially important in dealing with the "traditionalist" advocates of tradition, namely those who defend the "unchanging" or "perennial" character of a given tradition against so-called modernizing distortions; traditions are always-already selective, and their continuity over time requires selection as well.[52] From this follows that different emphases on different aspects of the tradition are perfectly natural within some general constraints. *Plurality* and *ambiguity*, then, are also key aspects of any long-standing and living tradition. No tradition is a single thing.[53] Hence, any attempt to deny the inherent plurality and ambiguity of tradition should be considered a selective emphasis itself often based on a somewhat arbitrarily *imagined* past.[54] This selective reconstruction of tradition comes, at best, from a desire to stabilize the tradition, giving its followers a sense of continuity and identity over time; at worst, it proceeds from a desire to manipulate people and accumulate power.[55] The latter point speaks to another important characteristic of any tradition, which connects to the prior normativity, continuity, selectivity, and plurality and ambiguity: *authority*.[56] Traditions, if they are living traditions, have power and authority over those who claim them. But, as with selectivity and normativity, the authoritative character of a tradition is merely a descriptive feature. The *truth value* of that authority, the question of whether it is well grounded or simply authoritarian, requires critical assessment.[57]

Therefore, the "modernization" of a tradition should be taken, prima facie, as a neutral phenomenon. *Change* and *innovation* are not antithetical to the idea of tradition. They are, in fact, inherent elements of it—so much so that even traditionalist interpreters who attempt to adhere "strictly" to the tradition often end up producing change. Sociologist Edward Shils writes: "'Strictness' itself opens questions which are not already answered and which must be answered . . . which will require new formulations [which] will entail varying degrees of modification."[58] Nonetheless, the inherent presence of change and innovation in traditions does not imply that all of them are appropriate, normative, or authoritative. Some may drastically contradict key tenets of the tradition, leading to the formation of something different. But that cannot be judged a priori; it requires the development of some basic criteria. Criteria, in turn, may well modify the tradition in unexpected ways, since the critical assessment of the ideals of a tradition may require its expansion and modification.[59]

Further, the traditional-versus-modern approach too easily presupposes "that ideas and patterns of simultaneous origin are consistent with each other: [whereas] those which originated at different times are necessarily in conflict."[60] But many ideals find their finest articulations in noncontemporaneous historical contexts. For instance, it is clear that some of the ideals presented in the New Testament regarding the sacredness of *all* human life find better articulation in the context of the democratic freedoms that started to emerge in the eighteenth century rather than in their contemporaneous highly hierarchical social structure of the first century. For similar reasons, as we saw in the previous chapter, Gutiérrez and Taylor interpret some key tenets of the process of secularization favorably. For them, only in a world in which ordinary life is fully affirmed we can see true transformational changes regarding questions of human rights, poverty, and injustice.

Another way to express all this is, in Shils's words, that "every orthodoxy in tradition is in incessant danger of breaking into heterodoxy."[61] And vice versa! Since traditions are never free from ambiguity, obscurity, and uncertainty, even the most well-intentioned attempts to maintain the core values of the tradition will naturally modify it in their effort to preserve it. In addition, we should note that the boundaries of a tradition are somewhat arbitrary and defined in different ways by people with varying degrees of authority. Often those holding positions of power in the tradition will define it "as homogeneous in composition and unilinear in interpretation."[62] However, this assessment is factually incorrect. Any, even superficial, examination of traditions like Catholicism, or liberalism, or Marxism will quickly be confronted with significant heterogeneity in each of them, although not without important family resemblances as well.

Another essential element of traditions is that they are inherently *pragmatic*. At first glance, this may appear counterintuitive since traditions tend to be associated with the retention of the past and, hence, with the attempt to maintain prior patterns of belief and action despite the emergence of new contexts. But this attempt, when we look at it closely, is grounded in the until-then practical efficacy of a tradition to respond to a problematic situation. In this sense, traditions should be understood as problem-solving interpretations.[63] But it would be a mistake to assume that this emphasis on the pragmatic dimension of traditions undermines their value, reducing our commitment to a tradition to its mere instrumentalization.

Traditions, especially religious traditions, attempt to provide a somehow coherent narrative that addresses some of the most fundamental questions about the orientation we give to our lives. Traditions deal with ideals, postulating values beyond their mere instrumentalization. And yet we cannot understand the stability and change of traditions if we do not pay attention to their pragmatic vein. Even the most precious *ideals*, like the Christian ideal of unconditional love for God and neighbor, must have some bearing in our *real* life. Otherwise, the tradition stops being a living tradition and becomes a mere object of the historical past. Selectivity, normativity, authority, change, and innovation respond to the need to provide a relatively adequate interpretation of the tradition that is able to speak to its practical needs. Moreover, as noted earlier, these are translated into *practices* that give life to the tradition. In the case of religious traditions, we can highlight some key practices: certain ways of reading and interpreting sacred texts, certain forms of celebrating the sacred mysteries, and certain ways of relating to the adherents of the tradition and to strangers.

It is this pragmatic stream of tradition that pushes its adherents to find new resources and conversation partners to resolve problems for which the tradition does not have an immediately available solution. As Shils notes, simply following and revering tradition is not the object of primary concern for most people.[64] Rather, their adherence to the tradition depends greatly on its problem-solving capacity ranging from the provision of resources to solve plainly everyday practical problems to the most fundamental questions about the meaning of life. If the tradition appears to have lost credit or capacity to give meaning to life, it may be abandoned altogether.[65] On other occasions, the perceived lack of relevance of the tradition may lead to a path of innovation that will reassure its contemporary value, but rarely without modification. In this latter process, the conversation or confrontation with other traditions is crucial and the outcomes vary greatly.[66]

Whatever the case, the exposure to other traditions is one of the most powerful driving forces of change and innovation in any given tradition. It may also be a main factor in the decline and extinction of a tradition, hence the frequent fear of exposure to alien worldviews among the strictest adepts of a tradition.[67] However, exposure to new methods, categories, and values may also be the saving grace of declining tradition and give it a new beginning.[68] Plus, the novelty brought to a given tradition should not be overstated; while innovations do take place, much of the tradition is often kept. Otherwise, the sense of continuity and of relative consensus over time is lost and, with it, the tradition itself.[69]

Lastly, this dialectic of continuity and innovation allows the emergence of *genuine* moments of creativity or re-creation.[70] Re-creation stands here for the process of creating something new *out of something we already had*. But re-creation also involves the imaginative, almost playful faculty that we tend to associate with creativity, so that the outcome is never fully predictable or teleological, despite the intentions of the interpreters.[71] The key aspect of these genuine moments of creativity in the context of a tradition is that they do not attempt to get rid of what is given to us by the tradition. Rather, genuine moments of creativity aim to include the otherness of the tradition within its own-ness.[72] This often happens by re-interpreting texts, ideals, and the role of certain figures in order to make their meaning more current or to assert the "original" meaning, allegedly lost or made opaque because of the passage of time, problems in the transmission of the ideas, or the intentional corruption of the tradition.

Jesus Christ: Tradition, Person, and Event

I conclude this brief taxonomy of tradition by returning to the Christian tradition and connecting our findings to its main figure, Jesus Christ. As has been established, traditions have among their main characteristics the following: *selectivity, normativity, authority, pragmatism, plurality and ambiguity*, and *continuity-in-innovation*. One of the main reasons why these features are constitutive of major traditions and, hence, of the Christian tradition, is that they originate in and permanently interpret events characterized by their surplus of meaning.

Theologian David Tracy has called these events "classics," assigning them two main notes: "permanence and excess of meaning," which, in turn, "always demand[s] interpretation, never mere repetition nor simplistic rejection."[73] He adds: "What we mean in naming certain texts, events, images, rituals, symbols and persons 'classics' is that here we recognize nothing less than the disclosure of a reality we cannot but name truth."[74] This permanent and excessive meaning not only demands interpretation but cannot ever reach a definitive one: the task of interpretation remains open, demanding that the interpreter enter the back-and-forth movement of disclosure and concealment of truth that takes place when we are confronted with a classic event.[75] In this sense, following Ricœur, Tracy sees in the manifestation-proclamation dialectic a paradigmatic form of articulation of the classics.[76] Further, although without using that name, Tracy acknowledges the importance of the institutionalization of meaning in that dialectic as well. We will see shortly that for Tracy the disclosing of the truth of the classic event depends on the capacity of each tradition of interpretation to stabilize meaning and develop certain correctives. Key among them, in Christianity, is the doctrinal genre, which is a paradigmatic form of institutionalization of meaning.

Drawing from this framework, Tracy argues that we can identify *religious* classics as "the self-manifestation (and concealment) of the whole by the power of the whole."[77] Tracy is well aware of the problems of providing a definition of religion, but after examining the issue in detail he concludes that religions tend to be marked by their concern "to articulate some sense of the whole" which, in turn, informs, transforms, and even forms all areas of life.[78] Moreover, this concern tends to emerge in limit-situations that pose limit-questions about the meaning of everything and that, often, point to what may well be its source ("the whole"; "God," for the monotheistic religions; etc.). It is in this context, with the already established permanence and excess of meaning, that we speak of "religious classics" as the self-manifestation (and concealment) of the whole/God by its own power. Hence, religious classics confront us with the *possibility* of revelation. Playing with Rudolf Otto's famous definition, Tracy maintains that religious classics may, at least, confront us with the tremendum; but they can also elicit faith and lead us to the fascinans.[79]

When we turn to Christianity, the general definition of a classic is further specified. In Tracy's view, the *Christian* religious classic is the *person* of Jesus of Nazareth and the belief in the *event* of the self-manifestation of the divine in him (the Christ-event).[80] This *person-and-event* piece is crucial; as the previous arguments have established, we only know the person *through the tradition* that believed and believes that Jesus was not only a man but the incarnation of the divine self. This means that our access to the Christian religious classic is conditioned by a process of distanciation from the original *manifestation* (the historical encounter with Jesus of Nazareth) through the oral and written *proclamation* of that experience (now turned, in faith, into the Christ-event). From this complex process follows that religious experience is characterized by both participation-nonparticipation in the self-manifestation of the whole and, in turn, that the religious *expression* (oral, written, or otherwise) of the originating experience can only be, at best, *relatively* adequate to the event of the self-manifestation of the whole/God.[81]

Yet relative adequacy is achievable. It is, in fact, crucial to guarantee both continuity-in-innovation in the midst of a tradition like Christianity, marked by its plurality and ambiguity. Reaching a relatively adequate expression of the Christian classic helps us also to correct two possible extremes. On the one hand are those moments in which certain forms of religious expression (dogma, for instance) attempt to suppress experience, especially new religious experiences. On the other are those instances in which the excitement for what appears to be novel leads to the abandonment of core values of the tradition. Overall, the always-only relatively adequate articulation of the Christian classic must remind the interpreter that the permanence and excess of meaning of all classics prevents them from being captured by once-and-for-all interpretations.[82] The Christian classic preserves its freedom to disclose itself anew. However, this never happens *totally* anew. The notion of relative adequacy suggests that some articulations of the Christian classic are better than others. But this determination requires the criteria I have been announcing for quite some time. To these I now turn.

The Search for Criteria and the Hermeneutical Role of the Option for the Poor

The plurality and ambiguity of the Christian tradition should not lead us to the belief that *all* is relative, and that this pluralism is inherently chaotic. The interpretation of the Christian classic is marked, instead, by certain *classic expressions* and *correctives* that have a normative role in the hermeneutics of the Christian tradition. As noted, the key normative role must be given to the Christian scriptures, since it is through them that we are acquainted with and are able to participate in the Christ-event: "an event that happened, happens and will happen."[83] Yet the Christian scriptures themselves are only a relatively adequate expression of the Christ-event:

They remain open to new experiences—new questions, new and sometimes more adequate responses for later generations who experience the same event in ever different situations. Yet throughout the Christian tradition these scriptures will serve as finally normative: as that set of inspirations, controls and correctives upon all later expressions, all later classical texts, persons, images, symbols, doctrines, events that claim appropriateness to the classic witness to that event.[84]

From this follows, again, that we can only develop relatively adequate interpretations. No final interpretation is possible because of the nature of the Christ-event, to which we must add the sociological and cognitive complexities described earlier. It is in this sense that Tracy prefers to speak of "canons within the canon" to emphasize the plurality of accounts of the Christ-event.[85] None of this implies giving up on the effort of producing better interpretations using a variety of tools, especially historical-critical, literary-critical, and social-scientific methods of analysis.[86] But even using those, the very nature of the event prevents the final fixation of meaning.[87] This, in turn, should make us suspicious of any attempt of suppressing plurality on both the progressive and conservative ends of the spectrum. Avoiding these extremes, the interpreter stresses both the importance of the event and the possibility of its permanent re-articulation over time. Furthermore, ecumenism within each Christian denomination, among the denominations, and, possibly, interreligious dialogue is fostered in this way.[88]

The past-present-future, disclosure-concealment dialectic of the Christ-event is the general norm for its interpretation. But the event allows different forms of expression, among which the following stand out: apocalyptic, proclamation-confession, gospel-narrative, symbol-images, reflective theology, and doctrine. Tracy argues that in this "basic compound" of forms of expression of the Christ-event we can find *correctives* that help us to find more relatively adequate interpretations.[89] Because of their importance, he highlights two of them: the *apocalyptic genre* and the *doctrines of early Catholicism.*

In Tracy's view, the apocalyptic is crucial because it operates through principles of intensification and negation that became "a major contextual presupposition of the intertestamental period and of the New Testament itself." The apocalyptic genre is a "challenge to remember the eschatological 'not-yet' in every incarnational 'always-already' and even every 'but-even-now' resurrectional transformation."[90] In short, the apocalyptic genre is a built-in reminder of the contingency of our articulations of the self-disclosure and concealment of the divine. Furthermore, we should not be misguided by the presence of the Book of Revelation (Apocalypsis, in the Greek original) in the Bible as if it could account for the entirety of the apocalyptic genre in the Christian scriptures. Rather, as Tracy notes, we should consider it as a fundamental premise in the articulation of *all* the books of the New Testament.

The doctrinal genre of early Catholicism has a different but equally important role. Its main function is to articulate and organize the *extraordinary* witness of the first disciples in the context of the *ordinary* world in which the new Christians must live. In turn, this demanded a process of stabilization of the extraordinary Christ-event through clarification and explanation, the development of ordered institutions and practices, and so on. This is precisely what I have called the institutionalization of meaning in my remarks on the triad of manifestation-proclamation-institutionalization. Yet, as Tracy notes, "What [doctrines, analogy, institution] mediate is none other than the same extraordinary event of God's self-manifestation in Jesus Christ to and for the ordinary: that the event also happens in the everyday, the stable, the measured, the ordered, the nonintensive, nonchaotic world of the ordinary."[91]

From these general considerations Tracy draws two main conclusions about the doctrinal genre. First, that the institutions, doctrines, and analogies produced by early Catholicism are "genuinely Christian and New Testament disclosures of the same event of Jesus Christ and merit the respect of all who honor that reality." Second, that the doctrinal genre implies a process of abstraction from the originating event and, hence, the relaxation (yet not elimination) of its original intensity. From this follows,

Tracy argues, that "the confessions and doctrines of early Catholicism are not the primary place to locate the most relatively adequate expression of the New Testament event. Like apocalyptic, though in an exactly opposite sense, doctrine plays a corrective rather than a central constitutive role in the New Testament."[92]

In contrast, the New Testament *proclamation-as-manifestation* of Jesus Christ has the central constitutive role in the interpretation of the Christ-event and the Christian tradition.[93] Here, proclamation has a two-fold meaning. On the one hand, "a word of address with the claim of nonviolent appeal to listen and receive its gift and demand; a questioning, provocative, promising and liberating word that the event happens now; a judging forgiving word." In this (primary) sense, proclamation is a word-event *from God.* On the other hand, a "word of preaching and response by the community and therefore also as a word of content in this Jesus as the Exalted One present now in word, sacrament and community, this Jesus Christ the Lord."[94] In this sense, its secondary sense, proclamation is a word-event *from the community* of believers *about God.*

Yet, to be able to proclaim to others the good news that God has proclaimed to us, we need faith. For it is only *in faith* that we can be compelled to share the good news. Moreover, it is only *in faith* that we can see it as such, and as good news being proclaimed by the divine itself. Lastly, it is only in faith that we can proclaim the good news to others with such intensity and devotion that the proclamation can become again a form of manifestation. From this follows that no interpretation that attempts to be relatively adequate will be so through bypassing the constitutive role of proclamation-as-manifestation. One could add: no interpretation that attempts to be relatively adequate will be so by disregarding the constitutive role of proclamation-as-manifestation-through-institutionalization.

Accordingly, approaches that attempt to interpret the Christ-event and the Christian tradition by reducing both to the faith *of* the historical Jesus are inadequate. Similarly, perspectives that aim to constrain the Christ-event and the Christian tradition to the boundaries of some official authority or some theologia perennis are also inadequate. In the first case, historical accuracy misses the constitutive role of faith-based proclamation, to which we should add the extreme difficulty of determining what Jesus's beliefs were. In the second case, in contrast, too much emphasis on orthodox interpretations of such faith undermines the manifestation of its originating, never fully understandable, event.

In addition to these somewhat formal considerations, Tracy provides further criteria that pay attention to the *content* of the proclamation-as-manifestation. In this sense, he stresses the centrality of three events in the life of Jesus, whom the tradition proclaims as the self-manifestation of God: the incarnation, the death on the cross, and the resurrection. These events have also become classic *symbols* for the interpretation of the Christian faith, going beyond the constraints of the historical context in which they originally took place.[95] Tracy expands:

All three form a dialectic unit to reveal the fuller range and meaning of [the event of God's self-manifestation in Jesus Christ]. The cross discloses the power, pain, seriousness and scandal of the negative: the conflict, destruction, contradiction, the suffering of love which is the actuality of life. The cross discloses God's power as love appearing as weakness to the powers of the world. It discloses the rejection incumbent upon the preaching and ministry of Jesus. . . . The cross discloses to the Christian the suffering love of God's own self by its intensified focus on that love as the ultimate, binding, internal relationship of the divine and the human.

The resurrection vindicates, confirms, and transforms that journey in and through its negations of the negations of a suffering love. The resurrection of Jesus by God grounds our hope in a real future for all the living and the dead where pain shall be no more. . . . Incarnation discloses the reality of the only God there is as here now, as here always, as here in past, present and future, through the decisive self-manifestation of that same God in the cross-resurrection of Jesus Christ. . . . The heart of the Christian symbol system is none other than the unbreakable dialectic of cross-resurrection-incarnation disclosing through its own internal tensions the fuller meanings of the event of Jesus Christ.[96]

Therefore, this *cross-resurrection-incarnation* dialectic operates both as the very content of the proclamation-as-manifestation of Jesus as Lord and as the norm that controls all relatively adequate interpretations of the Christ-event and the Christian tradition. However, two decades after the publication of *The Analogical Imagination*, Tracy adds a fourth symbol to these three. He develops his argument in an essay honoring liberation theologian Gustavo Gutiérrez, motivated quite explicitly by their common preoccupation with the situation of the poor and marginalized. Tracy's fourth symbol is the *apocalyptic of the Second Coming of Christ*,[97] which destroys at its core any Christian temptation to triumphalism, whether it be theological toward the Jews, as in supersessionism, or political, as in Christianity become Christendom and empire, ignoring the option for the poor and extending only special love. Without the symbol of the Second Coming, without apocalyptic, Christianity can settle down into a religion that no longer has a profound sense of the "not yet" and of God's hiddenness in history, a religion without any sense of the need for action for justice in the option for the poor.[98]

In Tracy's view, the symbol of the Second Coming has a decisive *fragmenting* role, *destabilizing* all Christian thought.[99] Even though this fragmenting power was already present in the dialectic tensions in the triad of cross-resurrection-incarnation, Tracy believes that the triad alone may have some limitations. The resurrection has always been interpreted in terms of the final triumph of Christ over the power of death. Yet this triumph has often led to triumphalism. Introducing the symbol of the Second Coming and putting it *at the same level* as the other three classic symbols reminds the Christian that the God of love, the giver of life, is also a judge. The tradition holds that, like the king in Matthew 25, God will come again to judge the living and the dead. And, in that final moment of eschatological judgment, the way we treated the poor, the sick, the hungry, and all others who have been forgotten by society will have a central role. Thus, Tracy writes: "Only the four symbols, united, of course, to the lives of Jesus they interpret, can bring Christian theology to the full-fledged option it needs now, the option for the poor."[100]

I would like to stress that this is not an anecdotal or arbitrary gloss to Tracy's theological project. The preferential option for the poor is a *fundamental hermeneutical key* to understand both Tracy's theology and his account of any relatively adequate interpretation of the Christian tradition. Since this is a central idea of liberation theology, I should further explore this issue before returning to liberation theology in the following chapter.[101]

The importance of the option for the poor emerges as a central issue in Tracy's oeuvre, at least, since his treatment of the matter in *On Naming the Present*.[102] In the opening chapter of that book, Tracy returns to the issue of the plurality and ambiguity, but this time he focuses on the *irruption of the other*. For him, one of the distinct features of our postmodern era is the disintegration of previously held assumptions about progress, reason, science, center and periphery, and so forth. In this context, many "others" have emerged, but those that stand out among them are the sub-jugated, those that even when there is no defined center remain at the margins of history.[103]

However, this situation offers an opportunity: the collapse of a uni-vocal point of view makes it possible for those who always assumed them-selves to be the center of the world to recognize the presence of the other. In this polycentric world, Tracy claims that "the others must become genuine others for us—not projections of our fear and desires. The others are not marginal to our centers but centers of their own. Their conflicts and their liberationist self-namings demand the serious attention of our center on their own terms."[104]

Indeed, the task of a Christian theology that attempts to be relevant today consists in being able to interpret our current situation in light of the Christian tradition, aiming to produce orderly Christian discourse and praxis. But as Tracy notes in conversation with Gutiérrez, one of the distinct features of our time is the persistent unjust suffering of millions, together with the progressive acknowledgment that such suffering is not fate and, therefore, can—and must—be eradicated. For Tracy, what we need is "a new theological understanding of both self and present time again. We need historical subjects with memory, hope, and resistance."[105] Tracy is explicitly thinking about the base communities that struggle for liberation. Tracy expands on the issue, this time focusing on the way the poor can teach us as *witness* of the Gospel's transformative power:

We must listen to other conversations, especially those of people in our own and other cultures who experience massive global suffering but have found new voices of their own and new historical actions to match those voices. Part of what one can hear in the voices of these "others," I believe, is the healing and transfor-mative message of the Christian gospel alive once again: a message neither mod-ern, nor antimodern, nor postmodern; a message to and for historical subjects in the concrete struggles for justice against suffering and oppression and for total liberation; a message also for our own time—a time that needs not merely better reflections on otherness and difference but needs above all to learn to listen and learn from others.[106]

As we can see here, Tracy's theology comes very close to Gutiérrez's under-standing of liberation and to the role the Peruvian theologian gives to the agency of the poor in both the process of liberation and the deepening of our interpretation of the Christian tradition. The poor, for Tracy and Gutiérrez, are not merely the receivers of the solidarity of the better-off or just the object of study of the progressive-minded theologian. The poor, through their organizing, witness, and reinterpretation of the role of faith in the process of liberation, are active producers of new articulations of the Christian tradition. In this new articulation—systematically presented in the work of Gutiérrez, among others—the preferential option for the poor takes a hermeneutical *normative* role: so much so, that in Tracy's theology—through the symbol of the Second Coming—it is elevated to the status of a fundamental, indeed classic, symbol to disclose the meaning of the Christian mystery as a whole.

The key issue to note here is the correlation between the experience of the poor and the normative role of the option for the poor in the hermeneutics of the Christian tradition. I do not hold some kind of "epistemological privilege" of the poor through which they can better disclose the truth of the Christian tradition. Such a position has been held by some liberation theologians, and I will critically turn to this issue in the following chapters. My point here is of a different nature. The point is that the faith-based organizing and activism of the poor allowed a return to certain values present in the Christian tradition, but not fully actualized by it. The poor and marginalized, by becoming more active in the struggle for their own liberation, and doing so motivated by their faith, brought attention to the very ideal of liberation in the biblical witness and the Christian tradition as a whole. In turn, this permitted the systematic reflection of theologians like Gutiérrez and Tracy who identified the centrality of the theme of liberation-salvation for the Christian faith, further providing resources for the faith communities already engaged in the process of liberation.

The importance of giving to the option for the poor the hermeneutical status that it has here cannot be overstated. We are not talking about a "special love for the poor," which leaves things at the level of the always important kindness and charity toward the needy. With Tracy and Gutiérrez, my claim is that fulfilling the promises of God's love for creation *requires* going beyond such "special love" to pursue social justice advocating for systemic change. Individual instances of charity, as important as they are, cannot deal with structural conditions that keep so many in the margins of society. Racism, sexism, homophobia, and the like cannot be overcome solely with kind gestures toward the victims of these abuses.

Legal, political, and cultural systemic changes are necessary to deal with these maladies. In turn this requires a reorientation of people's perspective. In the context of the Christian faith, this demands a fundamental option for the poor that gives to the ethical-political dialectic of love and justice "its proper Christian focus."[107] Naturally, none of this means that this option for the poor will look the same for all people. Not all of us are activists and organizers; not all of us are liberation theologians. Like with traditions themselves, plurality is always part of the option for the poor. Yet the key issue here is to emphasize the critical importance of such an option for the sake of a relatively adequate interpretation of the Christian faith.

This is why the symbol of the Second Coming—together with the incarnation, cross, and resurrection—is so relevant here. The Christian narrative is not one of a superficial "happy ending"; it ends, instead, "with a cry, a plea, a prayer, a passion, and 'Come Lord Jesus, come.'"[108] The expectation of the Lord constitutes an act of hope, indeed, but it also shapes the Christian imagination as an eschatological imagination more able to actively incorporate the preferential option of the poor in it. The "not yet" of the Second Coming—"once deliteralized and stolen back from the date-setting literalists," as Tracy notes[109]—reminds us that history is not just *this* history; it reminds us that there is a God in whom Christians trust, a God of love and justice who is coming to change our history. This hope reminds the believer that the story told by the powerful and the mighty can be challenged and must be subverted for the sake of those buried under layers of hatred, oppression, and indifference. The eschatological coming of the Lord restructures Christian hope, rescuing it from triumphalist readings of history and inscribing hope again *within* the horizon of salvation history—a history that Gutiérrez and Tracy understand as *one*, comprising both temporal liberation and eschatological salvation.[110]

The symbol of the Second Coming puts at the heart of the interpretation of the Christian tradition the question of social justice, especially the justice owed to the poor and most vulnerable. Tracy maintains that no relatively adequate interpretation of the Christian tradition can be produced if it does not listen to the cry of the poor. But this is not only a matter of love and compassion. It is a hermeneutical argument: through the symbol of the Second Coming, the option for the poor becomes a fundamental interpretative key of the Christian tradition and not only a matter of preference for the politically inclined. Though this becomes more explicit in the chapters in which I directly address liberation theology, the hermeneutical importance of this move for *all* Christian theology should not be neglected.[111]

Creative Fidelity: Constructive Theology and the Analogical Imagination

My previous considerations have been fundamentally methodological, focusing on criteria for relatively adequate interpretations of the Christ-event and the Christian tradition. However, important as method is, theology is fundamentally a *constructive* task. *Systematic* theology, especially, is a constructive task marked by the attempt to produce new meaning for the contemporary community of believers in fidelity to the tradition that has preceded them. Of course, this is exactly what liberation theologians attempted to do with their theological writings. As I have argued in the preceding chapter, this creative fidelity was at the basis of Gustavo Gutiérrez's new articulation of faith and politics.

The criteria developed before have the role of making us cautious in our God-talk. The excess of meaning and the incomprehensible nature of the Christ-event may even invite us to contemplative silence. But theology is a *language* about God; theology is fundamentally interpretative *discourse*. Even the mystical invitations to contemplative silence as the most adequate form of speech for religion depend on the possibility of discourse. Even "silence is possible as silence only to the speaker."[112] Hence the theologian must venture an interpretation; must *say* something beyond giving criteria for *how to say* or simply *not-saying*. Agreeing with Tracy, I believe that the most relatively adequate way to say something in Christian theology is via the language of *analogy*, finding similarity-in-difference.[113] This, in turn, requires establishing critical correlations between the sources of theological reflection. Again, this is precisely what Gutiérrez *did*. Here, the emphasis is on *how* he did it, so that we better grasp the originality of his thought and the theological legitimacy of his new articulation.

For Tracy, the two principal sources of Christian theological reflection are "the major expressions and texts of the Christian traditions" and "common human experience."[114] Both sources must be in permanent and critical conversation *if* religious claims are to become available to the wider public. Tracy, however, maintains that this publicness is not really a matter of choice. Publicness is inevitable. The theologian cannot avoid the wider public, even if they *imagine* speaking exclusively to their Church. In turn, this means that *some* form of conversation with common human experience—that is, not specifically Christian experience—will always take place and will always shape in *some* way the Christian self-understanding, even if this happens inadvertently. What varies is the willingness of the theologian to acknowledge this fact; what varies is the degree to which the theologian is aware of the influence of non-faith-based understandings in their theological views.[115]

If we use the image of the walls of a church or a cathedral, the real issue is not whether what happens *within* the walls relates to what happens *without*; intramural and extramural matters always relate. Not leaving the cathedral is not a real option. So-called traditionalists provide only a very selective interpretation of the tradition to depict it as stable and nonchanging, as if one could safely and permanently stay within the walls of an unshakable cathedral-fortress. But this is an imagined safety, a fictional stability. The real question is *how far* beyond the walls of this imagined cathedral the Christian theologian ventures in the process of providing a Christian interpretation of a particular subject. When is too far? At what point the theologian's interpretation is not recognizably Christian anymore? As noted earlier, the boundaries between orthodoxy and heterodoxy are quite tenuous and contingent on the changing nature of the Christian tradition's self-understanding.[116] And yet this is a risk that cannot be avoided if the tradition is to remain alive. As we saw before, traditions are the most preeminent frameworks we use to make sense of life. Inherently, they are problem solvers and practice-oriented. When a tradition stops providing relevant answers to new problems, the tradition dies.

For these reasons, the demand of publicness is not only the result of the liberal theologian's moral and intellectual commitment to a culture of "autonomous critical inquiry" in which there is a "duty to provide the proper kind of evidence for whatever claim he advances." "Rather, the task is primarily demanded for inner theological reasons." Since Christianity claims to express "an understanding of authentic human experience as such, the Christian theologian is impelled to test precisely that universalist claim."[117] How this is tested will naturally vary,[118] but the key issue will always be to show to the world that Christianity truly provides an answer to the most fundamental questions about meaning and truth. It is in this most fundamental sense that publicness cannot be avoided: it is inherent to the Christian tradition's claim to be the answer to those questions.

Now, in order to do so, Christian beliefs cannot work *unilaterally* as the only lens to interpret common human experience, what we may call "the world." In fact, as noted, they never do. The world has a role in the process of reshaping Christian beliefs too.[119] In this sense, Tracy advocates for a method of *mutual* critical correlations in which the two main sources of Christian theology are submitted to a careful assessment of their internal coherence and practical applicability, so that they can illuminate each other in the effort to respond to a given situation.[120] I fully agree.

The overall goal is the "refashioning of the original disclosure" through *analogy*, "a language of ordered relationships articulating similarity-in-difference."[121] Moreover, Tracy maintains that a *theological primary focal meaning* or *prime analogue* is required to proceed with the systematic task. Hence, the theologian requires a key concept or doctrine to analogically re-articulate the "permanence and excess of meaning" of the classic event. Further, the *Christian* theologian must do this considering the four classic symbols discussed earlier: incarnation, cross, resurrection, and Second Coming. However, this must be done always keeping in mind that the Christ-event is marked by the dialectic of *disclosure-and-concealment*, that is, by the impossibility of grasping the Christ-event fully because its own power of affirmation includes its power of negation.[122] Therefore, any articulation of the Christ-event will always have a tentative and only relatively adequate character marked by the dialectic of manifestation-proclamation-institutionalization discussed before. If this relatively adequate character is lost, "analogical concepts become mere categories of easy likenesses, falling finally into the sterility of a relaxed univocity and a facilely affirmative harmony."[123]

I conclude by sketching out how the analogical imagination operates in the context of the constructive theological work of liberation theology. Since the Christ-event is characterized by its permanence and excess of meaning, finding a primary focal meaning is crucial to develop a relatively adequate interpretation of the event. Of course, for Christians, the person and event of Jesus Christ *is* the prime analogue, the mediator in the interpretation of all reality. However, the Christ-event is also an object of interpretation for theology as a second-order discourse. In this sense, other more particular prime analogues can take primacy in order to refashion the original disclosure.[124]

In liberation theology, the prime analogue is liberation. Alternatively, we could also argue that the prime analogue is Christ-the-liberator, keeping the Christ-event as central, yet adding a crucial emphasis to develop a new set of ordered relationships. Now the primary focal meaning given to "liberation" cannot be a mere matter of theological preference; it must be appropriate to the original disclosure. In what follows, I show how that is indeed the case, appealing to the criteria developed in this chapter following Tracy's work. In a second move, I show how the use of analogy ad intra also operates ad extra, thus grounding the relationship in the political that is so crucial for liberation.

As noted, there are four fundamental symbols without which no relatively adequate interpretation of the Christ-event is possible: cross, resurrection, incarnation, and Second Coming. But the constructive theological task requires that we go beyond what those symbols disclose in general in order to produce an interpretation that responds to particular concerns and situations. In this sense, when we make liberation our primary focal meaning, a true moment of creative fidelity takes place by being both loyal to the tradition and yet innovative in its refashioning.[125]

Liberation theologians stress the importance of the cross, with its negativity and tragic meaning. Yet they advance the interpretation by focusing on the journey that led to that tragic end. Hence they disclose for us that Jesus was killed because he preached a message and lived a life that became a major challenge to the powers that be, both religious and secular. The message was indeed revolutionary in its challenge of the Jewish authorities' understanding of ritual order, mercy, and justice, and, overall, of their role as true messengers of God. This message of liberation became a major challenge and ultimately led to Jesus's execution. Thus, the focus on liberation discloses aspects that have often been overshadowed by more spiritual interpretations of the crucifixion; it discloses the historical and political context of Jesus's execution and gives people today a framework to understand their own "crosses" and "executions." Furthermore, as most liberation theologians maintain, this emphasis also allows people to see God in a greater relationship of solidarity with them: the cross becomes a symbol of shared suffering. In the crucified Jesus, the poor and marginalized can see their own experiences of negativity taken to the highest degree. Indeed, the divine, the very source of being, can suffer as we all suffer; can experience the brutality of humiliation, abandonment, and death as we all can. God knows about our sufferings and experiences them in God's very flesh.

However, the death on the cross does not represent the end of the story. The Christian tradition believes that Jesus was resurrected because his message of liberation was, more than anything, a life-giving vision. Hence, his resurrection is the fundamental sign of the triumph of liberation. Those who fight for the Kingdom of God and God's justice will not be defeated: that is the promise fulfilled in the resurrection. Certainly, there is suffering and negativity in the story of the cross, but the story keeps going. In fact, it is destined to a life of joy in communion with God that never ends. For we come from God and to God we shall return.

Cross and resurrection, in turn, cast light on Jesus's incarnation. The prime analogue of liberation allows us to stress Jesus's activity in the world instead of restricting the focus to the cosmological meaning of his incarnation *only* in terms of the salvation of the soul. Hence, great attention is given to his interactions with the poor, with the sick, with those who have been pushed to the margins of society because of their sexual impurity, but also with those, like tax collectors, who, holding economic and political power, were considered incapable of conversion. The overall message is clear: Jesus preached a life-giving vision that was for all, but one that announced the good news of God's Kingdom especially to the poor and marginalized. As with the cross and the resurrection, this new emphasis on liberation in the interpretation of the symbol of the incarnation allowed liberation theologians to give people today new resources to reinterpret their lives and organize themselves to find a better future.

Lastly, the focus on liberation in the interpretation of the Second Coming becomes a permanent reminder that the story is not over, especially for those who interpret the resurrection as ultimate triumph and disregard their responsibilities in *this* world. Here, as we noted, Tracy actually elaborates the point in direct conversation with liberation theology, Gutiérrez's in particular, arguing that those responsibilities are fundamental to the poor and marginalized. Thus, liberation becomes a key by which to read salvation history from beginning to end, but with a particular emphasis on concrete actions that bring the values of God's Kingdom closer to those who suffer the most.

What about the importance of Tracy's correctives for a relatively adequate interpretation of the Christ-event? The role of the apocalyptic genre should be already clear since the symbol of the Second Coming has a similar role. Yet we could expand upon it here in a way that also relativizes the primary focal meaning of "liberation." Since the apocalyptic genre is a permanent reminder of the not-yet, this should also apply to any liberationist interpretation that appears to be too certain about the path to follow. The prime analogue of liberation provides an appropriate focal meaning to refashion the original disclosure, but only *relatively*. The nature of the Christ-event does not allow fully adequate articulations, which in turn means that even those interpretations that advocate for the poor and the marginalized have limitations—all the more so when they identify the Christian message of liberation with partisan political agendas.[126]

But the other corrective, the doctrinal genre, is particularly important. For, as Tracy shows, doctrines as a genre allow the stabilization of the event over history, providing clarification and better understanding through a process of distanciation. The doctrinal corrective, therefore, allows us to identify better or worse interpretations of the Christ-event, a discernment that applies to the field of liberation theology as well. Thus, liberation theologies that overemphasize liberation as the primary focal meaning in a way that reduces the importance of the four fundamental Christian symbols, the apocalyptic, and the interpretation of all of them through the doctrinal genre would be less relatively adequate.

For instance, we may argue that the expression "Christ is the Che Guevara"[127] is quite inadequate as a refashioning of the original disclosure, among other reasons, because it completely disregards key doctrinal developments like the identity of Jesus with God. In contrast, the metaphors "Christ is black" or "God is black" are significantly more adequate because "black" in that phrase stands by "the oppressed" and the "is" has been always interpreted in the Black theology tradition as "identifies with." In this sense, "Christ is black" does not collide with the fundamentals of Christian self-understanding, although it requires some unpacking since the identity of God with blackness is not self-evident.[128] Therefore, I would argue that "Christ is the liberator" is a better relatively adequate articulation because it avoids some of the misunderstandings that the prior two examples elicit, stressing instead the key role of liberation in the Christian tradition that is perfectly compatible with its main symbols and correctives. If one adds, as I did in the previous chapter, a full account of the relationship between liberation and salvation, it becomes even clearer why "Christ the liberator" is indeed a relatively adequate way to refashion the original disclosure of the Christ-event.

The analogical imagination also operates ad extra. Indeed, Christians not only interpret the Christ-event *within* the Christian tradition. They also can explore—and have always done so—whether the Christ-event and its interpretations find some correlation, some analogue *beyond* the Christian imagination, in common human experience. I suggest that the prime analogue for this task is *human dignity* or *the dignity of life*—to also include nonhuman animals and the planet. Indeed, this is the position taken quite explicitly by the bishops gathered at the Second Vatican Council. In §40 of *Gaudium et spes,* they write that the defense of human dignity, human community, and the meaning of human activity "lays the foundation for the relationship between the Church and the world."[129]

We know well that one of the central concerns of the Christian faith is the dignity of life, especially human life. One of the most traditional ways to describe this concern is the Christian understanding of our being imago Dei (Gen. 1:27). The dignity we all share comes from God's loving, creating act. Thus, human dignity is inherent to our condition as children of God and cannot be taken away from us.[130] Nevertheless, such a dignity can be barely experienced when extreme poverty, violence, discrimination, and death are the everyday experiences of so many people. In traditional Christian vocabulary, all this is the consequence of *sin*. Therefore, Christ's passion, death, and resurrection represent God's greatest sign of love to overcome sin and restore in us the experience of our dignity of being God's children.

As noted, the focal meaning of liberation allows us to pay special attention to the content of Jesus's life-giving vision and his particular care for the poor and marginalized. His preaching and his actions stress the evils of their condition, call for the reign of justice and love, and promise rewards and punishments depending on the way we treated "the least of his brothers and sisters." Accordingly, liberation theologians argue, all Christians should make God's message of liberation, manifested in Jesus Christ, their own by fighting for the eradication of the consequences of sin and inviting all to the fullness of life in communion with God. In the traditional theological language of Latin Christianity, our fully being imago Dei implies an imitatio Christi.

My argument now is that these concerns are *analogically* present in other approaches to human dignity. Key among them are *political* approaches, since politics deals with the basic structure of society, with the institutions that provide the context for the existence of a just society in which the dignity of all people must be respected. My contention here, which I develop in subsequent chapters, is that these political approaches to social justice that focus on the dignity of life find important areas of agreement with the Christian concern for human dignity, especially as it has been articulated by liberation theologians.[131]

Of course, this by no means implies that the political approaches to human dignity present in the secular disciplines can exhaust the depth of the concept of human dignity in its Christian interpretation. Further, it does not mean that the Christian interpretation cannot elicit a better understanding of the political approach. But it *does* mean that an *overlapping consensus*—a relationship of analogy, we could say with Tracy—between political and theological approaches to the dignity of life is possible, as philosopher John Rawls claimed. Such is the case because Christians and other believers can see *some* crucial tenets of their faith *genuinely* represented in certain political conceptions.

Yet we should keep in mind that one of the key features of this attempt of analogical imagination is the presence of *mutual* critical correlations between the sources of theology. Accordingly, I will show in the next chapters how political approaches that I favor when it comes to the defense of the dignity of life can be expanded and corrected drawing from the articulation of the Christ-event produced by liberation theologians. Similarly, such theological articulation can benefit from secular, political approaches, drawing from these to think more clearly about the content of social justice. For one may pray to God to bring justice to the world, and one may protest the injustices of poverty and marginalization, but without an institutional framework for justice to be embodied in practices or everyday life, prayer and protest will not find ultimate fruition.

3

Theology on the Ground

FAITH-BASED POLITICAL ENGAGEMENT
IN PERÚ

I turn now to the experience of the basic ecclesial communities in Perú, the context of immediate influence of Gutiérrez's theology. My interest is to investigate how their members embraced Gutiérrez's contributions and creatively articulated the tension between political and religious values in their own experiences. Put simply, my goal is to move from the world of theological reflection to that of lived religion.[1] I do so to examine how the new articulation of faith and politics developed by liberation theologians was embodied in the concrete praxis of politically active Christian discipleship.

Here I rely on data and reflections on the Peruvian experience of political violence of the 1980s and 1990s. I focus on this period to highlight *the type* of political intervention developed by the communities influenced by liberation theology. To do so, I examine how the communities shaped by liberation theology understood the political and worked toward social change, under the context of political violence coming from the terrorist group Sendero Luminoso (Shining Path). Focusing on this moment rife with political violence allows me to stress that the communities influenced by liberation theology were *Christian* communities that fought for social change to defend the sacredness of life. Unlike Sendero Luminoso, liberation theology's commitment to radical political change fundamentally opposed treating human life like mere means to realize a political project. No utopian promises were worth the cost of real lives. No revolution should prioritize political strategy over human suffering.

I supplement these sources with material collected from interviews I conducted between December 2019 and February 2020. In these interviews, which include a long conversation with Gustavo Gutiérrez, I pursue the same basic question: that of the articulation of the possible tensions between the religious and the political. One additional advantage of this recent material is that—although in a rather limited way—it addresses what I see as a gap in scholarship devoted to liberation theology: the lack of information and reflection on what has happened to liberation theology in the last twenty or thirty years. My interviews with several of the key figures of *la corriente*—the name most people who are consciously related to liberation theology in Perú give to themselves—attempt to get at this question directly.[2] In the closing section, I step back and attempt to provide a more systematic view of the challenges ahead, arguing that liberation theology is well equipped to meet them.

"A Time of Small Heroic Acts:" The Response of the Faithful to Political Violence

I begin by addressing the relationship between faith and politics in the specific context of political violence in Perú during the times of vicious confrontation between Sendero Luminoso (Shining Path) and state forces (1980–1992).[3] My guiding question is this: How did the faithful respond to Sendero Luminoso, a self-proclaimed Marxist-Leninist party, allegedly fighting for the needs of the poor? In brief, the answer is that the communities of faith that were shaped by liberation theology's option for the poor did not embrace Sendero's project. Further, when Sendero Luminoso, facing the rejection of the most disenfranchised, started using terror against them to execute its political agenda, the supporters of liberation theology did not return Sendero's political violence. Rather, they relied on their faith to defend life and attend to the needs of the poor and marginalized. Ultimately, these were always communities of faith, not political cells. Their political activism was the *manifestation* of those deep faith commitments. Let me explore this matter in greater detail.

Background: Terrorism, State Repression, and the Role of Faith

On May 17, 1980, in the town of Chuschi, in the region of Ayacucho, the recent history of Perú changed dramatically. Chuschi was the first violent target of Sendero Luminoso. There, Sendero's members burned ballot boxes on election day, declaring open war against the Peruvian government and the democratic process.

Sendero Luminoso was founded in 1970. Its founder and historic leader was Abimael Guzmán, known by his comrades as Presidente Gonzalo. Sendero's initial area of immediate operations was Ayacucho, one of the poorest regions of Perú. There, Guzmán held a philosophy faculty position at the Universidad Nacional de San Cristóbal de Huamanga, a place that he turned into his ideological think tank. Guzmán conceived of Sendero as a revolutionary movement modeled after Mao Zedong's Cultural Revolution. Yet Sendero never really gathered a critical mass of followers to start a guerrilla-like military offense against the Peruvian state. Without the backing of the peasantry, Sendero quickly turned into a terrorist movement. Sendero permanently terrorized the poorest Peruvians—especially in Ayacucho and the most abandoned areas of Perú—with ruthless violence to obtain their support through fear. Over time, Sendero developed a strategy of targeted urban attacks (bombings, kidnappings, targeted killings of social leaders, etc.) that expanded its reign of terror for several years.[4]

Indeed, after a cruel war that lasted more than a decade (1980–1992), the magnitude of violence reached brutal levels. On August 28, 2003, the Comisión de la Verdad y Reconciliación (CVR), the Peruvian Truth Commission, presented its final report on the period of violence that began with the Ayacucho attack. The final death toll reached almost seventy thousand people. Of all deaths, 40 percent happened in Ayacucho. Eighty-five percent of all victims lived in the poorest regions of Perú. In addition, most of the victims were rural farmers (75 percent) who were disproportionally non-native speakers of Spanish. The picture this information draws is terribly grim. During the times of political violence, the poorest among the poor were the principal victims, despite Sendero's stance that they were confronting the state in order to improve the lives of the poor.[5]

What was the role of the faith communities in this context?[6] The CVR Report gives us a general sense of the answer:

Institutionally, the Catholic Church early on condemned the violence of the subversive groups as well as the human rights violations committed by the state. Its position materialized through actions defending human rights and condemnations of their violation. These actions and condemnations started very early through organizations like the Comisión Episcopal de Acción Social (CEAS) and others. The CVR concludes that many lives were saved, and many other violations were prevented due to the efforts of these organizations, as well as the actions of individual members of religious orders, the clergy, and the laity that went beyond theological and pastoral orientations. . . . [Their presence] contributed to the strengthening of social networks and to building a barrier that weakened the advancement of Sendero Luminoso and the "dirty war."

The CVR, however, has found that during most of the conflict the defense of human rights was not firm in the Archdiocese of Ayacucho. During a significant part of the conflict, the archdiocese obstructed the work of human rights organizations related to the church while denying the existence of human rights violations.[7]

Given the importance that the Peruvian Truth Commission gives to the role of the Episcopal Commission of Social Action (CEAS), I will turn to it in the following pages. I will especially focus on one of CEAS's key offices, the Coordinación de Pastoral de Dignidad Humana (Committee on the Pastoral of Human Dignity, CPDH).[8]

The history of CEAS is directly connected to the importance of Vatican II and the Medellín conference, both major events in the emergence of liberation theology, as I showed in Chapter 1. Vatican II's invitation to all people of faith to discern the "signs of the times" and to involve themselves directly in social and political matters elicited among the Peruvian bishops the desire to form an organization to address social issues. In 1965 they formed CEAS, but it was after the Medellín conference in 1968 that CEAS started displaying its real force under the leadership of Bishop Luis Bambarén SJ. Bambarén, a recently appointed bishop, was already known for his commitment to the poor in the peripheral areas of Lima and for his closeness to the ideas of liberation theology. Hence, his experience on the ground and theological commitments were key in guiding CEAS's mission of "advising the hierarchy of the church on issues relating to the social problems of the country and helping in the formation of the clergy, religious, and lay people on social issues." Historian Jeffrey Klaiber notes that soon "CEAS turned into the principal channel through which the concerns and problems of the marginalized classes became known to the hierarchy of the church."[9] CEAS was crucial, for instance, in the formation of the Comedores Populares (Popular Kitchens) in the late 1970s, which became—and still are—an indispensable resource to feed and organize poor families. The comedores have become a Peruvian institution among the poor, especially in times of great upheaval like the severe economic crisis and hyperinflation of the 1980s, the systemic adjustments of the 1990s to end the inflationary crisis, and the COVID-19 pandemic. Similarly, CEAS provided counsel and resources to help the to poor to organize themselves to fight for better health care and education, or against police or corporate abuses.

The CPDH: A Faith-Based Defense of Human Dignity

Pilar Coll, human rights lawyer and historian of the Coordinación de Pastoral de Dignidad Humana (CPDH; from now on, Human Dignity), locates the origin of Human Dignity in the 1977 national strike. The national strike—a massive halt of labor among thousands of workers—was led by the union leaders of the most important guilds and many community organizers in response to the severe economic crisis of the time and the increasing state violence against the labor movement. The military regime headed by General Francisco Morales Bermúdez responded by firing thousands of union leaders and workers involved in the strike, and with greater police brutality. Many people were arrested, and most union offices were searched without warrants. In such a context, several members of CEAS gathered to reflect on the increasing repression. Quite organically, Human Dignity formed between 1978 and 1979. About twenty people could be counted as its initial members. The goal was to provide a response to state repression and, more generally, to develop resources to ameliorate the suffering of many Peruvians whose jobs were lost and who were struggling with increasing poverty. Perhaps more importantly, the goal was also to use the credibility and institutional strength of the Catholic Church to support the cause of human rights, since civil society organizations like the Comisión Nacional de Derechos Humanos (National Commission of Human Rights) were perceived as too political and lacking legitimacy.[10]

In this early stage, Human Dignity's actions were modest but of great importance: bringing food and assistance to the strikers arrested and jailed by the regime and providing accurate information and legal assistance. All these actions were conceived as forms of *Christian* solidarity. This is clear in Coll's interview with Fr. Daniel Panchot, a Holy Cross priest with prior organizing experience in Chile. Panchot, who became a leading voice during this early stage of Human Dignity's work, made clear that the point was to awaken among the Christian communities the need to stand in solidarity with workers, teachers, and miners. Similarly, Fr. Felipe Zegarra notes in an interview with Coll that the interventions promoted by Human Dignity were not merely decided in administrative or coordinating meetings. Rather, he stresses the communal dimension of the organization. He notes that Human Dignity became for him his second spiritual community, the first being his parish.[11]

But things quickly became bleak. The already noted attack in Chuschi, Ayacucho, launched a time of great political violence marked by terrorist attacks perpetrated by Sendero and the repressive response of the state. This situation elicited a massive migration of people from the countryside to the cities, especially to the city of Lima, the capital. What started as the migration of individuals soon became the massive migration of entire families. Political violence rapidly created more poverty and displacement. Sister Natividad Ollo, then working in the newly established pueblos jóvenes (slums), shared with Coll her memories of a woman telling her: "Sister, take my child, I have no means to raise him." Similarly, Sister Juanita Kilduf—also interviewed by Coll—shares the tragic story of a boy she met in the county of Canto Grande who survived a massacre perpetrated by the military in his town in Ayacucho. The boy was able to survive because he spent the entirety of a night running away. Sister Kilduf noted, "I have never been to Ayacucho, but Ayacucho has come to Lima due to the violence."[12]

In this context, the members of Human Dignity took a more active role. Some of the interventions were "little heroic acts," as Hortensia Moncloa, a Human Dignity lay volunteer, notes. Among these actions were producing informative bulletins with news updates and social analysis and reporting information about the displaced, the disappeared, and those who were killed. Some of these reports were produced and compiled by volunteers like Moncloa on kitchen tables and carried to the post office in the same bags used for groceries. For people like Moncloa, these "little heroic acts" were conceived as a natural extension of their life of faith. The concerns of Human Dignity were always shaped by a sense of belonging to the Christian faith community. Similarly, all Human Dignity's interventions were an attempt to act on those commitments in a concrete historical and political context.[13] Coll maintains that one of the main reasons that explains the success of Human Dignity was that it was a community marked by friendship and emotional support, but especially by faith and hope: "Some of the interviewees affirm that [Human Dignity] was an authentic community and the place where the synthesis between professional work and their experience as Christians could take place, a place that allowed them to see the Gospel from a different perspective."[14]

Coll reminds us that at the foundations of Human Dignity was its commitment to a mystical and prophetic understanding of the Christian faith that was linked to a great concern for the poor. It is therefore not surprising that most of Human Dignity's actions were clearly "religious" in the sense of not having obvious "political" implications. Among the main tasks of Human Dignity we can count establishing networks of communication between bishops and parishes, celebrating masses to accompany the victims, planning days of fasting and prayer in response to violence, and providing biblical education on issues relating to human rights.

Even though the public interventions of Human Dignity were patently religious in the sense described, they were also moments of denunciation and protest. For this reason, both Sendero and the military interpreted them as being "political." Moreover, despite the pastoral motivation of its activities, Human Dignity was always open to working with non-Catholic organizations to defend the sacredness of human life.[15] This included cooperation with nonreligious groups politically active in the Left, which were normally the ones focused on human rights activism. However, despite the interpretations that attempted to frame this cooperation as the subordination of faith to politics, the members of Human Dignity saw their work as clearly theologically motivated. Ultimately, what motivated this radical defense of the dignity of life was their commitment to a God of Life who gives preferential attention to those lives most endangered and threatened. Behind these apparently politically motivated actions was a profound spirituality sustaining the option for the poor and marginalized.[16] Gutiérrez called it the "spirituality of liberation," a spirituality of solidarity with the marginalized and protest against their marginalization.[17]

The work of Gutiérrez and other liberation theologians was critical in establishing the spirituality of liberation behind the option for the poor. It built the theological foundations for the option for the poor that Human Dignity practiced every day. As Coll notes, it was a theology that "summoned us to encounter God in the thickness of social conflict and the suffering of a people, a theology that gave depth to everyday tasks related to the defense of life and human rights." Laura Vargas, a lay volunteer at Human Dignity, agrees: "Even though we did not talk about the theology of liberation, we were inspired by it, because we were nurtured by a great closeness to the suffering poor." Similarly, Moncloa shares: "In my whole process, the accompaniment of a live church, [walking] in the path of the theology of liberation, has been very important. I had three wonderful professors of theology at the Catholic University: Gustavo Gutiérrez, Felipe Zegarra, and Luis Fernando Crespo. They taught me about a religion committed to life."[18]

But liberation theology taught these people more than a sense of commitment to the poor and to the importance of social transformation. It also taught them to balance these qualities; it taught them spiritual discernment. For liberation theologians and those in Human Dignity it was clear that

The option for people's integral liberation demanded the mediation of a political and social project, which was not simply identified with the Kingdom [of God]. Christians wanted to be part [of that project], precisely because they were the church, because they were disciples of Jesus. Not for mere political reasons, but because this was a demand of their faith. They saw that the work of the church had political consequences, but that it was precisely the pastoral work of the church that allowed them to see that the political work was insufficient to transform reality. It was the work done as church that became a key factor in the affirmation of its identity and its mission of being a community at the service of the Kingdom.[19]

These testimonies point to a crucial idea—that despite the great importance of radical social and political transformation, people in la corriente understood the eschatological horizon of such transformation. Ultimately, liberation as salvation can only be accomplished in Christ. Gutiérrez's theology is quite clear about this. The relevance of these testimonies, coming from ordinary believers and activists, is that they confirm the critical importance of this eschatological orientation. They do so, though, *without* losing sight of the need to struggle for liberation in the present. What this shows is that the members of the communities shaped by the option for the poor were quite able to balance their political and religious commitments in organic ways, without reductionisms or oversimplifications.

Indeed, communities and organizations influenced by liberation theology—like Human Dignity—do not politicize the Christian faith. For these believers, their Christian faith demands that they commit to the construction of a more just society. Yet since social justice requires systemic changes in the basic structure of society, these believers felt—and still feel—compelled to intervene in the political arena through organizing, activism, lobbying, protest, running for public office, and the like. The link connecting their faith and their political participation is the profound conviction that the God of Life cares for all lives but especially those of the poor and marginalized.

Similarly, there is no reason to associate these practices with Marxism—as many critics have argued for years, including early documents issued by the Vatican.[20] Marxism was never the dominant force—although often a conversation partner—in the writings of most liberation theologians nor in the practice of the communities of faith shaped by the option for the poor. Further, as should be obvious at this point, there is no historical materialism or atheism in liberation theology.[21] In addition, there is no evidence at all that these faith communities conceived the process of social transformation as requiring a violent revolution. Quite the contrary: in Perú, they opposed Sendero Luminoso at the cost of their own lives and developed a vocal campaign in favor of life and against violence.

Lastly, liberation theologians and their faith communities in Perú articulated the balance between faith and politics *as Church*, as part of the spiritual body of believers in Christ. This is important because the focus of liberation theology on the poor and the occasional language of the "Church of the poor" has led some to believe that liberation theologians promote division within the Church and dissent from the authority of

Rome.[22] But the emphasis on the needs of the poor and marginalized refers to a theological and pastoral orientation, not to the desire to break away from the Church. As I have shown with the example of Human Dignity, people involved with its work very explicitly labored for justice as Christians, as members of the Church.

However, this should not erase the fact that the option for the poor taken by many of these Christians represents a moment of criticism of the Church and its authority. But notice that the problem is not authority itself, but *the kind of authority* exercised and the type of alliances it required. When authority was claimed in order to dismiss and displace the severe needs of the poor, and to defend the repression of the government or the military, liberation theologians protested. During the times of political violence, for instance, they protested against then-archbishop of Ayacucho Juan Luis Cipriani. Cipriani, as the Peruvian Truth Commission report shows, denied that there were human rights violations and obstructed the work of human rights activists while hundreds were killed in his diocese. Liberation theologians and practitioners did not attempt to break with tradition or disrupt the Church. Instead, they wanted to radicalize it, to make it return to its prophetic and mystical roots. Proof of this is that Human Dignity was a faith-based organization, after all. In fact, it was a branch of the Peruvian Conference of Bishops, the highest hierarchical organization of the Catholic Church in the country.[23] Gutiérrez and his colleagues did not have to break with the Church. They opted, instead, for transforming it from within.

The New Revolutions of Liberation Theology

In this section I present an interpretation of liberation theology that attempts to address its trajectory beyond the years of social revolution and political violence. My focus here is on the role of liberation theology during the convergence of democratization and modernization that started to shape Latin America in the 1990s. Since there is not much scholarship devoted to this issue,[24] I rely here on interviews I recently conducted with key figures of the movement in Perú, as well as other works that indirectly address the issue.[25]

The 1990s and the decades that followed represented a challenge for liberation theology and the faith communities that promoted the option for the poor. On the one hand, there were important changes at the ecclesial level with the appointment of new conservative bishops by Pope John Paul II and a backlash that started, at least, in the years between the conferences of Latin American bishops in Medellín (1968) and Puebla (1979). This created a hostile context for liberation theology but, more generally, it significantly wounded its institutional strength. There was significantly less support among the bishops, and thus less room to work within the structures of the Church. On the other hand, the sociopolitical context changed. From the time of social revolutions and political violence we slowly move to a new season, a season in which the goals of modernization and democratization started shaping the region and the Peruvian experience.[26]

Therefore, liberation theologians faced a twofold challenge: first, the need to expand and continue the struggle for social justice without the important institutional support of the Catholic Church; second, the need to do so in a postrevolutionary context in which the prevalence of the market economy, the spirit of entrepreneurship, the distrust of politicians and the political process, and the emergent but weak process of democratization became the new horizon for the option for the poor.

How did liberation theologians and faith communities address these problems? As mentioned in the previous section, they mobilized support for the cause of democracy and the defense of human rights. Yet some issues remain unanswered: How did they deal with the new economic and political horizon? What kind of new creative balance developed between religious and sociopolitical commitments? Where did they find the appropriate context to materialize them? In order to respond to these questions, I turn to the interviews I conducted between December 2019 and February 2020 with Gustavo Gutiérrez and some of his closest collaborators.

Two clarifications about them are warranted. First, this is a small sample of interviews. However, these are long conversations in which significant details were provided on the issues just raised. Therefore, although limited in the range of actors that they cover, these interviews give us insight about the process. Second, these interviews were conducted with some of the most important leaders of la corriente in Perú. I take this to be both an advantage and disadvantage. On the one hand, these conversations provide deep insight into the trajectory of liberation theology since the interviewees have accompanied and shaped the process from its very beginning. On the other, these conversations would benefit from being supplemented by further interviews conducted with people of the "base." Indeed, all the interviewees are either theologians, university professors, or professionals belonging to the middle class of Perú. They have been active participants in the struggle for liberation, standing in solidarity with the poor for decades. However, the perspective of working-class people would definitely enrich these reflections. Such a project will have to wait for now, but I feel confident that the reflections provided here are an accurate representation of the trajectory of liberation theology since they clearly overlap with those gathered by other works that have focused on the experiences taking place at the "base" level.

Before moving to my interviews, let me show this overlap by briefly focusing on the ethnographic and theological research conducted by Tom Powers with women in the poor neighborhood of El Agustino in Lima, Perú.[27] In this study, Powers conducts numerous interviews that provide great insight into the social, political, and economic context of these poor women and the role of faith in their lives. As we will see shortly, there is substantial overlap among these interviews, those conducted by Pilar Coll for her account of Human Dignity, and mine. In all three cases we see that people's intervention in political affairs was motivated by faith, by a belief in a God who loves all but especially the poor. Politics is a means, not an end. In the case of the women interviewed by Powers, they organized themselves through Servicios Educativos El Agustino (SEA, Educational Services El Agustino), a foundation created by the faithful of La Virgen de Nazareth Parish in 1978. Using SEA as their platform, these women created mothers's clubs, communal dining rooms, communal banks to support small businesses, occupational education centers, infant nutrition programs, health committees, neighborhood organizations, and other networks of support.[28]

Yet a second issue is also worth highlighting, and here we see an important element that does not appear as explicitly in my interviews or Coll's but was addressed in my discussion of religious traditions in Chapter 2: the eminently pragmatic, problem-solving nature of these women's articulations of their experience of faith, of their theologizing. As Powers notes, these women do theology because, faced with the massive problems created by internal displacement, poverty, and violence, they wanted to interrogate their faith to find answers.[29] In this process, their reading of the Bible and their retrieval of key biblical liberating themes is crucial. In many cases, such retrieval is directly influenced by the work of Gutiérrez.[30] Indeed, with him, these women ask: How are we to talk about a God of love in the midst of poverty and oppression, premature and unjust death, and the suffering of the innocent?[31]

In their reading of the Bible, these women find some answers, but they especially find hope, empowerment, and liberation. Not infrequently they do so with a critical attitude toward the Church, noting the limitations of its pastoral work, preaching, and its treatment of women.[32] In some cases, this has translated into a decline in attendance of regular church services. However, several women still strongly claim their Christian identity and see in their work to improve the lives of others and their own "the recognition of God's sacred gift of life."[33] Indeed, as we have seen before and will see again in my interviews, the theme of a life-giving God is central for these women as well. The sacredness of the person is a precious value to them, and the defense of this sacredness is one of their most fundamental commitments to the God of Life. Moreover, this is the case even if it takes place through less ordinary "religious" activities. Let me close with a citation that makes this explicit. Reflecting on her work at SEA and her spiritual journey, Relinda Sosa shares:

I think we all understand that there is a great deal about life that we do not understand. Why am I working here instead of trying to get a job that pays more money? Why was I dedicating more and more of my time to the *comedor* without really knowing whether it was good or bad? Why am I Catholic but I do not go to Mass? Why do I go to the church to cry and pray when I feel depressed? Why has my relationship with my children and my husband improved since I started working with the projects of SEA? Why do I feel closer to God than I ever have before?

I think the answer lies in the fact that, after years of fighting what I thought I should be doing, I have made myself available to Jesus. I am not perfect. I make many mistakes. But I keep on trying to hear the voice of God directing my work.[34]

Gustavo Gutiérrez: "What Saved this Project Was Our Persistence"

The witness of Human Dignity, the women in El Agustino, and many others should not make us believe that the work of liberation theology was properly understood. Despite the clarity with which many influenced by liberation theology describe the balance between faith and politics in their Christian discipleship, several critics preferred not to listen. For some of these critics, liberation theology was an unredeemable Marxist politicization of the Christian faith that had to be eliminated for the sake of religious orthodoxy. For other critics, liberation theology was not a threat to the Christian faith per se, but to their power and prerogatives as members of the ecclesial and social elites, accustomed to rule without challenge. Thus, liberation theologians became an uncomfortable presence that—for some—had to be eradicated.

Despite the already noted changes in the hierarchy of the Latin American Church since the election of Pope John Paul II, drastic transformations in Perú only started late in the 1990s when the former Opus Dei archbishop of Ayacucho, Juan Luis Cipriani, became archbishop of Lima in 1999. Before that, the two previous archbishops were either fully supportive of Gutiérrez and liberation theology (in the case of Cardinal Juan Landázuri Rickets, 1955–1990) or supportive or somewhat neutral (in the case of Cardinal Augusto Vargas Alzamora, 1990–1999).[35] Other bishops in Perú, most notably the former bishop of El Callao and former president of the Peruvian Conference of Bishops, Ricardo Durand, were quite hostile, but never to the point of having sufficient strength for a full-frontal attack on Gutiérrez and liberation theology. The appointment of Cipriani, however, changed things dramatically. Lima has always been one of the most important episcopal sees in Perú, so its influence should not be underestimated. In addition, at the time, Perú had an overrepresentation of Opus Dei bishops, who worked as allies of Cipriani in his quite open effort to eliminate or at least weaken the work of liberation theologians and the base communities.[36]

As Gutiérrez notes in his interview with me, Cipriani removed him and several other priests from their pastoral work in Lima. Cipriani made it increasingly difficult for them and for lay leaders to organize events, workshops, retreats, and the like. For Gutiérrez there is no doubt that "Cipriani really wanted to eliminate everything." He adds: "It definitely was a struggle. Undoubtedly, there was suffering." He continues: "We were on the edge. There were doubts about what to do next." Yet Gutiérrez also highlights that there were ways to persist in the struggle. Cipriani did not take away all their agency. Gutiérrez asserts: "He beat us but did not kill us."[37]

Indeed, Cipriani did not have control over everything. Some things were beyond his reach, like the fact that other bishops had autonomous jurisdiction over their dioceses. And although Cipriani had allies, he also had significant opposition in the Episcopal Conference. Other bishops defended Gutiérrez and the perspective of the option for the poor either explicitly or by opening their dioceses for the work done by him and his colleagues. In addition, Gutiérrez stresses that the theological and ecclesial current shaped by the preferential option for the poor was larger than the experience of the Peruvian Church. Such an approach was already widely disseminated in the Latin American Church, which prevented the possibility of all being lost despite Cipriani's efforts. In this sense, Gutiérrez does not see his work as an outlier but as a way of being a Church that was already part of important sections of the Church in Latin America. Thus, he notes, "we fought a battle from within."

Many things remained in place despite Cipriani's resistance. For instance, the famous Curso de Teología (Course of Theology), a gathering of theologians, lay leaders, and pastoral agents started by Gutiérrez and his colleagues in 1971, never really stopped.[38] Rather, it migrated to the Diocese of Chosica, just a few miles from Lima, where Cipriani lacked jurisdiction. Similarly, Cipriani's pressure forced Gutiérrez and his colleagues to reconsider how to practice and defend the option for the poor in this new, more hostile context. The protagonism of the Bartolomé de las Casas Institute (IBC) in this process should not be underestimated. Established by Gutiérrez in 1974 as a nonprofit, the institute was conceived from the beginning as a sort of think tank for liberation theology, supportive of the Church but independent of it.[39] When Cardinal Cipriani's hostility increased, such independence was crucial to produce resources that would defend the option for the poor as a sound theological perspective. In this sense, the institute's publisher, the Centro de Estudios y Publicaciones (CEP, Center for Studies and Publications) was crucial as well.

As Gutiérrez notes, his own books and the works of others, the publication of newsletters and magazines, all advocating for the option for the poor, were critical in the survival of this theological perspective. The newsletter *Signos* and the slightly more academic but still popular journal, *Páginas*, were and are still key parts of that publishing effort.[40] Similarly, his lectures all over the world, his academic position at the University of Notre Dame, and the fact that many of his colleagues were university professors, enabled la corriente to persist and survive in its darkest hours. Despite the fact that liberation theology was overall a basic ecclesial movement, in this new moment of greater hostility, the institutional and academic developments of this theological approach were decisive for its survival. In fact, Gutiérrez himself notes that he saw his intellectual production as a form of validation of this project, not so much as an end in itself. He has also shared with me that finally obtaining his doctoral degree in theology in 1985, a project he abandoned for decades after the conclusion of his coursework in France, was mainly driven by the desire to give scholarly and ecclesial validation to liberation theology.[41]

In this sense, against some critics, it is important to underscore that Gutiérrez and his colleagues did not decide to live comfortably in the academy and to dialogue merely among privileged minority scholars.[42] Instead, they saw academic production as a vehicle for social transformation, especially in the time of greater hostility and more limited contact with the base communities. But more importantly, at least for Gutiérrez, it was always crucial to produce social change as a member of the *Christian* community. After all, liberation was always understood as "integral liberation." Hence, it was never devoid of its Christian eschatological components.

Ultimately, liberation as salvation is only accomplished in communion with God through Jesus Christ. Therefore, criticizing liberation theology for its alleged failure to materialize "historical projects" for social change appears as a fundamental misunderstanding, both in its overlooking the changes that liberation theology actually produced and in terms of how liberation theologians and people in la corriente construed those changes. Change was never supposed to be fully accomplished in human history, although it should start here. Otherwise, this would not be a theological, Christological conception of the political intervention of the

Christian believer. We should recall—as some Marxist critics of liberation theology soundly do—that liberation theology is ultimately a *theological* project whose engagement in political activism and critique was always faith-based. Similarly, liberation theologians' engagement with Marxism was always partial and critical, permanently shaped by theological concerns and attentiveness to the faith of the people.[43] I return to this shortly.

The social and political context presented its own challenges. The 1990s witnessed a new landscape in Latin America. The neoliberal economic agenda started eroding certain forms of organization and solidarity. In Perú, this also overlapped with the collapse of Izquierda Unida (IU, United Left), the organization that gathered the most important parties of the Left. Such a context generated a sense of distrust in the traditional political parties and a loss of hope in the big structural changes promised by the Left. In part this is what explains the election in 1990 of Alberto Fujimori, a newcomer who had never previously held public office or belonged to a political party. According to Gutiérrez, the culture of entrepreneurship that started forming during these years came with important problems. In his view, a certain tendency to individualism and greed emerged, even among the poor. In our conversation, he referred to Luigi Zoja's *La morte del prossimo* (The Death of the Neighbor) to highlight that we may be in a situation where solidarity ties have greatly weakened.

A certain pessimism seems to have overcome Gutiérrez. He shares with me: "Some of the things we used to do, do not work as much anymore. There is less community." Yet he immediately continues in a more hopeful vein: "But we never know. What we do know is that life is not separated: the life of prayer from the life of politics. They are different, of course; but there is unity [between them] as well." In fact, Gutiérrez adds in the same interview that when we break the unity between faith and politics in the life of Christian discipleship, terrible things start happening. People want to limit the things God cares about just to those understood as traditionally religious, instead of believing that nothing escapes God's gaze and concern. "But people often resist this unity," Gutiérrez shares. He adds: "We tend to overstress themes like sin or the cross when we think about faith. Sin is, of course, important; but it has to be contextualized. Devotion is important, but [it is] not enough." Fully separating this from our political responsibilities appears to him to be a mistake, a theological mistake. "Yet," he adds, "we should acknowledge that there is lack of trust in the political process. And that lack of trust is legitimate."

Therefore, the new ecclesial and sociopolitical situation demanded a change of strategy. It also demanded new forms of articulation of our fundamental question, that of the relationship between faith and politics. As Gutiérrez stresses, the new situation required "a transformation of our way of living out our Christian faith. We kept the same beliefs, but there were changes: we had to find new meeting places and areas of outreach, we had to add nuances, some things [like their parishes] were taken away from us." A spirituality of resistance and persistence had to develop. Laypeople, for instance, migrated to nonprofits in which they continued to live out the values of their Christian faith. The Bartolomé de las Casas Institute was vital in that process. It became a place of resistance that gave resources to many people, lay and religious, to defend the option for the poor. One central aspect of such formation, Gutiérrez adds, was the study of magisterial documents so that people could understand that the preferential option for the poor was deeply embedded in the social teachings of the Catholic Church.

At a more personal level, Gutiérrez shares: "For me the question was if all this was worth doing. I decided to do it. But many friends in Latin America decided to leave [the Church, the project]. I tried to convince them to stay. But I do not blame them; the conditions were worse in other places." He adds: "What saved [this project] was our persistence. We learned how to be Christians in difficult times. We learned from the example of Jesus: there is suffering, but we can also have joy, hope, and celebration. That is the way you resist."

The Early Years: "Faith Leads to Commitment, and the Commitment Is Political"

The experience of some of Gutiérrez's closest collaborators over the years confirms and expands on his observations.[44] Based on interviews that I conducted between December 2019 to January 2020, the following testimonies reveal an experience of the articulation of faith and politics consistent with that of Human Dignity, the women of El Agustino, and Gutiérrez himself. I take these conversations to be of special importance because all my interlocutors have been part of the process of formation and development of liberation theology in Perú. All of them have worked closely with Gutiérrez as academic colleagues—all are or were professors at Pontifical Catholic University of Peru (PUCP), where Gutiérrez taught for decades. Similarly, all of them have worked closely with Gutiérrez as leaders of multiple faith-based initiatives within and outside the Catholic Church—some, for instance, participated in different capacities in the work of Human Dignity. They have all pursued scholarly projects in their own disciplines—theology, sociology, economics, psychology, and politics—shaped by the preferential option of the poor. They have all devoted their time to faith-based political activism for the sake of the poor and marginalized, a good deal of which took place through the Las Casas Institute that Gutiérrez founded. Lastly, they have all shared in prayer and reflection their commitment to the Christian faith, a commitment in which the influence of Gutiérrez and liberation theology has been paramount. Hence, they have been shaped and have shaped the development of liberation theology over the last five decades in ways very few others have done. To their reflections on faith and politics I shall now turn.

Fr. Andrés Gallego, a Spanish priest with decades of experience doing pastoral work in Perú, maintains that most students he advised in the Unión Nacional de Estudiantes Católicos (UNEC, National Union of Catholic Students) and the Movimiento de Profesionales Católicos (MPC, Catholic Professionals Movement) had some form of political affiliation. The conviction was that "faith leads to commitment, and that the commitment is political."[45] Gallego immediately adds: "But the theological basis [of this political commitment] always was that the Kingdom of God is larger than any political party." Later he adds: "In Perú being a Christian did not imply having a particular kind of political position. What led to such a position was the nature of [the Christian] commitment."

All interviewees agree on this. Catalina Romero, a professor of sociology at PUCP, recalls her time as a member of UNEC, stressing that in the faith communities

politics was always interpreted critically, from the perspective of faith. Liberation theology did not identify with any political party. What was central was the defense of life, especially during the times of terrorism. There were tensions

between faith and politics, and these were often discussed, but political affiliation itself was not discussed in community.[46]

Ultimately, these were first and foremost *faith* communities. On political
affiliation, Romero stresses, "there was no global or official view." Javier
Iguíñiz, an economics professor at PUCP, further confirms and contextualizes some of these remarks:

In UNEC there was great closeness to the ecclesial process [Vatican II], and great
spiritual dedication, with constant retreats, for instance; but there was also great
attention to politics. We paid attention to the political process, but it was always
critical attention. We were critical of [military junta chairman, General Juan]
Velasco,[47] critical of the Cuban Revolution, because we saw the poor as historical
subjects. So, we did not support any form of statism or authoritarianism despite
there [being] many Church-currents that favored Cuba.[48]

Drawing a contrast with the Chilean experience of Cristianos por el
Socialismo (Christians for Socialism), Iguíñiz adds:

Our Christian values always made us suspicious of any official political position.
There was a fear of identifying our faith with any concrete political project. We
rejected political labels and especially rejected the use of "Christian" in political
labels. . . . [We thought] that political affiliation must be totally plural, open,
although open to perspectives with a social orientation.

Carmen Lora, the director of CEP, the publishing house of all Gutiérrez's
books in Perú, confirms this point:

No [political] position had the monopoly over faith. We had long discussions
about this with our Chilean friends . . . in Christians for Socialism . . . for us
that was a kind of assimilation of faith into politics that we did not live in the
same way and did not perceive as the healthiest or most appropriate relationship. For us, faith had other dimensions, and that was key among us to maintain certain plurality, but also to have respect for people who, being conservative
from our political perspective, had an authentic experience of faith. . . . This was
very characteristic of the Peruvian experience. Here the contributions of Gustavo
[Gutiérrez] were very important to understand that religious experience cannot
be reduced to only one [political] option.[49]

In contrast, Lora adds that this plurality was not as common in certain
conservative circles that saw Left-leaning groups as inherently non-Catholic. The Sodalitium Christianae Vitae, a lay apostolic movement that was

antagonistic toward liberation theology since its inception, was the standard-bearer of this position. As Lora notes, things were aggravated with the emergence of Sendero Luminoso, which led to the identification of the Left with terrorism among many Peruvians, a problem that persists to this day.

Lastly, Rolando Ames, a former senator and magistrate of the Peruvian Truth and Reconciliation Commission (CVR), expands on some of these same issues.[50] In his view, "following Jesus means giving up one's life through active fraternity." But he sees in the Christian faith a "more comprehensive, long-term view . . . a greater awareness" than that of Marxism or even movements that appeared to be shaped by fraternity and solidarity, like the Cuban Revolution. For him, there were greater demands of personal consistency and intimate, personal sharing in the context of the Christian faith community. "We had political commitments, but our Christian community was that, Christian; it was nurtured by prayer, prayer was like our 'vitamin.'" Groups of Marxist orientation knew that and regarded this Christian commitment with suspicion, as lacking loyalty to the revolutionary project. Ames adds, "Marxists called it 'double affiliation' (doble militancia). Christians were somewhat rejected because Marxists believed they 'sugarcoated' class struggle."

Interestingly, Ames maintains that there was great respect for Christians as well. For instance, Ames recalls the admiration with which Javier Diez Canseco, one of the best-known leaders of the Left in Perú and a longtime congressman until his passing in 2013, spoke about left-wing Christians. Similarly, Gutiérrez, one of Diez Canseco's college mentors and a close friend, remembers many conversations with Diez Canseco in which he would repeat: "Most people leave [the struggle for justice], but you Christians stay."[51]

Why was this the case? Ames believes that the Christian horizon to understand the political realm was more comprehensive, wider. Christians in la corriente were not ideological; they did not consider themselves an "enlightened" group. Some orthodox Marxists did, trying to intensify social contradictions to bring about the revolution. In this sense, Ames claims that left-wing Christians had a mediating role among other groups in the Left. This was particularly true within IU—the coalition of the most important political parties of the Left. However, the mediating role of left-wing Christians remained crucial after the breakup of IU in 1995. Ames shares his memories of a conversation with a fellow ex-member of IU: "You [the Christians] were a small group, but you created the context for people to come together. There was something about your consistency, your behavior."[52]

Gallego believes that this mediating capacity and the less ideological stance in politics is connected to the importance of liberation theology in Perú:

In Perú people did not feel the need to leave the Church to engage in politics. Probably this was the case due to the strong theological accompaniment, to a type of theological reflection capable of accompanying the political commitment. . . . There was a lot of theological work on the notion of the Kingdom of God. . . . Being a Christian implies a commitment to the creation of social, historical conditions for the presence of the Kingdom. Gustavo [Gutiérrez] has always been very careful [about this issue]. He never said, "the construction of the Kingdom of God." [For him] we do not build the Kingdom. We build a church; the Kingdom we receive. Nevertheless, it is possible to create conditions for receiving the gift of the Kingdom through the struggle for justice, for truth. And these [struggles] are what many experienced in their political affiliations.

Iguíñiz agrees and expands on these issues:

We experienced great unity between our political and Christian identities. We combined commitment, prayer, and theological reflection. The central issue was that our Christian commitment must have relevance in our social life. . . . The openness of our Christian commitment was disconcerting for some on the Left. They had trouble understanding that we were not interested in taking over political power. . . . The work of Gustavo [Gutiérrez] was key in this regard, opening new possibilities. Thus, we avoided oversimplifications, theological or sociological. By reading social reality from the perspective of the Bible, we were able to see the poor in more complex ways than Marxists and without political instrumentalization.

All interviewees agree on this matter: their political commitment was less ideological and did not imply the embrace of any form of political orthodoxy about social change or power-building, Marxist or otherwise. Lora, discussing the importance of the Cuban Revolution, summarizes the position of Christian leftists at the time with a question: "Why would the revolution have to be an atheist revolution?"

The Middle Years: Hostility, Neoliberalism, Depoliticization, and Pentecostalism

The situation of liberation theology changed drastically starting in the 1980s. In the Peruvian context, the situation became especially aggravated during the 1990s and the long tenure of Cardinal Cipriani as archbishop of Lima (1999–2019). Yet some of the issues mentioned before had great importance in controlling the impact of what became a full-frontal attack. Key among them was the nuanced theological work of Gutiérrez and his colleagues. Gallego notes:

It was hard to theologically delegitimize liberation theology. So other attacks were put forward: they called us Marxists, for instance. . . . Gustavo [Gutiérrez] was theologically more thorough than others, but he was also wiser in his way of handling the internal politics of the Church. . . . We developed responses, mainly to avoid provocation . . . We kept in mind that we were part of a social fabric. So we became more careful, but without giving up on our ideals.

We should keep in mind that for Gutiérrez and la corriente, theology is a service to the church. He has called it an ecclesial function.[53] In this sense Gallego's comment on being part of a "social fabric" is particularly illuminating. For Gutiérrez and the faith communities influenced by his thinking, being part of the larger community of the Church is an essential component of their identity. As Gallego also notes, this does not mean giving up on their critical approach to the Church and society, but it does mean that finding balance between belonging and critical distance is essential. Breaking from the Church was never a desirable goal.

Nevertheless, the hostility toward the work of liberation theologians and the base communities did have an impact on the organization of pastoral work and on Christian identity. As Gutiérrez noted, many restrictions were imposed, and new creative responses were necessary. Key among them was the effort to give continuity to the option for the poor beyond the institutional Church structure. Romero highlights, for instance, that after the fall of several centers and missions that for years had been the institutional embodiment of the option for the poor,[54] the work of many committed Christians migrated to nonprofits: "In the NGOs we gave continuity to our practice of fraternity." Iguíñiz agrees: nonprofits, the state apparatus, and academia became new spaces, but not only because of the hostility of certain sectors of the Catholic Church. It was also because political affiliation started declining in the 1990s after the global collapse of socialism and the failure of the Izquierda Unida project in Perú.

Romero adds: "Christian values became secularized facing a Church that became more hierarchical and more focused on sacramental piety." Lacking a context to embody the preferential option for the poor through the means provided by the institutional Church, Christians did not give up their Christian identity or values. Rather, they found *new ways to express them* outside the institutional context, in the saeculum. *This* notion of secularization—not to be confused with Barger's "full secularization," discussed in Chapter 1—was already present in the work of Gutiérrez, but in this new moment it became more than a theological approach. It was forced by the circumstances because the "religious" spaces for the embodiment of the preferential option for the poor started to disappear. Hence the work *had* to migrate to the secular organizations of civil society.

For instance, in Perú several institutions and organizations were created during the time of political violence (1980–1992) and in its aftermath: AFAVIT (Asociación de Familiares Víctimas del Terrorismo; Association of Families Victimized by Terrorism), APRODEH (Asociación Pro Derechos Humanos; Association for Human Rights), IDL (Instituto de Defensa Legal; Institute of Legal Defense), the Vicariates of Solidarity, and some Evangelical institutions also focused on human rights. All these groups were gathered under an umbrella organization called CNDDHH (Coordinadora Nacional de Derechos Humanos; National Committee of Human Rights), whose first executive secretary was Pilar Coll—the human rights lawyer whose work on Human Dignity we studied earlier. What matters for my argument here is that, except for the Vicariates of Solidarity and the Evangelical organizations, none of the other organizations were religiously affiliated. Notably, however, 60 percent of the members of these organizations were connected to churches, the vast majority to the Catholic Church and to the groups influenced by liberation theology.[55]

In the interview, Gallego described this process quite tellingly as "learning to be Church outside the Church." Telling indeed, because this assertion *reframes* the religious-secular dichotomy. As I have argued all along, the key issue for Gutiérrez and the communities influenced by his theology was to produce a new articulation, a new balance between faith and politics, which in turn meant rethinking the relationship between sacred and secular. Instead of conceiving the sacred and the secular as fixed realms, Gallego's perspective implies that the creative agency of individuals and communities can sacralize experiences and institutions. In this sense, these secular institutions of civil society become sacred in some regard through the kinds of activities and goals they pursued, and the intentions behind the actors working in these spaces.[56] Romero adds: "The key intuitions were already present, in principle, in the Gospel, but they required updating. In this context, values like liberty and equality became central." Social theorist Hans Joas, using similar language, describes these new forms of sacralization as reflecting "the intensification of the motivation to put into practice a universalist morality that already exists in principle."[57]

Changes in the Church and the state, respectively, both forced and facilitated all this. The return to a more hierarchical and less democratic Church, on the one hand, and the slow but important democratic gains in Perú, on the other, created a new space. Romero notes that the presence of democratic deliberation, after years of military dictatorship, and the rebuilding of institutions allowed Christians to participate in the democratic process and become involved in government. Both Iguíñiz and Romero note that this transition took place almost in parallel to the emergence and expansion of Sendero Luminoso. Therefore, a large part of the work developed in this newly created democratic space focused on the defense of human rights and the defense of the democratic institutional framework required for that task. Iguíñiz adds, "The focus of 'liberation' changes from an emphasis on ending the dependency [on global economic and political oppressive systems] to an emphasis on human freedom and citizenship. . . . In this context, the notion of individual rights becomes central."

I suggested to Iguíñiz that such a shift of emphasis appears to overlap significantly with some of the key concerns of political liberalism. Was this the embourgeoisement of liberation theology, as some have argued? In what could be taken as a direct response to the critiques of theologian Ivan Petrella, one of the defenders of the thesis of the embourgeoisement of liberation theology, Iguíñiz elaborates quite insightfully. I cite in extenso:

Not if "liberalism" here stands for "individualism." In this sense, we should keep in mind that Gustavo [Gutiérrez] has distanced himself from [some aspects of] modernity but has always claimed to belong to it as well. [Remember that the notion of] "the individual as the subject of their own history" has been present in liberation theology from the beginning. . . . In this sense, such critique comes from those who were instrumentalizing liberation theology in order to advance a simplistic approach, an approach that still exists in Latin America according to which "liberation" is national liberation, liberation from imperialism, from transnational corporations, from economic systems. . . . But liberation theology inserted itself in the changes [dictatorship vs. democracy] that we were experiencing in reality. It was not held back by the theoretical framework of a prior moment. So, yeah, if [the defense of] democracy means embourgeoisement, sure, liberation theology adopted bourgeois values . . . it is not hard for me to imagine such a reading. But what this critique shows is a frustration . . . that liberation theology was not the tool that outlived the decline of socialism, the decline of Marxism in the political practice of Latin America. . . . Even though I am not familiar with this formulation of the critique . . . my provisional interpretation is that this possibly is the reaction of those who did not realize that liberation theology was not the replacement of the fervor, the militance typical of the traditional way to deal with the Latin American problem . . . [of those who did not realize] that liberation theology was not a conceptual framework dependent on the Cuban Revolution. . . . It became clear that liberation theology was not easily [politically] instrumentalized . . . because liberation theology did not reinforce the old way of doing things. In this regard, it also helps that in Gustavo [Gutiérrez] the more "Latin Americanist" social analysis of reality is present in 1971, but not after. . . . What really happens, more than changes at the theoretical level, is that the agenda becomes more complex after the end of the dictatorships. . . . I believe that [Gutiérrez's work on] Bartolomé de las Casas is an important intermediate moment in this regard . . . about claims of national sovereignty . . . and indigenous vindications vis-à-vis Latin American thought. [There we see] a liberationism with one foot on the classical [systemic, structural approach] and the other on more personal, spiritual approaches, on an inward experience of our solidarity with the oppressed.

I will return to these matters in the final chapter, but I would like to highlight two ideas. First, as noted all along in this book, liberation theology clearly distinguished itself from other liberationist projects, particularly those of political parties of Marxist orientation. It did so because this was a theocentric, faith-based, Christian approach to liberation. Such a distinct approach is obvious, and this is worth underscoring, *both* in the self-understanding of the members of la corriente and in the judgment about them passed by the secularly minded members of the Left.[58] As we saw with Human Dignity, this distinctiveness did not prevent cooperation with nonreligious activists. It simply shaped the goals and orientation of those fighting for justice from a faith-based perspective. Second, liberation theology has a "liberal" component, in the sense of the defense of liberty and fundamental individual rights. As Iguíñiz notes, this should not be confused with the embracement of individualism but should make us reconsider the relationship between political liberalism and liberation theology. Such reconsideration is the task of next chapter, in which we will study the correlation between political and theological accounts of the dignity of life. I return now to my historical reconstruction.

The religious and political landscapes changed in other regards as well; liberation theology's challenges were not only the emergence of a hostile conservative wing of the Catholic Church and the sacralization of certain forms of secular human rights activism. The 1990s was also the time in which Evangelical Christians started showing their true strength while the political process became more and more apolitical because of the failure of socialism and the triumph of the neoliberal economic model in Latin America. In fact, these two phenomena seem to be deeply interrelated. I focus first on the political dimensions, then turn later to the role of Evangelical Christians in the process.

Neoliberalism and Depoliticization

Lora notes that the breakup of Izquierda Unida—the coalition of left-wing parties—in 1995 deeply wounded the Left, but especially and negatively affected the relationship between politicians on the Left and the masses. This process of estrangement between the political Left and the masses, however, was already under way before 1995. Ames, who was actively involved in the Izquierda Unida project, agrees. The distance that emerged between the Left and the people created a political vacuum that was seized by then-president Alberto Fujimori. Indeed, facing the apparent failure of the socialist model of political organization, Fujimori presented a different model for personal success and social mobility. His was a model of individual entrepreneurship with a massive reduction of the role of government. In addition to Fujimori's neoliberal economic reforms of the 1990s, he was able to persuade the masses of the need of strong leadership to defeat the still-alive threat of Sendero Luminoso. Indeed, Fujimori gained great popularity among the masses with the arrest of Abimael Guzmán—the leader of Sendero—in 1992, which in practice meant the military defeat of Sendero, and the beginning of some economic recovery.

In his run for reelection in 1995, Fujimori won by a landslide—with almost 65 percent of the popular vote. He achieved this despite the growing corruption and authoritarianism of his regime—including the disbanding of Congress in 1992, targeted killings of civilians, and the kidnapping of political enemies, among other serious crimes. Most Peruvians, though, as 1995 election results show, either were not aware of these events or considered them inevitable collateral damages. What mattered most was the promise of pacification and economic opportunity, which, despite these serious issues, was perceived as somewhat fulfilled by the mid-1990s. Many among the poor believed in this promise.

For Lora, this political reality was somewhat replicated in the ecclesial context, which was already quite unfriendly toward liberation theologians. The Church started losing contact with the popular world, and pastors and pastoral agents had trouble understanding the new situation: "The people's option for Fujimori left many of us perplexed," Lora notes.[59] In agreement with Gutiérrez's interpretation about the growth of individualism, Lora maintains that people in la corriente had to find new ways to express their commitments. Pastoral work continued but focused on specific themes. Healthcare, for instance, became an important issue. The work on education remains central. Lora singles out the important contribution of the Jesuits and their vast network of projects in the whole country, key among them being the Fe y Alegría (Faith and Happiness) schools that offer quality education to kids in poor and underserved areas.[60] The prevention of violent social conflict is another area where people influenced by the option for the poor played an important role. The problem of inequality and the abuses of the government in tandem with big corporations always has potential for protest and conflict, so the Church uses its still-extant moral legitimacy to mediate and prevent violence.

In the last couple of decades, therefore, the members of la corriente and their allies have accompanied and helped those left behind by the economic "boom." Their preferential option for the poor has been constant and remains unwavering. For Lora, however, it is undeniable that important changes took place and that "the poor" do not have the same sense of solidarity that was typical in prior decades. Indeed, "poor" in the 1990s and still now is equated to being a "loser"; it is no longer an expression of class solidarity, she maintains. Nevertheless, here is where the theological work of Gutiérrez becomes important again. In his theology, "the notion of the poor is always multidimensional," Lora adds. Perhaps many are not economically poor any longer or conceive their poverty as solidarity-eliciting, but many of them are still left behind, marginalized. Liberation theology still has something to say to them.

In this sense, Ames suggests that Christians of la corriente must redefine their political activity. In fact, many are already doing so by working in government, trying to keep the ideals of the option for the poor alive but now with certain distance from the remaining parties of the Left. For Ames, this is important insofar as some of these parties remain too ideological, unable to recognize that despite all its crimes, the Fujimori regime was able to bring economic stability to the country and end terrorism. Agreeing with Lora, Ames stresses that a context like this is where the strengths of Gutiérrez's theology become more apparent; his approach does not depend on some ideological, political, or economic framework, such as Marxism or dependency theory. Rather, Gutiérrez's understanding of the poor is more complex: the poor are really the marginalized, the nonpersons. Hence, the option for the poor is an option for those who suffer. For Ames this has immense political potential because it allows us to read history against the grain, from the bottom up. Therefore, the same principles remain, but they can converse with a new situation. The option for the poor can still take place in a framework shaped by capitalist macroeconomics, for instance, but with the same critical distance it had from the socialist framework. Thus, liberation theology is well equipped to lead the anticorruption and antiplutocracy fights. More generally, it will continue fighting for a more just, less unequal society.

Pentecostalism: The Option of the Poor?

The growth of Evangelical Christianity is also an important phenomenon of this period. As a matter of fact, Evangelicals played a decisive role in the election of Alberto Fujimori in 1990 and have been an important force in the consolidation of neoliberalism and the culture of entrepreneurship in Perú since then. The most recent surveys suggest that Evangelical Christians comprise around 17 percent of Perú's national population, most of them Pentecostals and among the poor.[61]

Did liberation theologians opt for the poor and the poor opt for Pentecostalism? Some discussion of this apparent dissonance between the choices of the poor and those of liberation theologians is pertinent here. The answer to this question is complex, highlighting the transformation of the religious landscape of Latin America as well as the internal changes of both liberation theology and Pentecostalism. As Romero notes, what we start seeing in the 1990s, especially, is the opening of new political spaces together with the opening of the religious marketplace.[62] Of course, the opening of the latter is the consequence of the progressive growth of Protestant Christianity in the region since the late nineteenth century. However, the already discussed changes in ecclesial and secular politics elicited more rapid growth in the last few decades. From a negative point of view, the deliberate weakening of the base communities directed by the hierarchy of the Catholic Church and the little interest of the latter in a kind of evangelization that could go beyond the mere administration of the sacraments created a vacuum. As Lora notes, this also overlapped with the departure of many foreign missionaries who were clearly aligned with the option for the poor. Many of them were removed by unfriendly bishops, but some also finished their tenure and were sent to new missionary regions by the superiors of their religious orders.

More positively, the ecumenical orientation of la corriente, in line with the developments of Vatican II, did not elicit a countering reaction to religious pluralization. Hence, the emergence of alternative forms of Christian discipleship among the poor and marginalized, *in itself,* did not represent a problem. In fact, it was a natural and positive development of the pluralization of the religious marketplace facilitated by what sociologist José Casanova has called the voluntary disestablishment of the Catholic Church in Latin America after Vatican II.[63]

In sum, on the Catholic side, lack of religious personnel and lack of interest in attending to the problems of poverty and marginalization, in addition to ecumenism and the progressive disestablishment of the Catholic Church, fostered the growth of Evangelical Christianity in Perú. We must keep in mind that Evangelical Christians—because of the historical influence of Methodism and its emphasis on a "methodic" way of life and social cooperation—are traditionally well equipped for the creation of networks of solidarity and small businesses.[64] Moreover, in the context of the new economic model of Perú, they were especially well prepared to offer spiritual and economic support to those among the poor who were left behind by the institutional Catholic Church and the political parties. All this—in addition to its theological and transnational strengths—explains the exponential growth of Evangelical, especially Pentecostal, Christianity in Perú and the region.[65]

As noted, this growth, per se, does not represent a problem. However, liberation theology and Pentecostalism do have significant different ways to conceive the relationship between faith and politics. Further, despite their shared commitment to accompanying the poor, the groups approach poverty from significantly different points of view. On the negative side, Pentecostal Christianity tends to overlook questions of systematic injustice and institutional violence. On the positive end, Pentecostals tend to pay significant attention to microsocial change, in which personal healing, local leadership, solidarity, and entrepreneurship are key.[66]

Naturally, this new situation represents a challenge to which people in la corriente are still attempting to respond. Politics, particularly, remains an area of significant disagreement. Some of the most vocal Evangelicals in Perú, most of them Pentecostal, oppose systemic political and economic change, rehearsing old critiques that equate these changes with an inevitable path to become some version of Cuba or Venezuela. Further, they often see *this kind* of involvement with politics as misguided, since true change happens through the power of Jesus alone, through conversion.[67] However, some Pentecostal leaders do participate more actively in politics. Yet they tend to have a monopolistic approach to the political: they aim to accumulate political power via democratic means in order to enforce their religious agenda. The issues of gender equality, same-sex relations, and abortion are some of those that receive special attention. In these areas,

Pentecostal leaders have received important support from the conservative wing of the Catholic Church.

Yet we should not assume that the most vocal, conservative, and antagonistic voices represent the entirety of the Pentecostal movement in Perú. The same is true of Catholicism. Different streams exist within each, and this allows us to find areas of potential or actual agreement and room for mutual growth and learning. For instance, the Catholic Church can see in Pentecostalism a model of Church that is less hierarchical and more open to participation of the laity. Vatican II already made that invitation, but the Church is a complex entity, and some sectors still fight to see the prior system reign. However, the shortage of priestly vocations almost forces this faction to acknowledge that it is extremely hard to continue running the Catholic Church under the clerical model. Of course, this laity-focused model was already advanced by liberation theology, but the challenge of Pentecostalism may become an invitation for the expansion of a less hierarchical system.

But the Pentecostal experience casts light on some of the limitations of liberation theology as well. As noted, the arrival of democracy, the perceived failure of the socialist project, the massive expansion of the market economy, and the general distrust in the political process became serious challenges for la corriente. Pentecostalism and its Protestant ethic, in contrast, seemed especially well-suited to provide the kind of religiosity that this new moment needed. In this sense, liberation theology can learn from Pentecostalism to operate within a more limited framework for social change in which personal struggles and small forms of social organization take a more central role. Liberation can have a greater focus on personal regeneration, adding to its always important stress on liberation from oppressive structures an edge that was not as present in the initial years.[68]

Similarly, without losing its critical edge or the overall goal of big structural change, liberation theology can encourage and support entrepreneurial initiatives among the poor. In this way, social transformation is conceived as possible not only through grand-scale change, but also through the private initiative of the poor themselves to solve their immediate needs. Plenty of this is currently being done.[69]

In turn, globally and locally, Pentecostalism is facing the challenge of its own past and present mistakes, particularly in the political realm. Its antagonism with the Catholic Church and its desire to acquire a better public status has led some of its leaders to support political figures and regimes that appear to fundamentally contradict Christian values. The support for the dictatorships of General Augusto Pinochet of Chile (1973–1990) and General Efraín Ríos Montt of Guatemala (1982–1983) among some Pentecostal churches are only the two most shocking examples.[70]

From a theological and pastoral point of view, Pentecostalism faces the additional challenge of not becoming the "opium" of the people. It is true that many among the poor experience addictions, domestic violence, psychological trauma, and so on, and Pentecostalism has done very well providing moral compass and spiritual healing to so many. However, for a long time, it has overlooked structural issues that, in many ways, are the cause of the suffering of the poor that Pentecostal churches serve. Without rejecting its identity, Pentecostalism can revisit its social ethics by going beyond microsocial sanación (healing) to embrace the call for a misión integral (integral mission) that integrates spiritual depth and sociopolitical concerns.[71] As a well-known Guatemalan Pentecostal leader bluntly puts it: "Faith is more than just the music."[72]

Now, as noted before, not all Pentecostals are politically disengaged. Some are indeed public officials, political figures, and civil society activists. The common denominator between them—provided that honest religious piety is still on the table, which is not always the case—and those less actively engaged in politics is the sense of Christian moral responsibility to make the world a better place. The problem is that the call to be Christian citizens and to transform society into a City of God can feel like the weight of the whole world is on one's shoulders.[73] Dismissing the importance of the political process as a value in itself—not as mere means to Christianize society—puts all the responsibility of transforming society in the believer's faith, and this burden seems to be even heavier than the one advanced by liberation theology, in which big structural change is achieved through political action. Thus, Pentecostalism could see in the spiritually rich versions of liberation theology—like Gutiérrez's—a model in which faith and political action are organically connected. Paralleling the learning curve of liberation theology, this has also been happening for a while in the experience of many Pentecostal churches.[74]

In my view, the relationship between liberation theology and Pentecostalism underscores some of the distinct features of Latin American religion, while pointing to promising possibilities. On the one hand, beyond how much mutual learning has taken place between liberation theology and Pentecostalism, their persistent tensions and affinities make evident that Latin America is one of the contexts where the secularization thesis has been proven untenable. Modernization, democratization, and industrialization have not led to the decline or extinction of religion. Quite the contrary, they have elicited new narratives of sacralization that place the sacredness of human life, especially the life of the poor and most vulnerable, at the center of the Christian narrative of salvation. In this sense, the preferential option for the poor—in its liberationist and Pentecostal versions—has become a distinct feature of Latin American Christianity. On the other hand, the different approaches of liberation theology and Pentecostalism to the option for the poor point to the possibility of greater ecumenical dialogue and mutual learning. Indeed, deeper collaboration could lead to something more powerful than the already crucial acknowledgment of the sacredness of the poor. It could lead to a more integral way to deal with their situation by providing liberation *and* healing for the most vulnerable. I will return to these issues in the closing section of this chapter.

The Later Years: Aparecida, Pope Francis, and the Challenges Ahead

All interviewees agree that liberation theology has the theological and spiritual resources to face the challenges of our present situation. Yet they have slightly different interpretations of how those resources can be deployed to meet these challenges. Further, their different approaches seem to depend on their evaluation of the institutional Church. More independence from the Church often translates into a more optimistic tone. Less independence tends to translate into a slightly less hopeful outlook.

Iguíñiz points to the end of the 2000s as a place to find some answers. The Latin American and Caribbean Bishops Conference of

Aparecida, Brazil in 2007 is for him a key moment. There, the preferential option for the poor was praised and affirmed as a fundamental element of the experience of the Latin American Church. Pope Benedict XVI, the former prosecutor of liberation theology, was central in that moment of praise and affirmation.[75] Initially, Iguíñiz shares, people of la corriente approached the conference with suspicion, and understandably so. The previous Bishops Conference—held in Santo Domingo in 1992—was not at all representative of the values of the option for the poor, reflecting the already studied backlash against liberation theology that started in the late 1970s. Hence, without the vigorous liberationist leadership of the bishops gathered in Medellín or Puebla, and with the already disappointing experience of Santo Domingo, Aparecida did not appear to be a promising gathering. Therefore, when the conference unfolded and the documents started to become public, people of la corriente were gladly surprised. But then everything made more sense.

The results were the consequence of the type of work Gutiérrez and his colleagues pursued for decades, especially in times of hostility. Gutiérrez's sound theological work was able to become part of the theological consensus among a minority of the bishops. Indeed, Iguíñiz adds, his theology was deeply present, unanimously, among a minority who still had power in the hierarchy. Thus, without any prior coordination, when the bishops gathered in Brazil, this minority organically and spontaneously coalesced behind the prophetic perspective of the option for the poor, showing the consensus Gutiérrez and others were able to build over the decades. Pope Francis, then Cardinal Jorge Bergoglio, was part of that consensus.[76] The generational change and the loss of power among some of Pope John Paul II's appointees, especially those belonging to the Opus Dei, also favored such theological agreement. According to Iguíñiz:

They [the conservative group] only thought about the numbers because they had a bureaucratic understanding of the Church, whereas the vision of Gustavo [Gutiérrez] and many others was an inspirational, creative, principled, dedicated vision . . . that was meant to give meaning and orientation to the life of people. In this sense, Gustavo has been the vigilant guardian of the core of this vision. . . . Not everything is easy . . . but this [vision] continues to be what has given meaning to many lives in the Church . . . a little part of which became bishops . . . which is like, at the institutional level of the history of the Church, the ripening of a fruit whose seeds were planted [long time ago] and that was able to keep alive the motivations, enthusiasm, and dedication of an ecclesial commitment.

Iguíñiz sees the future with hope, but not naïvely. He believes that the papacy of Pope Francis has great potential for reform in the Church, to which we should add the importance of Francis's pastoral style. But many challenges persist; celibacy and gender relations are central among them. Iguíñiz believes that liberation theology has many resources to deal with these issues because, as all the interviewees noted, its subject is not merely the economic poor. Rather, its main concern is the unquenchable problem of exclusion and marginalization. However, he believes this is mainly in the hands of the laity since there is always great resistance to change in the hierarchy of the Church.

Romero and Lora agree, adding a more local perspective. According to Romero, the appointment of Fr. Carlos Castillo as archbishop of Lima in 2019 has created a new and favorable context. Castillo is a longtime friend of Gutiérrez, a theology professor at the Pontifical Catholic University of Perú, and very close to la corriente. In addition, Pope Francis has appointed several new bishops in Perú whose pastoral work, like Castillo's, has been shaped by the preferential option for the poor. Many of these bishops have reestablished connections with some of the pastoral agents who were central to the success of liberation theology in the past. Romero sees a quite productive context in this new moment. Lora notes also the global importance of Pope Francis and the local role of Archbishop Castillo and other authorities. Yet she highlights the presence of a generational gap between this generation of bishops and the newly ordained priests and lay leaders. Further, like Iguíñiz, Lora notes that there is a great sense of responsibility among the laity, but that their professional responsibilities are extremely demanding, leaving little time for pastoral work. In addition, because of the prior time of hostility, many spaces for such pastoral work do not exist anymore. Hence, there are new possibilities but also a lack of clarity about what is next.

Romero adds some perspective based on her scholarly work on religious pluralization in Perú. She uses the concept of diffuse religion to describe the kind of religious belonging common among Peruvians these days. By this she means a kind of religiosity that is passed on by family members, not by clerics or the institutional Church. Diffuse religion is fundamentally about cultural values and identity, not so much about doctrinal beliefs. For this reason, Romero sees it as the foundation of the faith of *both* Evangelical and Catholic Christians in Perú. In this sense, she believes that *this* is the basis for any kind of evangelization project. But if such a project were to take place, it must do so always respecting and trusting people's freedom, paying attention to the way communities organize their life instead of simply bringing something to them from outside. Romero's approach is somewhat pragmatic, noting that this diffuse religion is part of the new religious landscape in Perú. It is not necessarily a good or bad thing, simply a fact.

In contrast, Gallego's perspective is more somber and shows a certain degree of perplexity, not unlike Gutiérrez's own take. Asked about our present situation and the future, Gallego shares:

More than a prospective vision, I can share with you my concerns. I feel that in this moment we have a problem, a problem about how to make our faith explicit. We have progressively lost the contexts and the ways to express our religiosity, to express our faith. To give you an example, the Course of Theology was a way of making explicit our faith, the faith of la corriente, sometimes gathering two thousand people. Well, that has shrunk. But I think it has shrunk due to the strong penetration of neoliberalism, and [a] certain kind of secularization and egoism in our culture. . . . [In this context] it is very difficult to express the concern for a way to understand faith as shaped by community, by solidarity. I feel that to be community today is harder than before. And I also believe that there is less commitment. . . . We have a meeting this upcoming Saturday where I have to present on how to encounter God today, in these times and in the situation of our country . . . and I do not know what I am going to say. It is not an easy topic for me.

After a pause, Gallego elaborates:

When I refer to the problem that we have to make our faith explicit . . . what I am saying is that we have a problem [doing] theology today. Making faith explicit is not simply going to mass, although that [is important] too; making faith explicit is knowing how to pray, knowing how to confront your life with the practice of Jesus . . . this is what I see today as lacking . . . we do not have the appropriate ways to do this. And then we return to old formulations, but today they are empty.

An emotional pause follows, and then Gallego adds in a more hopeful tone: "I was recently reading about [Mario] Vargas Llosa's newest book . . .

Tiempos recios [*Tough Times*]. I do not know if he has read Saint Teresa [of Ávila], but that is a phrase of Saint Teresa: 'in tough times, strong friends of God.' And I believe that we are in tough times."

I bring this section to a close with some concluding remarks. First, the testimonies of the interviewees substantially agree on their assessment of the relationship between faith and politics in liberation theology. The central issue is to express their commitment to the Gospel and to the poor through the transformation of society, a transformation that requires political, systemic change.

Second, while their faith led supporters of liberation theology to pursue political engagement, there was ample room for disagreement and different political affiliations among them. The main reason for this is that most of liberation theology's advocates understood that the political was *only one area* for the manifestation of their commitment to the Gospel and the poor. Faith is always more profound and comprehensive than politics. Christians should create the conditions of the advent of the Kingdom of God. But ultimately, the Kingdom is always a gift; never something that can be produced by us.

Third, since there was no dogmatic political or theoretical affiliation, liberation theology was able to navigate different historical circumstances, modifying its strategies without giving up its core concerns. Plainly, this happens in the transition to a postrevolutionary moment in which the reconsideration of socialist hopes and the emergence of democratic alternatives in the region changed the political landscape. In this new era, liberation theologians and their communities focused on democracy building and the defense of human rights, first, against obvious violations and abuses, and later, against more subtle forms of abuse like the persistence of poverty, social inequality, gender and racial marginalization, and the destruction of the environment.

Fourth, liberation theologians have been particularly well-equipped to deal with intra-ecclesial conflict. On the one hand, this was possible because of their relative autonomy via the foundation of centers and institutes, their publishing and teaching, and so forth. On the other, a constructive response to ecclesial conflict was possible because liberation theology was able to shape the official teachings of the Catholic Church over the decades. In this sense, the key ideas of this theological tradition, the preferential option for the poor and the need to make such an option pay attention to systemic change, have become important parts of magisterial teaching, especially with Pope Francis.

Lastly, we can detect a slightly different approach to the future among the members of la corriente represented in my interviews. Interestingly, there seems to be a pattern of response depending on the ecclesial role of my interlocutor. Gutiérrez and Gallego, both priests, seem to have a gloomier but still hopeful approach to the future. It appears that their slightly somber tone is related to what they perceive as the erosion of certain forms of community, the progressive decline of the type of faith communities they were able to form and nurture in their pastoral work. Some sense of concern for the kind of communities that the institutional Church can foster appears to be important in their reflections.

In contrast, my other interlocutors, all of them laypeople, seem to see the situation with certain cautious optimism. Nobody denies the challenges that Gallego and Gutiérrez detect, but they do not seem to see the situation of the Church with similar concern. Instead, as Romero pointed out, there seems to be a more sociological approach that acknowledges the changes and sees in them opportunities for the formation of new communities and new forms of faith expression. Yet these new forms may look very different from the ones common among the base communities of the past century. The same may be true for the political, as Ames suggested in the interview. We may imagine that a "spiritual but not religious" model (or what Romero called "diffuse religion") can continue growing, but we should not necessarily see in this the death of community-oriented faith and political engagement. Rather, we may see them as new forms of expression and, perhaps, new forms of sacralization as well.

The Possible Futures of the Christian Option for the Poor

Let me elaborate on these issues in conversation with the work of Hans Joas on the articulation of Christian ideals in new historical situations. Some of the questions and challenges raised by my respondents are relevant not only for liberation theology but for the Christian faith as a whole. Although all the interviewees are part of the Church current, la corriente, shaped by liberation theology, they are first and foremost *Christians* and face the new challenges as such, not only as members of a theological school of thought or particular social movement. Fundamentally, they do so because they believe that the preferential option for the poor is not just a passing theological fashion. Rather, they believe it to be at the core of the Christian Gospel. Therefore, these are challenges for the Christian faith as a whole, not only for liberation theology.

Interestingly, liberation theology's radicalization of the Christian tradition may function as a blueprint of how to meet the challenges confronting the tradition as a whole.[77] The answers for the future may lie in interpreting the tradition as being in permanent revolution, permanently going back to its core values and reinterpreting them creatively in order to solve new problems generated by new historical conditions. I now turn to a more systematic identification of these challenges in dialogue with Joas's own discussion of the possible futures of Christianity initially addressed by theologian Ernst Troeltsch. Joas's focus is on Europe; mine is on Perú and Latin America. Yet the issues converge organically. Following Joas, I divide my account into sociological and cultural-intellectual challenges.

At the sociological level, Joas identifies three major challenges: the dissolution of traditional milieus, implicit religion, and globalization. The first two deserve consideration here. I will not discuss the question of globalization because its relevance in the context of Joas's study (Germany and Europe) is to present a challenge to the false equation of Christianity with European culture. Since my whole investigation is predicated on the idea that such equation is indeed false—showing the vigor and creativity of Latin American Christianity—I do not find it necessary to dwell on this topic.

As Joas notes, referring to Germany, "the dissolution of confessional milieus has indeed made it more difficult for families to pass on their faith. . . . But if we take account of differing degrees of the intensity of religious practice, a different picture emerges."[78] In my interviews with Gutiérrez and Gallego a similar concern emerged. Gallego offered a somewhat bleak assessment: we no longer seem to know how to express our faith, be a community, or do theology. But perhaps we should consider whether he is collapsing two different issues. Sociologically, it is certainly true that a more confessional Catholic milieu is in decline. This is true of Perú and Latin America, and importantly true regarding the poor. In Perú this can be partly explained by the process of neoliberal modernization and attributed to the growth of Evangelical Christianity, especially Pentecostalism. However, from the perspective of Christian value formation, this may offer an opportunity: "the question must be how values can be passed on in new ways amid such [a] change of milieu and how they can arise anew through new experiences. It may be that values and faith are sometimes poorly transmitted precisely because they are in a sense shut up in a milieu."[79] Therefore, the decline of certain forms of Christian life may be an opening for new options. Let us recall that this was Gutiérrez's assessment of the process of secularization-as-differentiation already in the 1970s. Further, the fundamental concern for the poor and marginalized can be an especially powerful thread to guide this transition.

This point directly connects to "implicit religion," which "refers to the multifarious values and practices that constitute an 'ultimate point of reference' . . . for those concerned."[80] We may connect this sense of implicit religion to what Romero calls "diffuse religion." In both cases what remains central is a fundamental sense of self-transcendence that is yet lived through spiritual practices and values that are not directly connected to formal religious affiliations. Now, the losses in formal Church affiliation are not balanced out by these new forms of casual piety. However, these new forms of spirituality do exist, and not only in Europe or the United States but also in Latin America.[81] Thus, the question is how this new implicit or diffuse religiosity affects the old forms of religiosity. Further, the question is whether the alleged individualistic tendencies of the new spiritualities are somehow related to the erosion of community and solidarity, a key concern of Gutiérrez and Gallego.

These questions take us to the cultural-intellectual challenges that Joas identifies in conversation with Troeltsch.[82] First, for Joas, two modern forms of egocentric individualism challenge the Christian ethos of love: utilitarian and self-expressive individualism.[83] Similar concerns have been raised by my interviewees. In contrast, Joas notes (drawing from Robert Bellah and colleagues) that there are two other viewpoints that focus on the individual in non-egocentric ways.[84] One is republicanism, understood as virtuous action for the common good of the political body. However,

Joas notes that republicanism has particularistic propensities, often deriv-
ing in nationalistic tendencies. For this reason, the biblical concern for the
individual—the other non-egocentric option—is a crucial alternative tradition. For in this tradition moral decentering is essential: "When making
decisions people are morally obliged to consider, not only those of their
fellows who belong to the same family, republic, nation, religion, or class,
but everyone, every human being, including future generations."[85] Philo-
sophically, this universalist intuition has been elaborated (among others)
by John Rawls, as Joas notes. I will return to Rawls and his contributions
in the following chapter.

What I want to highlight now is that individualism and chauvinistic
republicanism are true challenges for the Christian faith, but they are not
insurmountable—especially not if the preferential option for the poor is
stressed. The key to revealing the limits of individualism and chauvinistic
republicanism may lie in the way Christians articulate the interdepen-
dence of love and justice, as Joas maintains. I profoundly agree. In my
view, following the insights of liberation theology, we may reach a high
point of articulation of these two ideals. Jesuit theologian and martyr
Ignacio Ellacuría quite aptly expressed this by noting that justice is the
historical manifestation of love:[86]

> Abstractly, distinctions between what love is and what justice is can take place
> both as psychological and Christian outlooks. But, concretely, love must mani-
> fest itself as justice in a world of injustice. [Love] is not a prior stage or something
> that must be completed, as often happens in the social teachings of the church.
> Neither justice is prior to love, nor is love the supplement of justice. In justice we
> see the materialization of love, the realization of love in a historical situation.[87]

The unity of love and justice may also represent one of those exceptional
contexts in which norms (which are mostly restrictive) and values (which
are mostly attractive) converge.[88] In this sense, the Christian tradition,
especially with the radicalization of the ethos of love taking place in liberation theology, can produce such integration of the valuative dimensions
of love and the normative dimensions of justice.[89] But this requires further clarification, to which I will turn in the final chapter. The point for
now is that the integration of love and justice is indeed a challenge that
may require the formation of sui generis forms of community and a more
flexible approach to what we consider the Christian faith. However, the

craving for community and self-transcendence is always there, as is also the cry of the poor and marginalized. We have witnessed some of this during the global spread of COVID-19. New forms of community and solidarity formed and are forming. Perhaps they will give us a blueprint for what is next.

And perhaps the blueprint already exists, in principle, in the tradition, if we think about churches not so much in terms of confessions or denominations but as "networks of agape," as Joas suggests following Charles Taylor.[90] In *A Secular Age*, attempting to imagine a Church that is both modern and faithful to its Christian fundamental values, Taylor writes:

The life-blood of this new relation is agape, which can't ever be understood simply in terms of a set of rules, but rather as the extension of a certain kind of relation, spreading outward in a network. The church is in this sense a quintessentially network society, even though of an utterly unparalleled kind, in that the relations are not mediated by any of the historical forms of relatedness: kinship, fealty to a chief, or whatever. It transcends all these, but not into a categorical society based on similarity of members, like citizenship; but rather into a network of ever different relations of agape.[91]

Such an approach will definitely represent a challenge if we think about faith and community in terms of milieus, or in terms of fixed ritual rules or doctrinal securities. However, if a more diffuse understanding emerges, new spiritual possibilities emerge as well. According to Joas and Taylor, these new possibilities could be shaped by agape, the quintessential form of Christian love that manifests itself through our reverence for God and care for our neighbor.

From the perspective of a network of agape, confessional differences become less relevant. What remains central is the values that all Christians share.[92] Further, it also matters greatly what Christians share with other religions and nonreligious worldviews. In this sense, the Church can still hold to be one, but not uniform; holy, but also sinful, and in need of permanent reform; missionary, but in a dialogical, inclusive, and inculturated form; and Catholic in the sense of embodying moral universal values in concrete situations.[93] Therefore, a new spirituality of agape may develop as an alternative to egocentric forms of individualism and nationalistic forms of solidarity.[94] Again, liberation theology seems to be particularly well equipped to meet this challenge since its history has always been one of ecumenism and collaboration with nonreligious people, bringing people together around the values of love and justice for all, but especially for the poor and marginalized.

Joas also highlights the challenges to the Christian understanding of the sacredness of the person. Here, again, the perspective provided by liberation theology is particularly illuminating. Beyond the different forms of reductionist naturalism often attacking Christian personalism, the real issue is Christianity's own historical failure in defending the sacred core of every human being. We may say that this is a challenge related to the legitimacy of the Christian faith, about its moral authority and credibility. In this sense, the long-standing defense of the rights of all, but especially of those of the poor and marginalized, puts liberation theology in a strong place. Further, liberation theology historically emerged as a form of immanent critique of the Church's betrayal of its own commitments to the values of the Gospel. In this sense, it became a radicalization of values already existing in the tradition, but rarely fully embodied.

Therefore, a Christian faith oriented by the preferential option for the poor can meet this challenge twofold: first, by giving orientation to the Church through its example of a long-standing commitment to the sacredness of life, going even beyond the person to include the sacredness of all creation. Second, by remaining a self-critical voice that condemns any form of triumphalism, it reminds the Church of its failures, and keeps it accountable. But in doing so, a faith shaped by the notion of liberation could also become a strong defense of the idea of transcendence understood as the "radical desacralization of all structures of political domination and social inequality."[95] Joas has in mind such a defense of transcendence vis-à-vis the totalitarianisms of the twentieth century, but the same is true in the context of terrorist attacks of Sendero Luminoso in Perú. A Christian faith shaped by the notion of a God of Life who unconditionally loves all, but especially the poor, appears to be particularly well equipped to advocate for the transcendent sacredness of life against all those who instrumentalize it for political, ethnic, or any other reasons.

4

The Struggle for Social Justice

BETWEEN PUBLIC RELIGION
AND PUBLIC REASON

One of the key contributions of sociologist José Casanova to the sociology of religion is the development of the concept of public religions, and the correlative idea of the deprivatization of religion in the modern world. The two concepts can be summarized as follows:

Religions throughout the world are entering the public sphere and the arena of political contestation not only to defend their traditional turf, as they have done in the past, but also to participate in the very struggles to define and set the modern boundaries between the private and public spheres, between system and life-world, between legality and morality, between individual and society, between family, civil society, and state, between nations, states, civilizations, and the world system.[1]

One of the key examples of public religions studied by Casanova is Latin American liberation theology. Indeed, as I have shown in previous chapters, liberation theology does not enter the political arena to defend the traditional turf of the Catholic Church—as previous models of religious-political participation did. Instead, liberation theologians in Latin America entered the political arena to defend the rights of the poor and marginalized. In the context of political violence studied in Chapter 3, this also implied a strong defense of democracy and the democratic ideals of liberty, equality, and peaceful coexistence. A defense of democratic

ideals developed—and this is worth noting—against a political movement, the Shining Path, whose *stated* ideals were to bring justice to the
poor and marginalized.

The cruelty and terror spread by the Shining Path in its unsuccess-
ful attempt to take over the Peruvian state made crystal clear, for liberation theologians and many of their allies in the progressive movement,
that liberty, equality, and peaceful coexistence were nonnegotiable ideals.
Democracy became a must for liberation theology. Yet this did not mean
a naïve idealization of democracy. Distinctions had to be drawn between
the ideals of democracy and their quite defective and unfinished material-
ization in Peruvian society. In this sense, as Casonova suggests, the publicness of liberation theology became both a challenge *and* a development of
the foundational ideals of liberal democracy and its understanding of the
public sphere.

What is at stake here is our interpretation of which may be the most-
just social arrangements of our living together in a political community
(the question of social justice) and the correlative question of which may
be the most adequate forms of intervention in the public sphere (the question of public reason). But since we are discussing the intersections of
public religion, public reason, and social justice, one central issue we must
reckon with is that of the *role of religions* in the very formation and development of a society's conception of social justice.

Casanova, again, gives us a hint of what may be taking place in this
dynamic relationship between public religion, public reason, and social
justice in our time:

Western modernity is at a crossroads. If it does not enter into a creative dialogue
with the other, with those traditions which are challenging its identity, modernity will most likely triumph. But it may end up being devoured by the inflexible,
inhuman logic of its own creations. It would be profoundly ironic if, after all the
beatings it has received from modernity, religion could somehow unintentionally
help modernity save itself.[2]

What if religion, indeed, is the key to save the ideals of liberal democracy
from its more than occasional illiberal tendencies? What if *certain understanding* of religion is the key to retrieve the emancipatory core of modernity and democracy? What if certain *religious ideals* can enrich, challenge,
and keep honest the aspirations behind our frail modern democracies?[3]

I would like to suggest that this is indeed the case. But this requires, in turn, that we think about religions as complex and multifaceted, identifying the streams of religious thought and belief that embrace the emancipatory thrust of modernity and democracy. That is, religious communities that embrace *as their own* "the cognitive critique of traditional religious worldviews, the moral-practical critique of religious ideologies of legitimation, and the subjective-expressive critique of religious asceticism and alienation—while upholding publicly the sacred values of modernity, that is, human life and freedom."[4]

My argument so far should have made clear that these values are at the heart of liberation theology. Liberation theology is, by its own genesis, an immanent critique of traditional Christian views of how to relate to the question of poverty and injustice. It is a critique of the legitimation of a status quo—both political and ecclesial—that allows the hunger, marginalization, and suffering of so many. And it is, lastly, a critique of religious mindsets whose disproportionate emphasis on spiritual matters leads to the vanishing of any serious concern for the need of the most vulnerable here and now. In turn, as we have discussed in Chapter 1, liberation theology, through its understanding of the unity of history, is fundamentally committed to the defense of freedom and the affirmation of life. But this requires further development, especially if we want to understand both the overlap with and the critique of modernity at the center of liberation theology.

I propose approaching these issues in three steps. First, I consider the question of public reason and the conception of social justice behind it. Second, I examine the advantages of this understanding of public reason and social justice, especially when it comes to clarifying liberation theology's own conception of justice. Lastly, I close by sketching what I call an *inclusive* conception of social justice that incorporates religious intuitions, thus offering a more realistic and potentially successful account of the kind of alliances necessary to pursue a more just society.[5]

Public Religion and Public Reason: Reframing the Problem

One of the most definitive statements of the meaning of public reason in contemporary political thought has been developed by John Rawls. Studying his position on the topic will prove to be illuminating for our purposes. However, there is an added advantage in focusing on Rawls's treatment of the topic. Several scholars maintain that Rawls—and liberalism, in general—has some kind of hostility toward religion or, more precisely, toward religious arguments in the public sphere.[6] If these scholars are correct in their assessment, this will totally undermine the legitimacy of a public religion like liberation theology from a Rawlsian perspective. All religious argument in the public sphere—Rawls would argue, according to his critics—should be precluded for the very sake of democracy.

But, as noted earlier, my position is the opposite: the presence of religions and religious arguments in the public sphere not only is healthy, but *may* help to strengthen democracy and the struggle for social justice. Rawls, in turn, has provided one of the most sophisticated and influential theories of social justice. Therefore, if such a theory were to be opposed to the public presence of religion, it would follow that, according to Rawls, social justice is achievable only by circumventing religious faith. Or put differently and more bluntly: religion must not be part of our public debates because religion undermines social justice. As I noted in the introduction to this book, this is the position held by many still today. But it is not mine. As I shall argue, neither it is Rawls's. Moreover, I take this position to be both theoretically and practicably untenable.

These common misconceptions are derived from the fact that the content of our personal beliefs is excluded from what Rawls calls the "original position." As it is well known, this is a device of representation designed by Rawls in *A Theory of Justice* to establish the principles of justice on which reasonable people can agree. In turn, this means that the principles of justice must be determined *without* appealing to concrete religious beliefs or, in fact, to any kind of comprehensive doctrine of the good.[7] It is not my interest here to discuss the hundreds of pages devoted to the study and critique of Rawls's theory, something I have done elsewhere.[8] But a few considerations seem in place to discard some clearly incorrect readings of Rawls's approach.

The first is that "the original position is not, of course, thought of as an actual historical state of affairs, much less as a primitive condition of culture."[9] It is a *purely hypothetical* situation."[10] From this follows the idea that the original position does not attempt to produce a full philosophical anthropology or to depict people as they truly are. Rawls comes closer to a full philosophical anthropology in Part III of *A Theory of Justice*, when he discusses what he calls his "full theory of the good." Many critics overlook this crucial section of the book, directing their ammunition against the original position as if Rawls did not supplement his "thin" theory of justice with a "thick" one, in which solidarity, benevolence, and community are crucial.[11] But let us focus on the original position for the purposes of my argument.

The following are the main features of the original position: no one knows their place in society, nor do they know their fortune in regard to natural assets, nor their conceptions of the good, nor their psychological propensities. Rawls calls this state of unknowing the "veil of ignorance." In short, the principles of justice must be chosen behind the veil of ignorance so that nobody enters the decision-making process with advantages or disadvantages. In such a way, "since all are similarly situated . . . the principles of justice are the result of a fair agreement or bargain."[12]

Now, the knowledge the parties *do not* have is as important as the knowledge they *do* have. The representative individuals entering the social contract do so knowing what Rawls calls "the circumstances of justice," namely, that there will be differences of class, income, ethnicity, and so on, as well as differences of ends and purposes. This implies that in all likelihood the society they are shaping would be marked both by identity of interest *and* by competing claims that can create conflict, especially if we grant their mutual disinterest[13] and the condition of moderate scarcity.[14] But, as noted before, because they decide behind the veil of ignorance, "they do not know how the various alternatives will affect their own particular case."[15] Reasonable people, then, would agree to terms of cooperation that would allow them to further their interests and well-being *and* would abide by them willingly.[16]

For Rawls this is crucial because even though the agreement reached in the original position is not historical but hypothetical, it has the potential to have binding force in concrete historical situations. Put differently, "the conditions embodied in the description of the original position are ones that we do in fact accept. Or if we do not, then perhaps we can be persuaded to do so by philosophical reflection."[17] When people assess their *actual* terms of cooperation in their *current* societies, they can use the principles of justice of the original position as a point of reference.[18] Hence, if current arrangements can be referred back to basic principles on which we would all agree in ideal conditions of equality (the original position), then those arrangements are just and we can justly demand cooperation from one another. Note also that given that this is a device of representation and not a historical situation, it can, in principle, be simulated by anybody as an exercise of their moral imagination.[19] I will return to the strengths and weaknesses of this line of argument later in this chapter.

All this considered,[20] Rawls believes that the parties behind the veil of ignorance will choose two basic principles.[21] In his words:

the first requires equality in the assignment of basic rights and duties, while the second holds that social and economic inequalities, for example inequalities of wealth and authority, are just only if they result in compensating benefits for everyone, and in particular for the least advantaged members of society.[22]

Rawls believes that given the conditions examined here, it makes sense that prima facie people will choose equal distribution of social goods: they know there is so far no reason to receive more than that and they have no reason to settle for less. This equal distribution includes equal liberty and equal opportunity, of course.

But the parties can also consider an alternative view. Given that they know that inequalities will arise because they know the "general facts of human society," they can consider the regulation of inequalities in such a way that they could "make everyone better off in comparison with the benchmark of initial equality." The way to do that, Rawls argues, is to consider the position of the least advantaged in society: "inequalities are permissible when they maximize, or at least all contribute to, the long-term expectations of the least fortunate group in society." He calls this the maximin rule, for it maximizes the minimal share. From this follows that injustice is "simply inequalities that are not for the benefit of all,"[23] especially the least fortunate. Perhaps the reader has already noticed that this second principle seems to overlap, in philosophical parlance, with the notion of the preferential option for the poor advanced by Gutiérrez and his colleagues. But drawing this connection more clearly is the task of later sections of the chapter.

For now, let us stress that the remarks supplied earlier should suffice to dismiss charges that argue that Rawls defends a philosophical anthropology that uproots or dislocates the self.[24] What Rawls defends is the capacity that each of us has to use our moral imagination—the capacity to interpret and reinterpret critically, constructively, and comparatively the moral resources we have available[25]—to consider what the conditions for a just society should be. Rawls presents to us a moral ideal—expressed in his ideal theory—whose practical implications are enormous. As with any ideal, what matters most is the normative and subjective orientation that ideals give to our lives, not their literal realization in reality. His position certainly has some problems, to which I will turn shortly. But a deliberately truncated philosophical anthropology and the postulation of an impractical moral ideal are not some of them.[26]

My central interest here, though, is not to get entrapped in debates about Rawls's oeuvre, but to pay attention to aspects of his work that can help us advance an account of justice in which religions enter the public sphere to advance the ideals of democracy. In this sense, it is undeniable that Rawls does not ground the principles of justice in any religious conception of the good life. The main reasons for this have already been explained while discussing the formulation of the original position. But does this mean that religion has no role in public debates or in the defense of the principles of justice? Let us turn to these questions by discussing Rawls's take on religion and public reason.[27] I will address first his approach in *A Theory of Justice* and later his account in *Political Liberalism*.

A Theory of Justice: What Is the Role of Religious Freedom?

In *A Theory of Justice*—especially, in §§ 33–35—Rawls examines religion and public reason focused on the question of liberty of conscience/religious freedom. First, he defends the centrality of equal liberty of conscience. From the perspective of the original position, he argues, "it seems evident that the parties must choose principles that secure the integrity of their religious and moral freedom." Of course, they do not know what their views are or how they will fare in society. Precisely for that reason, they will seek fair terms of cooperation. In Rawls's view, "it seems that equal liberty of conscience is the only principle that the persons in the original position can acknowledge. They cannot take chances with their liberty by permitting the dominant religious or moral doctrine to persecute or to suppress others if it wishes."[28]

Rawls also has something to say about those who believe that equal liberty is an imposition on their beliefs:

A person may indeed think that others ought to recognize the same beliefs and first principles that he does, and that by not doing so they are grievously in error and miss the way to their salvation. But an understanding of religious obligations and of philosophical and moral first principles shows that we cannot expect others to acquiesce in an inferior liberty. Much less can we ask them to recognize us as the proper interpreter of their religious duties or moral obligations.[29]

From this argument, Rawls moves to the limitations on the equal liberty of conscience. His basic point is that the limitations should serve "the common interest in public order and security." Here he is extremely careful to stress that this "does not imply that public interests are in any sense superior to moral and religious interests; nor does it require that governments view religious matters as things indifferent or claim the right to suppress philosophical beliefs whenever they conflict with affairs of state." He clearly states that "the notion of the omnicompetent laïcist state is also denied."[30]

So, when *can* the state intervene? Only when there is reasonable expectation that the freedom of some will affect the public order, meaning by this that it will affect the conditions "for everyone's achieving his ends whatever they are (provided they lie within certain limits) and for his fulfilling his interpretation of his moral and religious obligations." Such expectation must be based on evidence and ways of reasoning generally recognized as correct—the question of public reason, to which I will turn shortly. Rawls adds: "Now this reliance on what can be established and known by everyone is itself founded on the principles of justice. It implies no particular metaphysical doctrine or theory of knowledge." In sum, "the limitation of liberty is justified only when it is necessary for liberty itself, to prevent an invasion of freedom that would still be worse."[31] Of course, those limits can also be reassessed if the general principles of justice remain standing.

In sum, Rawls has a careful understanding of the role of religion in the public sphere from both the level of the ideal theory and the level of actual public deliberations. Religious freedom is heavily encouraged and only limited when it wants to limit the freedom and well-being of others. Obviously, sometimes the lines are hard to draw, and the judiciary will have to make some ad hoc decisions. But this does not invalidate the core of the argument.

Political Liberalism: Can Religious Argument Enrich Public Reason?

One difficult and representative case puts some extra pressure on Rawls's account of religion. The example at issue is Abraham Lincoln's second inaugural address. The reason why Lincoln's address presents difficulties for Rawls's framework is that the speech brings up religious premises in order to defend principles of basic justice.[32] Here we are closer to the issue that concerns us, namely, public religions and public religious arguments.

Rawls has two different lines of reasoning for the Lincoln speech. Both approaches address public religious discourse from a *normative* perspective; that is, both responses to the Lincoln address consider what *ought* to be the case for the sake of good democratic citizenship. But Rawls obviously knows that, at the *descriptive* level, religious arguments are always going to have a place in the public sphere simply because religious people inhabit the public square too. So, the point is never to pretend that we can or should live in a world in which religion disappears from the public arena. The question is whether certain forms of religious intervention are more or less conducive to strengthen good democratic living, that is, a kind of living together in a political community that honors equal liberty and pays special attention to the needs of the least advantaged among us.

But before getting into these matters, we should further clarify what is meant by public reason. For Rawls, this is directly related to having a public conception of justice. In such a society, people know and accept the principles of justice, and the basic social institutions generally satisfy them.[33] Of course, not all societies have the same principles of justice. But, generally speaking, Rawls believes that most democratic modern societies embrace some form of the two principles of justice discussed earlier. Asserting that these two principles constitute a *public* conception of justice means that the rules and structures to adjudicate different claims are publicly available and that people appeal to them to resolve their possibly competing needs.[34] Accordingly, public reason is public in three ways: "As the reason of citizens as such, it is the reason of the public; its subject is the good of the public and matters of fundamental justice; and its nature and content is public, being given by the ideals and principles expressed by society's conception of political justice, and conducted open to view on that basis."[35]

Let us return to Lincoln and to Rawls's first take on public religion. In the 1993 edition of *Political Liberalism*, Rawls considers Lincoln's speech appropriate for an *inclusive* understanding of public reason.[36] In that context, Rawls argues that in societies marked by conflict it may be necessary to include arguments coming from comprehensive doctrines when dealing with issues of the basic structure. Rawls has in mind the work of the abolitionist and civil rights movements, heavily religious in both their motivations and the articulation of their motivations. On this account, comprehensive arguments are allowed *only* if these arguments advance the cause of a public reason that will not depend on them in the future.[37] One should add to this, as Rawls does, that, strictly speaking, Lincoln's speech does not have direct bearing on constitutional essentials (in contrast with a Supreme Court decision, say).[38] Thus, even if it violated the provision of offering publicly available reasons, the violation would have had no major consequences on questions of basic structure. Or, alternatively, it could have *indirect* bearing on the basic structure, becoming a source of inspiration for constitutional changes, as in fact was the case. But the key piece of the argument is the former, namely that, when required, a more inclusive understanding of public reason is in place for the sake of public reason itself.

The second line of reasoning appears in the preface to the 1996 edition of *Political Liberalism*. In Rawls's view, this is a yet more permissive approach. Here Rawls drops the conditions stated earlier (conflict and need of nonpublic arguments for the sake of the development of public reason). He defends, instead, the idea that comprehensive reasons, religious or otherwise, can be introduced in public discourse *at any time*.[39] Rawls simply adds a proviso and asks that in due course public reasons be presented *as well*. In his view, this is important to make explicit the common ground—overlapping consensus[40]—between these comprehensive doctrines and the principles of justice, so that the public alliance to the latter is strengthened and, with it, the stability of democracy as well.[41]

Bracketing the details for a moment, one immediate conclusion can be derived from these two lines of reasoning about public religious argument: religious discourse can be—and historically has been—a fundamental source of motivation in the struggle for social justice. The civil rights movement led by Martin Luther King Jr. or the resistance to the terror of the Shining Path led by Gutiérrez and his colleagues made decisive contributions to the cause of social justice in each of their societies. The United States and Perú became more peaceful and more just societies—however unstable these gains are—because of the religious advocacy of King, Gutiérrez, and many others. Public religions have a key role to play in democracy, and Rawls does not deny it. He rather recognizes it openly, calling the *religious* support of the *political* conception of justice its "vital social basis."[42]

Now, some scholars have taken issue with Rawls's approach because the *religious* dimension of public discourse seems to be treated as an accident that can be tolerated but must later be overcome.[43] Let us examine this more carefully, putting aside the admiration that Lincoln, King, Gutiérrez, and others deserve. Is Rawls's position—as philosopher Jeffrey Stout suggests—that Lincoln's addresses and King's speeches are mere "placeholders for reasons to be named later"?[44] I do not believe so. Rawls's point is that in certain contexts, the religious nature of these speeches can be a source of misunderstanding, confusion, or disagreement. But this is also true of any comprehensive doctrine that appeals to ideas that are not generally available to most people.

An argument for social justice based on, say, Karl Marx's metaphysics of class conflict in history would provoke similar reactions in Rawls. Would it not be wise to suggest that *when needed* ("in due course"), more widely available forms of argument are used? Such a shift does not imply denying the importance of Lincoln's address or the fact that it deploys religious rhetoric and arguments. It only means that the lines that define what is publicly available shift over time and depend on the history of each society. It is perfectly conceivable in the future, or even today, that Lincoln's appeal to God could become a source of division or simply an idea without any currency. In such a scenario, out of respect for different views or just as a matter of political strategy, it does not sound absurd to suggest that more widely available forms of argument can be used to advance the same goal. I believe this is all that Rawls is saying.[45]

Certainly, there is some room to interpret Rawls as demanding too much from religious people who use religious arguments in the public sphere. According to some critics, Rawls is asking them to detach themselves from their core beliefs, undermining their capacity to live a "religiously integrated life."[46] But there is another way to interpret this: a more charitable, accurate, and productive way, I would argue. As with the original position, I believe that Rawls is not asking us to deny who we are, dislocating ourselves. Rather, I see here an invitation to use our moral imagination. Rawls expects that the members of the political community can—and want to—communicate with each other in ways that are understandable to each other. Often this will require from us that we change our register, using different images, alternative concepts, and so forth. It will require finding common ground, both by trying to see things from the perspective of our interlocutors and by appealing to general and widely recognizable reasons and experiences. Interestingly, all this is something most of us do on a regular basis when we meet a stranger, travel to foreign place, or start learning a new language. Clearly, Rawls's point is not mere philosophical speculation. Indeed, this capacity for role taking and generalization are essential elements of our human sociability, but they are also essential for democracy.[47] Without the willingness to entertain alternative views and understand their context of emergence, we are condemned to misunderstanding and conflict or to live in isolated clusters without communication with each other. Arguably, the combination of conflict and isolation is one of the greatest current threads to democracy in the United States.

But Rawls *actually* goes beyond mere tolerance of religious discourse. In "The Idea of Public Reason Revisited" he considers some important examples that make this plain. First, he recommends ("it is wise"[48]) that people introduce their religious-comprehensive views when some contentious political issues are at stake—for instance, public support for religious schools. This is necessary for the sake of justice and understanding. Bracketing religious views here is unwise, since we would not understand the nature of the disagreement. The same could be said about abortion. A different matter is to judicially decide these cases—if and when this happens—using comprehensive arguments, something that Rawls, and, I imagine, most of us oppose. Yet this example shows that Rawls's position clearly encourages the public presence of religious views and arguments in the public sphere.

Another form of public presence of religion is what Rawls calls *declaration*. Declaration consists in openly stating the religious values behind a person's or a community's support for the principles of justice at the basis of the political conception of a given democracy. For instance, he writes: "Citizens of faith who cite the Gospel parable of the Good Samaritan do not stop there, but go on to give a public justification for this parable's conclusions in terms of political views."[49] Not surprisingly, and in agreement with my interpretation in this book, Rawls himself acknowledges the affinity between his political principle of difference—that of the special attention to the needs of the worst-off in society—and the Christian care for the poor.[50]

Rawls also considers *conjecture*, which he defines as the kind of public engagement with our fellow citizens where we argue based on what we believe to be their basic, comprehensive beliefs. We could even slightly modify Rawls's point here and imagine that we *know* what those beliefs are, a case closer to my previous example about abortion or public funding of religious schools. What matters here, though, is to engage in conversation using arguments internal to our interlocutor's comprehensive views to point out that they can still—on the grounds of their own religious views—endorse the political conception. This may imply detecting inconsistencies, suggesting the reorganization of the hierarchy of certain religious values, and revisiting forgotten ideals of our own traditions in order to find better forms of understanding each other as citizens. Thus, conjecture can certainly make religious arguments more intelligible to nonreligious people, or, in other words, more *public*.[51] But it can *also* make religious people reconsider the very nature of the beliefs they hold.

In addition, it can make them realize that they can express their religious beliefs in alternative or nonreligious language for the sake of better understanding. It is a two-way street.

Critics seem to assume that such creative new forms of expression do not take place, as if we were all rigidly able to express our main religious concerns solely through monistic means. But that is surely not always the case. The whole point of Rawls's overlapping consensus regarding a political conception of justice depends precisely on maintaining that that is not always the case. Indeed, Rawls conceives of people being capable of seeing themselves and their own comprehensive doctrines represented in *that* consensus. Now, this is precisely what we saw in Chapter 2, especially through my study of the work of David Tracy.

The Christian tradition—but this is true of all traditions—is a self-interpreting tradition that is constantly and creatively reinterpreting itself. Most certainly, not all interpretations are equal, but the fact of revision and reinterpretation vis-à-vis new developments is undeniable. For Tracy, this is directly related to the *public character* of the Christian faith in a twofold way, due to interrelated practical and theological reasons. On the one hand, practically, the Christian faith is public—à la Rawls—insofar as it aspires to *public intelligibility*. The goal is to make Christian claims understandable to others, not only to Christians. On the other, theologically, the Christian faith is public because at its core it has the duty of proclaiming a mystery that it holds as the source of salvation for all. Hence, for the believer, presenting their beliefs to others in understandable ways is a *responsibility* of their faith. In that process, though, the believer may learn to speak different "languages," depending on need and context, learning that some of the claims of their faith may need revision as well.

Lastly, Rawls considers the case of *witnessing*.[52] Using the example of Quakers' pacifism, he argues that in some cases people who generally accept the political conception of justice may feel compelled to express their disagreements about specific issues *on comprehensive grounds*. We can say the same of multiple other forms of *religious* criticism of the present political order. As noted before, liberation theologians—in Perú, in the United States, and in many other places in the world—have been some of the strongest defenders of freedom and equality, while paying special attention to the needs of the most vulnerable. Therefore, the religious critique is not against the political conception of justice itself, since equal liberty and attention to the needs of the most vulnerable are the two principles of justice at the core of most democratic societies. The critique is, rather, against the fact that these principles are so rarely realized in our modern democracies. Rosa Parks, Martin Luther King Jr., Dorothy Day, Abraham Joshua Heschel, Gustavo Gutiérrez, James Cone, Delores Williams, and so many lesser-known people of faith have appealed and continue appealing to the language and ideals of their religious traditions to make the world more just. In the name of God, they denounce the injustices of the present political arrangements by giving witness that the God they believe in opposes injustice and wants the flourishing of all creation.

Now, having demonstrated that Rawls gives ample room to religious argument in the public sphere is not an attempt to overlook some problems in his understanding of public reason.[53] In a recent chapter, for instance, philosopher Jeffrey Stout revises and expands his critique of Rawls in *Democracy and Tradition*, targeting Rawls's convoluted development of the notion of public reason.[54] Stout rightly points out that Rawls seems to have at times a more inclusive and dialectical understanding of public reason, and other times a more restrictive approach to it.[55] I agree with Stout's critique regarding Rawls's "murky" account of the concept, granting that there are inconsistencies in the multiple angles through which Rawls approached the topic. However, following my prior remarks, I support a more holistic approach and embrace what I take to be the essential components of Rawls's notion of public reason: that, ideally, people should do their best to produce arguments that are as publicly available as possible, but without any restriction to religious arguments and values in the public sphere.

In this sense, I disagree with Stout's interpretation of Rawls's position vis-à-vis the figure of the hypothetical "Great Orator."[56] For Stout, this is a paradigmatic figure of ethical social change (he models it after Gandhi, King, and others) that uses nonpublic reasons to make society more just. The Great Orator does so by inspiring people and often by challenging the public consensus about just social arrangements. Stout suggests that Rawls's more restrictive understanding of public reason would not be happy with such a figure. Moreover, it also implies that Rawls's approach has trouble accounting for creative innovations like this, since they would not proceed through public argument alone. Ultimately, Stout implies, Rawls's model could end up justifying the status quo.

But this is a quite uncharitable reading of Rawls's point, although *hypothetically* possible based on some of the inconsistencies Stout highlights. Beyond the arguments already presented, I would like to point out that Stout overlooks in his critique the *actual* content of *justice as fairness*. Stout seems to forget that the thrust of the project is to create just social arrangements based on the principles of equality and difference, not to validate *any* kind of public consensus just because it follows from widely accepted modes of reasoning. Equality and difference *normatively* define the most basic meaning of social justice. If a society violates these principles, it is unjust. It does not matter if injustices are widely accepted and validated through public reasoning.[57] Therefore, Stout's suggestion that Rawls's model of public reason would indirectly endorse slavery or other forms of abuse if the arguments against it are not public strictu sensu appears to me as untenable. *Formal* publicity is not what really matters. What matters is the ultimate goal of public reason; what matters is justice. Hence, Stout's reading is only possible *if* one takes public reason in its narrowest, most formal sense *and* isolates it from the content and goals of Rawls's project.

But the thrust of Stout's critique is well taken. Rawls's model appears to be rigid at times and some of its parts do not seem to be fully connected, which leaves room for the criticism of those who are not interested in connecting the pieces and tend to generally reject formal and too-theoretical approaches to justice. Stout's pragmatist orientation and focus on grassroots organizing puts him in that camp.[58] But I have suggested another view. Indeed, it is possible to develop an approach based on Rawls that gives great emphasis to our moral imagination and to the formation of ideals, to our role-taking in moral reasoning, and to the creative process necessary to produce an overlapping consensus. In my view, this perspective allows the achievements of Rawls's theory to come into sharper focus. *Justice as fairness* does not offer a once-and-for-all answer to all issues about social justice, but "at least provide[s] guidelines for addressing further questions."[59] Yet these are key guidelines, for they give us a blueprint to adjudicate among conflicting claims about the good, the most pressing issue in pluralistic societies.

Now, the purpose of my discussion of Rawls is to expand and clarify our understanding of public religions like liberation theology. The role of this examination of his account of public reason is to show that religious believers can enter and actively participate of the political arena as *religious* people, without having to bracket their beliefs or pretending that their commitment to social justice does not have religious or theological roots. Indeed, I have shown that Rawls does not expect that. In fact, his notion of "overlapping consensus" presupposes that the political conception of justice developed by one's society must be socially validated through different means, often appealing to religious comprehensive doctrines. In other words, the active participation of religious believers in support of the principles of justice is a *necessary*—although not sufficient—condition for the development and stability of a just society.

From this follows that liberation theology can be construed as an example of Rawls's "overlapping consensus." What Rawls only discusses at the theoretical level is powerfully realized in liberation theology. As we have seen in previous chapters, liberation theology, through its creative interpretation of the resources of the Christian tradition, puts forward a conception of justice that very much overlaps with Rawls's, as Rawls himself recognized. Moreover, in practice, this movement was always able to navigate organically the demands of public reason and the demands of the Christian tradition. But this requires moral imagination and creativity.

Let us turn now to this exercise of the moral imagination by considering how these political and theological conceptions of social justice relate to each other. What can they learn from each other? What are the theoretical and practical advantages of examining this overlapping consensus? The contributions of the work of David Tracy, studied in Chapter 2, will help us frame these issues in terms of analogy and critical correlation.

The Critical Correlation Between Liberty and Liberation

My contention is that there is a strong analogy between Rawls's and Gutiérrez's accounts of social justice. We can see this by examining Rawls's two principles of justice in dialogue with Gutierrez's threefold account of liberation. Rawls's *principle of equality*—that of the equality in the assignment of rights and duties—finds its analogue in the second dimension of liberation discussed by Gutiérrez in *A Theology of Liberation*. There, Gutiérrez writes: "Liberation [is the process of] humankind assuming conscious responsibility for its own destiny. . . . The gradual conquest of true freedom leads to the creation of a new humankind and a qualitatively different society."[60] In my view, Gutiérrez's oeuvre should be considered an elaboration of this idea in terms of equal liberty and equal respect, the key two elements of Rawls's first principle of justice.

In turn, Rawls's principle of difference—that social and economic inequalities are just only if they result in compensating benefits for everyone, and especially for the least advantaged—finds its theological analogue in the preferential option for the poor. As shown earlier, this is explicitly acknowledged by Rawls.[61] Indeed, for both Rawls and Gutiérrez no just society can exist if its basic structure does not guarantee access to basic social goods for the "least advantaged members of society." The principle of difference is Rawls's political-philosophical articulation of this issue. The preferential option for the poor is a political-theological articulation of the same problem.

Indeed, for Gutiérrez, liberation from oppression—the first dimension of liberation[62]—operates through the option for the poor, through the conscious decision of the poor, and of those standing in solidarity with them, to fight against poverty and subjugation. But we must underscore that the goal of liberation is to achieve a life of fulfillment in which we can experience the fullness of our liberty while being treated with respect. In this sense, liberty and liberation—like the principle of equality and the principle of difference in Rawls—are in a *lexical* order for Gutiérrez as well.[63] Freedom from oppression cannot be pursued at the expense of freedom itself. Doing this simply betrays the ultimate goal of liberation. As I have shown, this is why liberation theologians in Perú opposed so strongly the Shining Path and became fierce defenders of democracy and human rights. In turn, liberation must always qualify liberty, not unlike the way difference qualifies equality in Rawls's conception of justice. Otherwise, we are left with a naïve defense of liberty that does not acknowledge how so many people rarely experience true freedom because of poverty, racism, and sexism, and how necessary it is to make institutions and the law sources of liberation.[64]

Of course, since this is an analogy, we should not dismiss the differences found amid the already noted similarities. The most salient difference is that Gutiérrez's is a Christian theological project that interprets history eschatologically. Therefore, as he often argues, his is a theocentric approach. The option for the poor is not *merely* a political approach to social change. Rather, it is a perspective based on and motivated by a belief in a God who loves humanity and the believer's love for God. Hence, the fullness of liberation is experienced only in the ultimate communion with God—the third dimension of liberation.[65] Yet liberation theology is a political approach as well.

In fact, this is exactly the kind of comprehensive doctrine Rawls had in mind when explaining his notions of overlapping consensus and reflective equilibrium. Rawls's goal with his theory of justice is to create the appropriate conditions of possibility for a plurality of "thick" conceptions of the good. Gutiérrez's theocentric approach is one of those thick conceptions, a comprehensive doctrine. Nevertheless, it is a comprehensive doctrine that understands that the creation of just social arrangements is the precondition of any thick conception of the good. Without these conditions, no integral liberation is possible. For this reason, Gutiérrez does not interpret the Christian faith as one whose trust is only in a God who saves in the eschatological future. Rather, Gutiérrez offers a new and revolutionary theological articulation of the Christian tradition that shows us a God who liberates now, creating the conditions for the ultimate eschatological liberation. In this sense, political liberation from all forms of oppression is key. It is key as a political end in itself, but it is also crucial as the precondition for any thick conception of liberation, theological or otherwise.

Addressing the Problem of Moral Motivation in Rawls's Theory

When we move from identifying the points of similarity-in-difference to a more active sense of critical correlation, we can also find spaces of mutual correction and illumination between Rawls's and Gutiérrez's projects. I begin with *justice as fairness.* Rawls's theory of justice has some important limitations, although not those often alleged by some of its most well-known critics. For the purposes of my argument, the most important limitation is Rawls's excessive emphasis on philosophical argumentation, to the significant detriment of his treatment of moral motivation. Put differently, Rawls gives us a powerful philosophical account of why social justice should be based on the two principles he develops, but only scarcely explores the emotional and valuative dimensions required to commit to those principles. Social justice, after all, is not merely a matter of clean arguments. It requires commitment, especially when justice is threatened constantly by egoism, nativism, racism, sexism, and the like. I would like to suggest that these aspects missing in Rawls's theory are strongly present in liberation theology.[66]

Liberation theology gives to Rawls's principles of justice a powerful narrative, inserting them not only in the trajectory of the democratic tradition but in the past and current history of struggles for justice that had religious values at their core. Moreover, liberation theology shows how certain religious ideals can be creatively reinterpreted over time to produce new developments facing new situations. In the case of liberation theology, this meant confronting the values of the Christian tradition with the situation of extreme poverty and marginalization of millions of people. In doing so, liberation theologians and their faith communities produced a new interpretation of the notion of social justice that saw in the transformation of social structures the natural extension of the old commandment to love God and neighbor.

In this sense, we should consider my account of liberation theology in previous chapters as an *affirmative genealogy*. By this I mean, following social theorist Hans Joas, a contingency-conscious method of historical reconstruction whose main goal is the affirmation of certain values. Such an affirmation creates the context for these values to call upon us, and, thus, the revitalization of the possibility of realizing them in history.[67] This *affirmative* dimension is crucial when it comes to the question of moral motivation. One of the great advantages of movements like liberation theology vis-à-vis the ideal of social justice is that the people who have committed their lives to walk with the poor and to fight against oppression do not do so only for philosophical or political reasons. Certainly, philosophical and political reasons are quite present as well. But one of the strengths of liberation theology, especially after decades of censorship, persecution, and even the torture and death of many of its followers, is that the source of motivation of this movement was its belief in a God of love, a God of Life who wants justice and peace for the world. This is the source of liberation theology's sensibility to suffering, not argument alone.[68]

Put differently, the commitment to social justice that I am discussing is based on affective, intense experiences of self-transcendence. Such experiences—witnessing the killing of George Floyd due to the abuses of law enforcement, for instance—take ourselves outside of our own small world, confronting us with the scandal of unjust suffering and death, and create a deep sense of subjective certainty about the evil in front of us. For many religious believers, this also elicits a deep subjective certainty that such horrors are not wanted by God. In liberation theology, this is grounded in a reading of the sacred scriptures of the Christian faith that presents a God who creates and loves all of us but who especially cares about the poor and those who suffer unjustly. In turn, this profound affective and subjective certainty reorients people's lives and inspires them to join the struggle for liberation based on their love for God and their neighbors.[69]

As Charles Taylor suggests, this is a superbly powerful idea that may go far beyond any form of philanthropy or solidarity driven by secular humanism. The notion that we should love each other unconditionally because each of us at our core is made in the image and likeness of God can hardly find a comparably strong source of motivation to treat each other justly.[70] Sure enough, this is a millennia-old idea in Judaism, Christianity, and several other traditions, that has only been imperfectly practiced. *But the ideal is there*, and when it finds even partial realizations, it can produce profound change. I maintain that liberation theology has produced some of those partial realizations, but so have several prior movements inspired by religious ideals, like the abolitionists and the civil rights movement in the United States. Further, conceiving of the process of social transformation in an eschatological perspective becomes itself a source of motivation not only for action but for endurance and sustenance in the face of human failure.[71] Let us not forget that liberation theologians and members of the base communities have suffered a great deal of censorship and persecution, often at the cost of their own lives. The brutal assassination of the Jesuit community led by liberation theologian Ignacio Ellacuría (El Salvador, 1989) is just one of the most notable examples, but many lesser-known lives have been taken by the enemies of justice.[72] Yet the faith in a God of Life who will not abandon God's creation has nurtured faith-based activists' persistence in the past and still does so today.

Refining Liberation Theology's Conception of Justice

But Rawls's theory also helps us to improve important underdeveloped aspects of liberation theology. Perhaps the most important issue in this regard is that liberation theologians have not offered a fully developed theory of justice. Arguably, this underdeveloped account of justice is one of the reasons that led to some of the well-intended criticisms that liberation theology has received. For instance: Is liberation theology's understanding of social justice dependent on socialism? If so, does it align with democratic socialism, Marxism, or a different stream of socialist politics? These matters have been rarely addressed and have left many scholars in the dark in terms of how to assess liberation theology's position on social justice. Furthermore, this lack of clarity about how to understand justice became even more evident when liberation theology transitioned to a postrevolutionary era in which the framework of socialist politics became less relevant, as shown in Chapter 3.

For instance, these tensions become clear when one examines Gutiérrez's account of the preferential option of the poor. As theologian Stephen Pope has argued with careful textual evidence, Gutiérrez does not have a clear political-philosophical stance regarding the problem of distributive justice. Hence, when it comes to the question of a system of justice that could stress some form of preference ("partiality," in Pope's language) for the most vulnerable, Gutiérrez simply appeals to God's love and its radical discontinuity with human justice. For Gutiérrez, the foundations of the option for the poor are ultimately theocentric.[73]

But, if this is true, we face issues regarding the capacity to communicate this claim to others who do not share such a theocentric belief, not to mention how to create a system of justice in a pluralistic society whose public policy cannot be grounded in religious reasons. Is Gutiérrez giving up on our capacity to create just social institutions? Is he making the option for the poor an exclusively Christian claim? The tensions do exist in Gutiérrez's work, as I also acknowledged in regards to Stout's critique of Rawls. However, these are not unresolvable issues. As Pope writes: "A theory of justice that acknowledges the importance of need, however, would not conflict so strikingly—indeed, at all—with the intended point that God favors the poor."[74] Surprisingly, Pope never mentions Rawls's theory, perhaps the most important systematic effort to acknowledge the role of need in the context of distributive justice.

Unfortunately, in the development of their ideas and their response to their critics, liberation theologians addressed theoretical issues about justice only in piecemeal fashion. Moreover, most of them left behind the project of developing a more systematic theory of justice in order to focus on more classical theological themes or simply because they decided to focus on improving the lives of the poor on the ground. Despite the importance of these tasks, I believe that this has left both a theoretical and a practical gap that must be filled. Gutiérrez, in one of his most recent public addresses, seems to agree. The title of his lecture is telling in this regard: "There Is Nothing More Practical than a Good Theory."[75] But his commitment—and invitation to others—to clarify theoretical matters of liberation theology is a long-standing practice of his work,[76] against other anti-theoretical currents of liberation theology.[77]

In my view, a theory like Rawls's gives to liberation theology the systematic approach to justice that it requires. This is especially true in our present situation, when the focus of liberation theology has increasingly turned to democracy building and the defense of human rights. Javier Iguíñiz, a development economist and a collaborator with Gutiérrez for several decades, has already hinted toward a similar answer, stressing Gutiérrez's emphasis on the importance of liberation understood as the freedom to develop one's life plans, to pursue a life of flourishment. In a carefully exegetical comparative study with the influential work of Amartya Sen, winner of the Nobel Prize in Economics, Iguíñiz argues that Gutiérrez and Sen advocate for a conception of development that implies expansion of freedoms and capabilities.[78] By doing so, Iguíñiz maintains that Gutiérrez's notion of liberation and Sen's understanding of liberty overlap because both conceive of human development as requiring a basic threshold without which no freedom or real justice can emerge. At the end of the day, as Iguíñiz underscores, poverty is a fundamental impediment in our capacity to experience equal liberty and equal respect.[79] Philosopher of liberation Enrique Dussel makes similar points, advocating for an understanding of liberty as liberation in which the subjective satisfaction of our capabilities is essential.[80]

In fact, careful study of the early development of liberation theology shows the same basic intuitions. In agreement with my initial point, theologian Ismael García takes as his starting point the lack of an "explicit, complete and well-argued statement of what [liberation theologians] mean by the term justice."[81] Noting this, García undertakes a meticulous reconstruction of liberation theology's theory of justice as presented in the works of Hugo Assmann, Gutiérrez, José Míguez Bonino, and José Porfirio Miranda. Interestingly, García's research, which covers only the early development of liberation theology (up to 1982), demonstrates that even then liberation theologians defended a conception of justice in which formal freedom is expanded and given material content through an understanding of equality that takes into account the needs of the worst-off in society. Like Iguíñiz's interpretation of Gutiérrez's work, García's study underscores that liberation theologians defend that true freedom requires greater socioeconomic equality in order to fulfill our capabilities.[82] Considering the normative role of basic need in liberation theology's conception of justice, García writes:

A human need, thus, is defined in terms of what is necessary for a person to . . . be *capable* of fulfilling his/her plan and share in that of his/her community. It is defined in terms of what will make it possible for a person to have some control over his/her destiny and that of his/her community. Not to have them, thus, would be injurious to the person's sense of self-respect, dignity, and freedom.[83]

In this sense, the unearthing of liberation theology's early theory of justice already shows its great concern for an expansive sense of liberty that is expressed though the need of liberation from unjust limitations of our capabilities. Moreover, like Rawls, liberation theology rejects the idea that access to social goods should be based on merit or desert.[84] Rather, the basic needs of survival, self-respect, dignity, and freedom are sufficient warrant for this access.[85] Since the goal, theologically and politically, is the enhancement of life, access to basic social goods cannot be conditional; it is required in order to have a just society.[86] In order to make this happen, social institutions must be developed so that they can further elaborate and enforce the conception of justice we are discussing, a conception in which freedom and well-being, especially that of the most vulnerable, is guaranteed.[87]

My contention here is that the most compelling theory of justice developed in the last few decades that systematically addresses all these issues through the connection between liberty and liberation is Rawls's.[88] Such a theory can be expanded in many different directions; I have suggested some here. Yet the core elements for a theory of justice are present in Rawls's account: the principles of equality and difference must be respected to prevent any violation of our human dignity. The task now is to make these principles more tangible, so that even at the philosophical level, justice appears to us as more concrete.

Further, from a Christian perspective, these principles must be fleshed out so that we may understand *how* justice may become the historical embodiment of love in a world full of injustices, a key idea of liberation theology developed in the work of Ignacio Ellacuría.[89] Indeed, one of the key challenges for contemporary Christianity is how to connect justice (understood as a concept of legal and moral universalism) with love (a key concept of the Christian ethos). The Christian belief in a God who loves human beings unconditionally has the potential to solve this issue, as we have also shown in previous chapters. However, as Hans Joas underscores, this Christian belief "does not provide us with complete instructions on how to strike the balance between 'love' and 'justice.'"[90] What follows is my attempt to "strike the balance."

Reclaiming Religion: Toward an Inclusive Account of Social Justice

After exploring the areas of critical correlation between Gutiérrez and Rawls, my final task is to offer an integrated approach. The goal here is to build on their accomplishments producing an account that can deal with the question of social justice while leaving ample room to include religious argument and motivation.

I propose doing this by focusing on philosopher Martha Nussbaum's Capabilities Approach, one of the most compelling expansions of Rawls's theory.[91] Nussbaum's approach to justice is important because it takes seriously the normative core of Rawls's principles, yet expands them.[92] She does so by not only giving the principles more specific content (going beyond Rawls's "indexes"[93]) but considering them in the context of non-ideal theory, in the context of societies marked by their failure to meet the moral core that these principles embody. Further, Nussbaum expands on Rawls, paying great attention to the key role that our emotions play to produce moral motivation to act justly.[94] Hence, the Capabilities Approach gives us a blueprint to consider the question of the specification of the principles of justice that keeps the core of Rawls's ideas and, therefore, *analogically*, shares some of the fundamental concerns of liberation theology.

Nussbaum puts forward a list of ten "central capabilities" to flesh out her understanding of social justice. She defines capabilities as "a set of opportunities to choose and to act . . . ; [which] are not just abilities residing inside the person but also the freedoms or opportunities created by a combination of personal abilities and the political, social, and economic environment."[95] Her list includes living a normal-length life; enjoying bodily health and adequate shelter; bodily integrity, which entails free mobility and freedom from violence; using our senses, imagination, and thought; freely experiencing our emotions; using our practical reason, which may allow us to develop a conception of the good life and to plan accordingly; the right of affiliation, both in terms of living with and toward others and in terms of having the social bases for self-respect and nonhumiliation; concern for other species; being able to play; and control over our own environment by having access to political participation and having property and labor rights on an equal basis with others.[96]

For Nussbaum, all these capabilities are interconnected and necessary. They operate as a threshold, an ample social minimum, below which a society cannot be considered just—at least in the context of modern democracies. Now, as a minimum, the logical implication is that richer conceptions of justice are possible. In line with Rawls, Nussbaum's approach is not a comprehensive doctrine.[97] *But liberation theology is.* Hence, the inclusive theory of justice that I am sketching here builds on approaches like Rawls's or Nussbaum's by providing a fundamental threshold. Such a threshold operates as the foundations of any comprehensive conception of justice—religious or otherwise—that values equal freedom and special attention to the needs of the least advantaged in our societies. As I have demonstrated throughout this book, this is the case with liberation theology.

The great advantage of considering a relatively tangible threshold while thinking about social justice is that public religious leaders can go beyond prophetic admonitions, turning to a set of principles and actions that can be more easily operationalized in the struggle for justice.[98] Naturally, this is of immense practical value when public religious actors working for the poor and marginalized have to establish interfaith alliances or alliances with nonreligious actors. Having a common language that is meaningful to all parties—despite the different theological or nontheological interpretations each give to such meaning—is crucial.

Further, we should underscore that, for both Rawls and Nussbaum, meeting the threshold represented by the basic capabilities is *required* to produce just social arrangements. We have already examined this in the context of the formulation of Rawls's theory of justice: the principles of justice produce the most fair organization of a society in which people have a plurality of comprehensive doctrines. Now, this point is central in the formulation of an *inclusive* theory of social justice, since this gives additional and decisive strength to a public religion like liberation theology. In this inclusive approach, honoring equal liberty and respect and the needs of the most vulnerable should not be construed as a mere invitation to charity or as the result of the benevolence of good political authorities—as sometimes happens in public religious discourse.[99]

In this sense, the "thin" understanding of justice provided by the *political-philosophical* foundations of the inclusive theory gives to liberation theology additional grounds to establish the soundness of the *theological* preferential option for the poor. In doing so, this theory allows a more concrete balance between justice and love in liberation theology, and for Christian theology in general. Such an inclusive view stresses the crucial role of the formation and reformation of social institutions (whether this is legislation, the economy, education, or anything else) understood as moral spaces through which we are held accountable to, and express care (we may say "love") for, each other, especially the most fragile among us. In this sense, social institutions become both moral spaces for responsibility-as-imputation and responsibility for the fragile other.[100] After all, this is exactly what Rawls's principles of justice do, further expanded through

Nussbaum's central capabilities. They give content to justice—show us what it must look like, quite concretely—but, in doing so, through their analogical relation with the ideas of liberation and the option for the poor, they give us a glimpse of what love may look like.

Consider poverty as an example to which the Capabilities Approach can be applied as a framework to embody the balance between justice and love. When we construe life as a capability, it becomes clear that life is not mere subsistence. It must be a life worth living. Hence, when we consider that in many places living conditions are so precarious that the worth of life can barely be perceived, this central capability invites us to examine critically a series of political and economic issues ranging from the flaws of free-market economy, the quality of the social services provided by the state, possible problems of corruption, the priorities of the allocation of money in national and local budgets, issues of international trade and geo-politics, and so forth. A similar argument can be made regarding bodily health and bodily integrity. Severe poverty certainly undermines people's health and often makes them vulnerable to different forms of violation of their physical integrity. Therefore, to consider the quality and nature of the healthcare system becomes a central policy issue. In the United States and around the world we have seen this play out because of COVID-19, the unpreparedness of the health system, and the way the virus (and its repercussions, economic and otherwise) more severely affects the poor. Naturally, this is even worse among the nations of the global south.

Consider now the senses, imagination, and thought. Further, consider them in tandem with practical reason as the capability articulating them all. Good education is often inaccessible to poor households. Moreover, the possibility of expanding one's imagination through music, art, literature, and play (another central capability) represents a chimera for many children and adults in situations of poverty. Recognizing these capabilities as necessary in order to live a life with dignity may lead us to push for educational reform in terms of formal education in schools but also in terms of the importance of public museums, libraries, and parks as spaces for leisure *and* the development of the imagination. Here we could include the emotions as well. Poverty is emotionally disruptive for individuals and families. Hence the issue is not only lifting people out of poverty but also providing the conditions for healing and regaining self-respect. Self-respect is a key dimension of affiliation and relates also to control over our environment. People must be able to associate freely and to participate effectively in the political process. Acknowledging these as rights may lead us to work on electoral reform, challenge gerrymandering and voter suppression, and ensure that the political system represents fairly the will of the people.

In addition, respect for other species and the environment deserves attention. Animal farming, for instance, is fundamentally an economic and political issue based on demand and the lack of ethical regulation of the state. Yet immense amounts of food are wasted every day, especially in the United States, while the poor cannot even know when they will have their next meal. Similarly, we are becoming more and more aware of the devastating presence of environmental racism. Indeed, in addition to the immense threat of global warming, deforestation, water pollution, and the like, it has become increasingly clear that these threats affect the poor and racial minorities at disproportionately greater rates than the rest.

This brief sketch does not attempt to be exhaustive but should suffice to stress my original point: Making justice more tangible allows us to *analogically* see what liberation and the option for the poor—key expressions of Christian love—may look like. Christian love-made-justice is, of course, more comprehensive than any political conception of justice, even if it expresses love as well—through values like fraternity, benevolence, and solidarity.[101] Yet in making sure that all people meet the threshold of justice, believers can allow their neighbor to experience a glimpse of God's unconditional love, while waiting for its fullness in the ultimate communion with the divine. Further, the point is that many religious believers can see their *religious* values partly represented in a *political* conception of justice that cares for equality and the least advantaged among us. If such a conception is framed in an inclusive way—as I am trying to do here—this sketches a theory of justice that welcomes and encourages public religions, because these religions, as Casanova suggests, may well enrich democracy and strengthen the fight for a more just society.

Certainly, not all religious people defend a conception of justice that defends equality and the concern for the least advantaged among us.[102] Precisely for this reason, it is essential to develop an inclusive conception of social justice. Such a conception would allow the religious people who do defend these values to have a strong presence in the public sphere, build alliances among each other and with nonreligious actors, and counter attempts to take over the religious public conversation by anti-democratic, exclusionary religious groups.[103] We must remember that the United States and Latin America are still heavily religious societies, and there is no reason to believe that this is going to change any time soon. Yet, quite often, the public religious sphere appears dominated by vocal religious conservatives, many of whom have strong exclusionary rhetoric (against reproductive rights, same-sex relations, immigrants, the poor, and so forth).

One of the key errors of many liberal theories of justice—at times an error of Rawls himself—has been to try to limit the presence of religion in the public sphere as if *all* religions inherently have exclusionary tendencies. Clearly, this is not the case. An inclusive theory of social justice takes note of this basic insight and fosters a conception of justice that builds on the principles of liberal theories like Rawls's, but openly encourages religious presence and argument in the public arena. Plus, as I have argued all along, such encouragement does not assume a rigid interpretation of religious actors themselves, as if they could only express themselves using religious language, rhetoric, and premises. Religious people are also people and have common, nonreligious experiences that they can share with others. This brings people together. This is essential for social justice.

None of these somewhat optimistic considerations about public religion, public reason, and social justice should make us naïve. Millions are still disenfranchised, living paycheck to paycheck, if not unemployed and lacking a safety network. Tremendous amounts of wealth have been produced in the last few decades, but the distribution of this wealth has become scandalously unequal. Contradictions like these remind us of the contingency of our human achievements and perhaps alert us to more fundamental questions about the meaning of human existence and the inescapable presence of evil. I have discussed the focus on democracy and the defense of human rights in liberation theology, but this should not suggest that these are taken as already realized ideals. We are far from that; we will always be. Moreover, these are by no means stable gains. We see their contingent nature all over the globe. No political victory or economic improvement should lead to naïve triumphalism. The struggle continues; it never ends.

However, the never-ending nature of the struggle should not lead us to despair either. In fact, it can and should be a source of profound hope. Yet to speak of hope only vaguely and somewhat romantically will not do; hope must be created. It is true that victories are feeble and that backlash seldom disappears, but it is also true that the capacity of people to organize themselves to struggle for a better future is always there, creating hope. And when people come together, organize, and mobilize, they can win, even if the gains are modest and temporary. Liberation theology has been part of these struggles for decades, proving the strength and depth of its vision by listening to the cry of the poor and giving them resources to become subjects of their own destiny. Among those resources, perhaps the greatest is the simple yet daring idea that God does not forget the sufferings of the most vulnerable, that God loves them, and that God stands by their side while they tirelessly fight for God's Kingdom to come.

Notes

Introduction

1. Without trying to be exhaustive, these are some of the key recent, and relatively recent, works dealing with the matter: Phillip Berryman, *The Religious Roots of Rebellion: Christians in Central American Revolutions* (Maryknoll, NY: Orbis Books, 1984); Christian Smith, *The Emergence of Liberation Theology: Radical Religion and Social Movement Theory* (Chicago: University of Chicago Press, 1991); Talal Asad, *Genealogies of Religion: Discipline and Reasons of Power in Christianity and Islam* (Baltimore: Johns Hopkins University Press, 1993); José Casanova, *Public Religions in the Modern World* (Chicago: University of Chicago Press, 1994); Gayraud S. Wilmore, *Black Religion and Black Radicalism: An Interpretation of the Religious History of African Americans*, 3rd ed. (Maryknoll, NY: Orbis Books, 1998); Omar M. McRoberts, *Streets of Glory: Church and Community in a Black Urban Neighborhood* (Chicago: University of Chicago Press, 2003); Saba Mahmood, *Politics of Piety: The Islamic Revival and the Feminist Subject* (Princeton, NJ: Princeton University Press, 2005); Catherine E. Wilson, *The Politics of Latino Faith: Religion, Identity, and Urban Community* (New York: New York University Press, 2008); Martha C. Nussbaum, *Liberty of Conscience: In Defense of America's Tradition of Religious Equality* (New York: Basic Books, 2008); Steven H. Shiffrin, *The Religious Left and Church-State Relations* (Princeton, NJ: Princeton University Press, 2009); Kevin Lewis O'Neill, *City of God: Christian Citizenship in Postwar Guatemala* (Berkeley: University of California Press, 2010); Gary J. Dorrien, *Breaking White Supremacy: Martin Luther King Jr. and the Black Social Gospel* (New Haven, CT: Yale University Press, 2018); Gary J. Dorrien, *The New Abolition: W. E. B. Du Bois and the Black Social Gospel* (New Haven, CT: Yale University Press, 2015); Matthew Bowman, *Christian: The Politics of a Word in America* (Cambridge, MA: Harvard University Press, 2018); Lilian Calles Barger, *The World Come of Age: An Intellectual History of Liberation Theology* (New York: Oxford University Press, 2018); Karen J. Johnson, *One in Christ: Chicago Catholics and the Quest for Interracial Justice* (New York: Oxford University Press, 2018); Felipe Hinojosa, *Apostles of Change: Latino*

Radical Politics, Church Occupations, and the Fight to Save the Barrio (Austin: University of Texas Press, 2021).

2. In this book, I use the concept of *articulation* in its standard meaning in English. So, notions like "expressing oneself coherently" or "producing clear ideas about something" meet the mark and suffice to understand my use of the concept. However, behind *articulation* is also a more complex philosophical stance present in the work of Charles Taylor and Hans Joas that I fundamentally share. In this sense, articulation is the attempt to produce a coherent narrative of oneself, or one's community, or tradition. Such a process is especially complex because it requires finding balance between ideal and real selves, aspirations and flaws, what we do not know about ourselves, and what we may never be able to articulate. Since this book is focused on liberation theology's development of a new faith-based political identity, keeping in mind this more complex philosophical understanding of articulation seems pertinent. On these issues, see Charles Taylor, *Sources of the Self: The Making of the Modern Identity* (Cambridge, MA: Harvard University Press, 1989); Hans Joas, *The Genesis of Values* (Chicago: University of Chicago Press, 2000).

3. In the context of the United States, we can see some of the issues described in my characterization of the progressive-conservative debates in the disputed narratives about the meaning of *Christian*. On this issue, see Bowman, *Christian*, whose epilogue summarizes these tensions very well. For a long-term and transnational account of these tensions, with particular attention to the process of secularization, see José Casanova, "Public Religions Revisited," in *Religion: Beyond a Concept*, ed. Hent de Vries (New York: Fordham University Press, 2008).

4. I will use the categories *progressive* and *conservative* as ideal types, without dealing with highly controversial debates about the plurality within each group. Noting that these are not absolutely accurate depictions of each self-defined progressive or conservative, I do hold that this basic typology is representative of a vast sample of people in each group.

5. Karl Marx, "Contribution to the Critique of Hegel's Philosophy of Right: Introduction," in *The Marx-Engels Reader*, ed. Robert C. Tucker, 2nd ed. (New York: Norton, 1978), 53.

6. For the classic iteration of this argument, see Max Weber, *The Protestant Ethic and the "Spirit" of Capitalism and Other Writings*, trans. P. R. Baehr and Gordon C. Wells (New York: Penguin Books, 2002). See also Harvey Cox, *The Market as God* (Cambridge, MA: Harvard University Press, 2016); Elizabeth L. Hinson-Hasty, *The Problem of Wealth: A Christian Response to a Culture of Affluence* (Maryknoll, NY: Orbis Books, 2017).

7. See Martha C. Nussbaum, *From Disgust to Humanity: Sexual Orientation and Constitutional Law*, Inalienable Rights Series (Oxford, UK: Oxford University Press, 2010).

8. Of the works cited earlier, Wilson, *The Politics of Latino Faith*, and Barger, *The World Come of Age*, come closest to the theological rationale I focus on. Unlike most sociological pieces on religious activism, Wilson notably pursues the path of trying to understand the theological framework behind the activism of the Latinx faith-based organizations that she studies. However, her study is rather schematic (only parts of Chapter 3) and overstresses contrasts between Latin American and Latinx liberationists regarding capitalism and popular religion. Barger's case is different since she has written a comprehensive and capacious "intellectual history" of liberation theology. I will discuss her book in Chapter 1. For a critical review of Barger's book, with which I strongly agree, see J. Matthew Ashley, "To Change the World: An Intellectual History of Liberation Theology," *Commonweal*, January 31, 2019, https://www.commonwealmagazine. org/change-world.

9. The turning point in this area of scholarship was Casanova, *Public Religions in the Modern World*, although the work of the British sociologist David Martin had already questioned this assumption by distinguishing patterns of secularization and noting that in many regions of the world the privatization-decline of religion hypothesis does not hold. See David Martin, *A General Theory of Secularization* (Oxford, UK: Blackwell, 1978).

10. The focus of my book will be on Christian liberation theology and on Gustavo Gutiérrez's oeuvre. Liberation theology has developed non-Christian streams and covers the work of many different theologians. My emphasis, however, follows practical and methodological concerns. Practically, the Christian stream of liberation theology is the most influential and the one on which most scholarship has been produced. Methodologically, despite the many common themes among the different currents of liberation theology, the differences matter, especially when it comes to the balance-without-reduction that I propose.

11. It may be argued that figures like Bartolomé de las Casas anticipated the contributions of liberation theology, an argument that could deemphasize the radical change I attribute to liberation theology. Even though it is true that Las Casas was a man ahead of his time, there are important differences between Las Casas's project and that of Gutierrez and his colleagues. Las Casas does not fundamentally challenge the colonial system or the existence of fixed social locations. Indeed, Las Casas criticizes how the colonial system has brutalized the native inhabitants of the Americas. He sees the preaching of the gospel as an excuse for an extractive project and asks for a moratorium until new ways of sharing the gospel can be sorted out. *But* he does not question the legitimacy of preaching the gospel through a colonial project; he only rejects its current form. Similarly, Las Casas deeply cares about the situation of indigenous people in the Americas, but he accepts the standard medieval cosmology of fixed social locations: some people are placed in the world to be wealthy and powerful, and some

are poor and vulnerable. His call is for the powerful and wealthy to be compassionate toward the poor, emulating the kindness of Christ. He is not arguing for the upending of the medieval hierarchical system. Therefore, the difference of approach with liberation theologians is substantial. And naturally so. There are five hundred years between them. Gustavo Gutiérrez acknowledges these differences in his study of Las Casas; see *Las Casas in Search of the Poor of Jesus Christ* (Maryknoll, NY: Orbis Books, 1993). For this reason, my argument in Chapter 1 of *La subversión de la esperanza* (Lima: PUCP, IBC, CEP, 2015) is that Las Casas is better paired with philosophies of radical compassion for the other, like that of Emmanuel Levinas, instead of with liberation theologians. Radical compassion for the poor and marginalized is at the core of Las Casas's thinking, not systemic, structural change, even if he probably was the most radical critic of colonial rule and extractivism in his time.

12. The most systematic account of the issue is Ismael García, "The Concept of Justice in Latin American Theology of Liberation" (PhD dissertation, University of Chicago, 1982). Stephen J. Pope, "Proper and Improper Partiality and the Preferential Option for the Poor," *Theological Studies* 54 (1993): 242–271, has also underscored key issues relating to the position of Gutiérrez and others regarding social justice.

Chapter 1

1. See Gustavo Gutiérrez, "The Option for the Poor and Christian Theology" (presented at the Catholic Social Tradition Conference, Center for Social Concerns, University of Notre Dame, March 23, 2019), https://youtu.be/6G8xBPN-8o0. The relevance of this keynote address should be underscored since this is Gutiérrez's most recent presentation on liberation theology and its fundamental concerns. Here Gutiérrez decides to rearticulate those concerns using the notion of "one history" as his guiding threat and calls it "the foundation" of the preferential option for the poor.

2. My work in this and the following chapters is limited mainly to Catholic and contemporary theology. So even though I briefly engage some contemporary Protestant theologians, my contention is neither that this is a comprehensive account of all forms of contemporary liberation theology nor that my work exhaustively studies liberationist insights throughout the history of all Christian theology. Such task is beyond my competence but also beyond the interests of this book. It is clear, nonetheless, that the *major* shifts regarding the identification of the causes of poverty and the subsequent cry for the reorganization of society, politics, and the economy are twentieth-century developments. If we limit the discussion to Protestantism and Catholicism, we only start seeing them in full force with the emergence of the Social Gospel (but even here with

limitations) and the civil rights movement, and with important developments in Catholic social teaching and the emergence of liberation theology, respectively. On this, see Lillan Calles Barger, *The World Come of Age: An Intellectual History of Liberation Theology* (New York: Oxford University Press, 2018), especially chapters 7 and 8.

3. This brief account is mine but draws freely from the work of Gustavo Gutiérrez, Leonardo Boff, Ignacio Ellacuría, Jon Sobrino, Maria Pilar Aquino, James Cone, J. Deotis Roberts, Delores Williams, and Elisabeth Schüssler-Fiorenza, among others. For a more comprehensive approach that is focused mostly on the Latin American case, see Leonardo Boff, "Libération," and Pierre Sauvage, "Genèse, évolution et actualité de la théologie de la libération," in *Dictionnaire historique de la théologie de la libération: les thèmes, les lieux, les acteurs,* ed. Pierre Sauvage, Luis Martínez Saavedra, and Maurice Cheza (Brussels: Lessius, 2017). See also Barger, *The World Come of Age,* chaps. 4–6. However, Barger's account has some flaws—to be discussed later—produced by her blending together the ideas of liberation theologians who disagree on significant theological doctrines.

4. For a couple of examples on the last two topics, see Charles Robert Pinches and Jay B. McDaniel, eds., *Good News for Animals? Christian Approaches to Animal Well-Being* (Maryknoll, NY: Orbis Books, 1993); Daniel P. Castillo, *An Ecological Theology of Liberation: Salvation and Political Ecology* (Maryknoll, NY: Orbis Books, 2019).

5. On this topic, see Miguel A. De La Torre, ed., *The Hope of Liberation in World Religions* (Waco, TX: Baylor University Press, 2008).

6. In this sense, accounts that focus too much on the role of the "intellectuals" (the theologians) can be misleading. Such is the case, at times, with the otherwise excellent book by Christian Smith, *The Emergence of Liberation Theology: Radical Religion and Social Movement Theory* (Chicago: University of Chicago Press, 1991). The case of Barger, *The World Come of Age,* is slightly different, because hers is a history of ideas. But the point stands: a more capacious account of liberation theology cannot exclude the "base" level. Some go a step further to argue that liberation theology maintained a top-down organizational system. For example, see David Martin, "Thinking with Your Life," in *David Martin and the Sociology of Religion,* ed. Hans Joas (New York: Routledge, 2018), 169. But there is little evidence for this, and Martin himself has argued the opposite in his earlier writings.

7. For a history of the way Christianity related to poverty and wealth in antiquity, see Peter Brown, *Through the Eye of a Needle: Wealth, the Fall of Rome, and the Making of Christianity in the West, 350–550 AD* (Princeton, NJ: Princeton University Press, 2012). For a brief history that focuses on the centuries that followed the period studied by Brown up to the end of the Middle Ages, see Jorge V. Pixley and Clodovis Boff, *The Bible, the Church and the Poor: Biblical, Theological and Pastoral Aspects of the Option for the Poor* (Tunbridge Wells, UK: Burns and

Oates, 1989), 159–184. For the Modern period and beyond, see Philip F. Mulhern, *Dedicated Poverty: Its History and Theology* (Staten Island, NY: Alba House, 1973), chaps. 5–6. See also Leen van Molle, *Charity and Social Welfare*, vol. 4, The Dynamics of Religious Reform in Northern Europe, 1780–1920 (Leuven, Belgium: Leuven University Press, 2017).

8. For the classic study of this transition, see Max Weber, *The Protestant Ethic and the "Spirit" of Capitalism and Other Writings*, trans. P. R. Baehr and Gordon C. Wells (New York: Penguin Books, 2002).

9. On the philosophical, sociological, and theological ideas shaping this transition, see Barger, *The World Come of Age*.

10. For a history of democratic Christian socialism, see Gary J. Dorrien, *Social Democracy in the Making: Political and Religious Roots of European Socialism* (New Haven, CT: Yale University Press, 2019).

11. On this, see Lester R. Kurtz, *The Politics of Heresy: The Modernist Crisis in Roman Catholicism* (Berkeley: University of California Press, 1986); Marvin Richard O'Connell, *Critics on Trial: An Introduction to the Catholic Modernist Crisis* (Washington, DC: Catholic University of America Press, 1994).

12. For a history of the nouvelle theologie, see Rosino Gibellini, *La teologia del XX secolo* (Brescia, Italy: Queriniana, 1992).

13. For this notion of "voluntary disestablishment" and its sociopolitical consequences for the global and Latin American churches, see José Casanova, "Parallel Reformations in Latin America: A Critical Review of David Martin's Interpretation of the Pentecostal Revolution," in *David Martin and the Sociology of Religion*, ed. Hans Joas (New York: Routledge, 2018).

14. David J. O'Brien and Thomas A. Shannon, eds., *Gaudium et spes*, in *Catholic Social Thought: The Documentary Heritage*, expanded ed. (Maryknoll, NY: Orbis Books, 2010), §1, my emphasis.

15. See Felipe Zegarra, "Juan XXIII: Temas centrales de su teología y espiritualidad," *Páginas* 255 (March 2012): 12. Zegarra's piece also gives more context to explain Pope John's theological and ecclesial commitments and his concern for the poor.

16. See John W. O'Malley, *What Happened at Vatican II* (Cambridge, MA: Belknap Press of Harvard University Press, 2008), 122–123.

17. For the document and some context, see Maria Clara Bingemer, *Latin American Theology: Roots and Branches* (Maryknoll, NY: Orbis Books, 2016), 46–54.

18. Smith, *The Emergence of Liberation Theology*, 17. "CELAM" stands for "Consejo Episcopal Lationamericano" (Latin American Episcopal Council).

19. Smith, *The Emergence of Liberation Theology*, 153.

20. Smith, *The Emergence of Liberation Theology*, 14.

21. Smith, *The Emergence of Liberation Theology*, 14.

22. See Smith, *The Emergence of Liberation Theology*, 15; Todd Hartch, *The Rebirth of Latin American Christianity*, Oxford Studies in World Christianity (Oxford, UK: Oxford University Press, 2014), 130–34.

23. Gustavo Gutiérrez, *A Theology of Liberation: History, Politics, and Salvation*, 2nd ed. (Maryknoll, NY: Orbis Books, 1988), 29.

24. Gutiérrez, *A Theology of Liberation*, 34.

25. Gutiérrez, *A Theology of Liberation*, 30.

26. Gutiérrez, *A Theology of Liberation*, 31.

27. Gutiérrez, *A Theology of Liberation*, 34.

28. On the historical and theological flaws of integralism, see Massimo Faggioli, "A Church Within the Church: Behind the New Integralism Is the Old Intransigentism," *Commonweal*, January 8, 2019, https://www.commonweal-magazine.org/church-within-church.

29. David Martin partially disputes the "voluntary" nature of this disestablishment in a recent exchange with José Casanova. But I take Casanova's point to be quite subtle: the Catholic Church resisted disestablishment in the decades that followed the great social revolutions. However, when the "battle" was lost it could have simply tolerated the new democratic developments without affirming them. Vatican II, in this sense, was much more than mere toleration; it was a radical affirmation of the value of the secular world, the separation of church and state, the salvific power of other religions, and the value of democracy and human rights, among other issues. Therefore, a qualitative leap took place in the second half of the twentieth century that cannot be explained solely based on exogenous factors. On this, see Casanova, "Parallel Reformations in Latin America," 85–88, 99–100; Martin, "Thinking with Your Life," 169.

30. See Jacques Maritain, *True Humanism* (New York: Scribner, 1938), 23–26.; J. Dean Brackley, "Salvation and the Social Good in the Thought of Jacques Maritain and Gustavo Gutierrez" (PhD dissertation, University of Chicago, 1980), 30–38. For a similar view, see Benedict XVI, *Values in a Time of Upheaval* (New York: Crossroad, 2006).

31. We will see shortly that despite the similarities, this position differs in significant ways from Gutiérrez's and from Charles Taylor, "A Catholic Modernity?," in *Dilemmas and Connections: Selected Essays* (Cambridge, MA: Belknap Press of Harvard University Press, 2011).

32. See Maritain, *True Humanism*, "Appendix," 288–304; Maritain, *Man and the State* (Chicago: University of Chicago Press, 1951), 153; Brackley, "Salvation and the Social Good," 40–60.

33. We should note that the background of Maritain's argument is his defense of democratic values against the experience of the European totalitarianisms. In this sense, his rejection of the idea that the Kingdom of God may find any realization in history is a response to what he sees as the implicit goal of Marxism

and other forms of socialism (see *True Humanism*, 47–52.). Maritain sees the communist iteration of Marxism, with its atheist commitments and its rejection of true humanism, as especially dangerous. Gutiérrez's approach is rather different because of his chronological and geographical distance from the tragedies of World War II and the different impact of Marxist thought in Latin America.

34. Brackley, "Salvation and the Social Good," 71–80. Maritain conceives his approach as a rejection of old forms of Christian dualism. His is an attempt at a new Christian synthesis (see Maritain, *True Humanism*, 112). However, as these pages show, the synthesis is rather tense and has important limitations to explain the role of Christians in the political realm.

35. On this distinction, see *Summa theologiae*, I–II, Q. 109–114, in Thomas Aquinas, *Summa theologiae: Latin Text and English Translation, Introductions, Notes, Appendices, and Glossaries*, vol. 30 (Cambridge, UK: Blackfriars, 1964). For more background with special reference to the scholastic theory of natural law, see Jean Porter, *Nature as Reason: A Thomistic Theory of the Natural Law* (Grand Rapids, MI: Eerdmans, 2005).

36. Brackley, "Salvation and the Social Good," 80–110.

37. Brackley, "Salvation and the Social Good," 99.

38. See Maritain, *Man and the State*, 164–165.

39. In this sense, we should distinguish Maritain's approach from that of John Howard Yoder, *The Politics of Jesus: Vicit Agnus Noster*, 2nd ed. (Grand Rapids, MI: Eerdmans, 1994). Maritain has trouble articulating his call to action in the world, but never denies the relevance of direct intervention in politics, especially when the dignity of the human being is under threat. In contrast, Yoder's approach represents one of the most extreme expressions of the Distinction of Planes model. For a similar position, but without its most dangerous conclusions, see Stanley Hauerwas, *A Community of Character: Toward a Constructive Christian Social Ethic* (Notre Dame, IN: University of Notre Dame Press, 1981). For a powerful critique of both Yoder and Hauerwas in light of the abuses committed by the former and their relationship to his theology, see Janna Hunter-Bowman, "The Opportunity Stanley Hauerwas Missed," *Christian Century*, accessed November 11, 2017, https://www.christiancentury.org/blog-post/guest-post/opportunity-stanley-hauerwas-missed.

40. Maritain, *True Humanism*, 114.

41. Maritain, *True Humanism*, 115.

42. Maritain, *Man and the State*, 164.

43. Maritain, *True Humanism*, 291–298. Maritain adds a third plane (although, as he indicates, it is really part of the spiritual plane, and only accidentally distinct): "the spiritual as adjoining the temporal." To this realm pertain those matters that, affecting the earthly city, directly concern the good of the soul. Although Maritain maintains that in this intermediate plane the Christian can

act in the temporal order "as a Christian as such," this does not really solve the problem. For it remains unclear where one should draw the line that distinguishes "religious interests" from secular ones (293–294).

44. Gutiérrez, *A Theology of Liberation*, 35.

45. Gutiérrez, *A Theology of Liberation*, 37.

46. Gutiérrez, *A Theology of Liberation*, 36.

47. Gutiérrez, *A Theology of Liberation*, 39.

48. Gutiérrez, *A Theology of Liberation*, 39–40. For a comprehensive study of this moment focused on the basic ecclesial communities, see Catherine Ferguson, "The Poor in Politics: Social Change and Basic Church Communities in Santiago, Lima and Mexico City" (PhD dissertation, University of Denver, 1990).

49. Gutiérrez, *A Theology of Liberation*, 40.

50. Gutiérrez, *A Theology of Liberation*, 41.

51. In this sense, Gutiérrez implicitly rejects the "secularization thesis" and is close to the positions developed by David Martin in *A General Theory of Secularization* (Oxford, UK: Blackwell, 1978) and José Casanova, *Public Religions in the Modern World* (Chicago: University of Chicago Press, 1994), 6ff. Gutiérrez also comes very close to Martin in saying that the secularization process in Latin America is "uneven and combined" (*A Theology of Liberation*, 43). Martin describes it as "mixed" or even speaks of "religious reconfiguration" instead of "secularization." See David Martin, "What I Really Said About Secularization," and "Has Secularization Gone into Reverse?," in *Sociology of Religion: A David Martin Reader*, ed. Dedong Wei and Zhifeng Zhong (Waco, TX: Baylor University Press, 2015), 218, 250.

52. Barger, *The World Come of Age*, 152.

53. Similarly, Hans Joas argues that "most experts now consider [the secularization thesis] wrong" and yet that "overcoming the thesis of secularization does not, of course, mean ignoring secularization, but rather seeing it in all its diversity" (*Faith as an Option: Possible Futures for Christianity* (Stanford, CA: Stanford University Press, 2014), 3).

54. Casanova, *Public Religions in the Modern World*, 6.

55. Casanova, *Public Religions in the Modern World*, 6. They were not, then, just "new" religious movements, but their novelty had to do with their interest in participating in the public sphere (see *Public Religions in the Modern World*, 5, 19, 57–56 for the conditions of that participation, and 64–66 for an assessment of the legitimacy of the conditions).

56. Casanova, *Public Religions in the Modern World*, 7; also 19ff.

57. See Casanova, *Public Religions in the Modern World*, 213–215. The American case, however, made evident from the outset the problematic nature of (a) and (c). See Casanova, *Public Religions in the Modern World*, 28–29.

58. For the most compelling—and earliest—account of these patterns of secularization, see Martin, *A General Theory of Secularization*.

59. On the question of the permanent presence of the sacred and new forms of sacralization, see Hans Joas, *The Sacredness of the Person: A New Genealogy of Human Rights* (Washington, DC: Georgetown University Press, 2013); Hans Joas, *The Power of the Sacred: An Alternative to the Narrative of Disenchantment* (Oxford, UK: Oxford University Press, 2021).

60. See Casanova, *Public Religions in the Modern World*, 17ff, 39. However, theoretical bias can also show the interest of some of the defenders of the secularization thesis in making religions publicly irrelevant by accusing them of "trespassing illegitimately on the public sphere or of crossing systemic boundaries by assuming nonreligious roles" (*Public Religions in the Modern World*, 212). For a genealogy of these theoretical biases and an alternative account emphasizing new forms of sacralization, see Joas, *The Power of the Sacred*.

61. Casanova, *Public Religions in the Modern World*, 212. David Martin, to whom Casanova refers as one of the first challengers of the secularization thesis (*Public Religions in the Modern World*, 11), is of the same mind: see his "What I Really Said About Secularization," 215. Casanova has revised his argument about public religions, especially after some of the criticisms provided by Talal Asad, *Formations of the Secular: Christianity, Islam, Modernity* (Stanford, CA: Stanford University Press, 2003). Two main areas of reformulation matter here, although neither of them affect the core of my argument about Gutiérrez's take on the secularization process. First is the stress on the Western trajectory of secularization. In his revision of the argument, Casanova takes a more global approach, supporting the concept of "multiple modernities" and hence the diverse patterns of the process of secularization. Second, he acknowledges that the differentiation of the religious sphere from the political sphere is quite different in non-Christian societies. In turn, this affects what public religions look like in places where Islam, for instance, is the dominant religion. For these revisions, see José Casanova, "Public Religions Revisited," in *Religion: Beyond a Concept*, ed. Hent de Vries (New York: Fordham University Press, 2008).

62. Casanova, *Public Religions in the Modern World*, 233, my emphasis.

63. Casanova, *Public Religions in the Modern World*, 234.

64. Liberation theology represents *one possible articulation* between faith and politics, one that, following the voluntary disestablishment of the Catholic Church after Vatican II, mostly constricts the role of religious activism to civil society. However, as Casanova acknowledges in a revision of his argument in *Public Religions in the Modern World*, that is *not the only way* in which faith and politics, church and state, the religious and the secular, do or must interact. On this topic, see Casanova, "Public Religions Revisited."

65. See Charles Taylor, *A Secular Age* (Cambridge, MA: Belknap Press of Harvard University Press, 2007). For a more focused account of the optional nature of belief in contemporary societies, see Joas, *Faith as an Option.*

66. Barger, *The World Come of Age*, 165.

67. Casanova, *Public Religions in the Modern World*, 13.

68. Casanova, *Public Religions in the Modern World*, 15.

69. Barger, *The World Come of Age*, 172, my emphasis.

70. Barger, *The World Come of Age*, 173, my emphasis.

71. For a similar critique, highlighting some additional issues, see J. Matthew Ashley, "To Change the World: An Intellectual History of Liberation Theology," *Commonweal*, January 31, 2019, https://www.commonwealmagazine.org/change-world.

72. Barger, *The World Come of Age*, 150.

73. Here I understand the "anthropological turn" in terms of Taylor's "affirmation of ordinary life," that is, the ethical concern for the enhancement of life and the avoidance of suffering here and now, see Taylor, *A Secular Age*, 13ff. For the "historical turn," I refer to an epistemological shift based on the acknowledgment that our historical context decisively shapes the task of understanding. On the historical turn and its influence in theology, see H. Richard Niebuhr, *The Meaning of Revelation* (New York: Macmillan, 1941).

74. Brackley ("Salvation and the Social Good," 11ff.) insightfully notes that Maritain and Gutiérrez generally fit with the description given by Niebuhr of the "Christ above culture" and "Christ the transformer of culture" types, respectively. See H. Richard Niebuhr, *Christ and Culture*, (New York: Harper, 1951).

75. Gutiérrez, *A Theology of Liberation*, 43. Indeed, for Gutiérrez, one of the key dimensions of the process of liberation is the critique of the old state-church alliance, moving from a reactionary or "ghettoized" church to a church engaged in the process of liberation that stands in solidarity with the poor (58ff.).

76. Karl Marx, "Contribution to the Critique of Hegel's *Philosophy of Right*: Introduction," in *The Marx-Engels Reader*, ed. Robert C. Tucker, 2nd ed. (New York: Norton, 1978), 53.

77. Gutiérrez, *A Theology of Liberation*, 43.

78. Taylor, "A Catholic Modernity?," 169–170.

79. Liberation theology clearly defends a form of "theological humanism," that is, the mutual affirmation of the need to enhance ordinary life (humanism) and the faith in a God of love who would ultimately heal and redeem what the human being cannot (theology). I substantially agree with the account of theological humanism developed in William Schweiker, "Humanism and the Question of Fullness," in *Aspiring to Fullness in a Secular Age: Essays on Religion and Theology in the Work of Charles Taylor*, ed. Carlos D. Colorado and Justin D. Klassen (Notre Dame, IN: University of Notre Dame Press, 2014). On

"humanism open to transcendence", a slightly different position, see Taylor, "A Catholic Modernity?"

80. Gutiérrez, *A Theology of Liberation*, 44.

81. Gutiérrez, *A Theology of Liberation*, 45.

82. But not without ambiguities, as always happens in these church documents. See Gutiérrez, *A Theology of Liberation*, 195, fn. 38.

83. Several decades earlier, Ernst Troeltsch developed this point compellingly in "Historical and Dogmatic Method in Theology," in *Religion in History*, Fortress Texts in Modern Theology (Minneapolis: Fortress Press, 1991). In this essay, Troeltsch rejects dualistic understandings of history, which, in his view, insert dualism into God's will. Instead, he argues for the idea "that history is not a chaos but issues from unitary forces and aspires towards a unitary goal." (27) Further, he defends "a conception of history as a disclosure of the divine reason." (27). Yet we should note that Troeltsch does not conceive this process naïvely, as a pure progression. Rather, he conceives of it as a trajectory where there is plenty of "struggle and error" (27).

84. O'Brien and Shannon, *Gaudium et spes*, §47.

85. O'Brien and Shannon, *Gaudium et spes*, §57.

86. David J. O'Brien and Thomas A. Shannon, eds., *Populorum progressio*, in *Catholic Social Thought: The Documentary Heritage*, expanded ed. (Maryknoll, NY: Orbis Books, 2010), §14, §13.

87. O'Brien and Shannon, *Gaudium et spes*, §40.

88. Gutiérrez, *A Theology of Liberation*, 46.

89. Gutiérrez, *A Theology of Liberation*, 63. For his account of the social process of liberation taking place at the time, and the role of the clergy and laypeople, see part 3, "The Option Before the Latin American Church."

90. We should not conclude from this that the majority of the bishops, clergy, and laypeople were involved in the process of liberation. As Gutiérrez notes, the situation of Latin America in the 1960s and 1970s was one of intense conflict and division within society and the church. In fact, his work is an attempt to find unity amid conflict. See Gutiérrez, *A Theology of Liberation*, 75.

91. On the history that preceded the publication of James H. Cone, *Black Theology and Black Power* (Maryknoll, NY: Orbis Books, 1997), originally published in 1969, and James H. Cone, *A Black Theology of Liberation*, 20th anniversary ed. (Maryknoll, NY: Orbis Books, 1990), originally published in 1970, see Gayraud S. Wilmore, *Black Religion and Black Radicalism: An Interpretation of the Religious History of African Americans*, 3rd ed. (Maryknoll, NY: Orbis Books, 1998). See also James H. Cone and Gayraud S. Wilmore, eds., *Black Theology: A Documentary History*, 2nd rev. ed., 2 vols. (Maryknoll, NY: Orbis Books, 1993).

92. Gutiérrez, *A Theology of Liberation*, xiii.

93. Gutiérrez, *A Theology of Liberation*, 85. For a recent statement of this theological consensus, see David Bentley Hart, *That All Shall Be Saved: Heaven, Hell, and Universal Salvation* (New Haven, CT: Yale University Press, 2019).

94. Gutiérrez, *A Theology of Liberation*, 85.

95. Gutiérrez, *A Theology of Liberation*, 85.

96. Gutiérrez, *A Theology of Liberation*, 86.

97. Gutiérrez, *A Theology of Liberation*, xxxiv, my emphasis.

98. Gutiérrez, *A Theology of Liberation*, xxvii. Yet these remarks should not suggest that the liberation of the poor and the construction of a more just society are not worthy ends in themselves. Gutiérrez's point simply is that, from the standpoint of the Christian faith, justice is only completed in God's Kingdom.

99. Joas, *The Sacredness of the Person*, 90. Yet, as Joas also notes, this process could not have been set in motion without certain structural preconditions. In the case of liberation theology, at the ecclesial level, these were the preconditions created by the trajectory of Catholicism in the twentieth century, especially after Vatican II.

100. Joas, *The Sacredness of the Person*, 85.

101. Note that Gutiérrez advances a biblical theology of salvation without accounting for the status of the biblical text, simply assuming its authoritative role. In following chapters, I develop a comprehensive account of the formation of religious traditions, including the Christian tradition, in order to supplement what I see lacking in Gutiérrez's argument.

102. Gutiérrez, *A Theology of Liberation*, 86–87. Here we see a reason to focus on the work of Gutiérrez instead of the otherwise remarkable oeuvre of Cone when it comes to the question of liberation. Even though Gutiérrez and Cone agree on the basics, Cone's treatment of salvation history or eschatology is rather brief. Consequently, in my view he has some difficulties at the level of *theological* articulation to defend his otherwise sound *ethical* claim that liberation must be a "Black event." (On his eschatology, see Cone, *A Black Theology of Liberation*, 135–142.) In addition, Cone has a more tense relationship with the Christian tradition and what he often calls "white theology," which leads to some debatable choices that Gutiérrez avoids. One of them is to prioritize "blackness" over everything else in his theology, at least in his later writings. In contrast, Gutiérrez does not make "the poor" the primary source of his work, but one among several others. On this issue, see James H. Cone, *God of the Oppressed*, rev. ed. (Maryknoll, NY: Orbis Books, 1997), "Preface to the 1997 Edition," especially x–xi. On some of the problems associated with the prioritization of blackness, see Victor Anderson, *Beyond Ontological Blackness: An Essay on African American Religious and Cultural Criticism* (New York: Continuum, 1995).

103. James Cone's reflections on sin, especially on the sin of "whiteness," are more comprehensive and insightful than Gutiérrez's. However, the rhetoric of

Cone's criticism of whiteness leads him at times to collapse whiteness (white supremacy) with being white (a phenotypical feature) in ways that suggest that both should be rejected. Such an approach makes Christian reconciliation difficult to understand but also appears to make blackness dependent on whiteness. On the first issue, see J. Deotis Roberts, *Liberation and Reconciliation: A Black Theology*, 2nd ed. (Louisville, KY: Westminster John Knox Press, 2005). On the second, see Anderson, *Beyond Ontological Blackness*.

    104. Gutiérrez, *A Theology of Liberation*, 88. I have amended the translation, which instead of "fraternal" uses "comradely."

    105. Gutiérrez, *A Theology of Liberation*, 88. The critique that Delores S. Williams, *Sisters in the Wilderness: The Challenge of Womanist God-Talk* (Maryknoll, NY: Orbis Books, 1993) provides to Black theologians on their interpretation of Exodus is equally valid for Gutiérrez and his Latin American colleagues. In this sense, with Williams, we should advocate for a "hermeneutic of identification-ascertainment" (144–149). In doing so, we become keenly aware of our position as interpreters of biblical texts and of the position of those producing the texts so that, unlike Black and Latin American liberation theologians, we will not overestimate the liberating power of certain narratives without considering who are the oppressed in those very same narratives. Indeed, Cone and Gutiérrez give great importance to the liberation from Egypt but have nothing to say about the genocide of the Canaanites in the taking of the Promised Land.

    106. Gutiérrez, *A Theology of Liberation*, 89.

    107. Gutiérrez, *A Theology of Liberation*, 90. Gutiérrez's treatment of "Christ the liberator" is rather brief in his oeuvre, often stating the key ideas I will note in this section and then inserting them into a larger account of the process of liberation-salvation. For more on the "Christology of liberation," see Ignacio Ellacuría, "The Crucified People," in *Ignacio Ellacuría: Essays on History, Liberation, and Salvation*, ed. Michael Edward Lee (Maryknoll, NY: Orbis Books, 2013); Jon Sobrino, *Jesus the Liberator: A Historical-Theological Reading of Jesus of Nazareth* (Maryknoll, NY: Orbis Books, 1993).

    108. Gutiérrez, *A Theology of Liberation*, 91.

    109. Gutiérrez, *A Theology of Liberation*, 91–92.

    110. Gutiérrez, *A Theology of Liberation*, 92.

    111. On this, see Gutiérrez, *A Theology of Liberation*, chapter 2, and Gutiérrez, *The God of Life* (Maryknoll, NY: Orbis Books, 1991). The latter book is Gutiérrez's articulation of a faith in a life-giving God in the midst of the times of political violence in Perú, when the terrorist group Sendero Luminoso (Shining Path) brutally killed thousands of Peruvians, most of them poor.

    112. On this issue, see David Tracy, "The Christian Option for the Poor," and the insightful response of J. Matthew Ashley, "The Turn to Apocalyptic and the

Option for the Poor," both in *The Option for the Poor in Christian Theology*, ed. Daniel G. Groody (Notre Dame, IN: University of Notre Dame Press, 2007).

113. Gutiérrez, *A Theology of Liberation*, 24.

114. Gustavo Gutiérrez, *On Job: God-Talk and the Suffering of the Innocent* (Maryknoll, NY: Orbis Books, 1987), xiii. Gutiérrez also notes here, and especially in *We Drink from Our Own Wells: The Spiritual Journey of a People* (Maryknoll, NY: Orbis Books, 1984), that this methodological distinction is a sign of a spiritual commitment. The distinction between the first and second acts, however, requires refinement. I will provide a more nuanced account in the following chapters.

115. Gutiérrez, *A Theology of Liberation*, xx.

116. Gutiérrez, *A Theology of Liberation*, xxi. Here, precisely for the importance of the dialogue with the tradition, is important to see how Gutiérrez expands the Christian understanding of poverty. He distinguishes three forms. First, "material or real" poverty, the one described earlier. For him, this poverty is always a sin and Christians must work toward its eradication. Second, "spiritual" poverty, the most emphasized in the tradition. We see it in the gospels, especially in Jesus's beatitudes. For Gutiérrez, this is the fundamental idea at the root of all Christian spirituality: it calls for our full trust in and dependence on God. Lastly, poverty as "solidarity and protest": a lifestyle of simplicity in solidarity with the poor and active engagement in the eradication of poverty. The first and last definitions expand the tradition by making solidarity and protest a form of deep spirituality that nurtures the struggle against injustice. (See *A Theology of Liberation*, 162–173).

117. Gutiérrez, *A Theology of Liberation*, 24–25.

118. Gutiérrez, *A Theology of Liberation*, xxvi. For a defense, but also critical analysis of the ethical and theological underpinnings of the "preferential option for the poor," see Stephen J. Pope, "Proper and Improper Partiality and The Preferential Option for the Poor," *Theological Studies* 54 (1993): 242–271.

119. Gutiérrez, *A Theology of Liberation*, 25. In this chapter, Gutiérrez critically engages the concept of development. He discusses the concept as it was understood in the context of the theories of development of the 1960s, widely applied in Latin America. However, the new approach to human development, focused on the expansion of freedom and capabilities coheres with the proposal advanced by Gutiérrez. On this issue, see Raúl E. Zegarra, *La subversión de la esperanza: diálogo contemporáneo entre teología de la liberación, filosofía y opción por los pobres* (Lima, Perú: PUCP; IBC; CEP, 2015), chap. 6, "¿Desarrollo o liberación? Repensando los alcances de la *Populorum progressio*."

120. Martha C. Nussbaum, *Creating Capabilities: The Human Development Approach* (Cambridge, MA: Harvard University Press, 2011), 20. The language of capabilities is not explicitly used by Gutiérrez. Yet, as I will show in Chapter 4,

it not only is congenial with his theology but helps to articulate the implicit conception of justice behind liberation theology.

121. Historically, the nurturing and sustenance provided by religious values and practices had great importance in the struggles of liberation. The same can be said of more relatively recent struggles like those of the civil rights movement in the United States or for democracy and poverty-eradication in Latin America. However, as the editors of Vincent W. Lloyd and Andrew L. Prevot, eds., *Anti-Blackness and Christian Ethics* (Maryknoll, NY: Orbis Books, 2017) argue, this may be changing today with movements like Black Lives Matter. In this sense, Lloyd and Prevot maintain that the new more "secular" movements would do well to pay attention to their religious counterparts, and learn from their history, institutional resources, and spiritual practices. Plus, paying attention to religion may also give them resources to address anti-Blackness since, arguably, its genesis may be connected to religion (xviii–xix).

Chapter 2

1. In addition to my discussion of secularization in Chapter 1, even though *secular* and *religious* may refer to relatively identifiable objects, it is by no means clear that we can easily delimit their content and absolutely distinguish one from the other. Further, within each realm we can find a variety of forms of religious and secular expression. *Religion* may include views that range from New Age eclecticism to very strict forms of Tridentine Catholicism. Similarly, *secular* may refer to different forms of humanism that can easily coexist with religious views or can refer to active efforts to suppress religious beliefs, as happened with the Soviet "state atheism." On the complexities related to defining these terms, see Talal Asad, *Genealogies of Religion: Discipline and Reasons of Power in Christianity and Islam* (Baltimore: Johns Hopkins University Press, 1993); Talal Asad, *Formations of the Secular: Christianity, Islam, Modernity* (Stanford, CA: Stanford University Press, 2003).

2. On this issue, see Matthew Bowman, *Christian: The Politics of a Word in America* (Cambridge, MA: Harvard University Press, 2018).

3. H. Richard Niebuhr, *The Meaning of Revelation* (New York: Macmillan, 1941), x, 133ff.

4. I understand the notion of "relative adequacy" as having two key components. On the one hand there is *general, public intelligibility* for which we consider ordinary criteria like internal coherence and intersubjective validation over time. On the other there is the *appropriateness to the object of study*. We cannot apply to poetry or painting the criterion of simplicity that is often used for logic and mathematics. Similarly, if our subject is an inherently metaphysical question like "the ultimate meaning of life" or "God" we cannot apply criteria solely from

the empirical sciences. My main interlocutors here are Paul Ricœur, *Interpreta-tion Theory: Discourse and the Surplus of Meaning* (Fort Worth: Texas Christian University Press, 1976), 75ff.; David Tracy, *Blessed Rage for Order: The New Plu-ralism in Theology: With a New Preface* (Chicago: University of Chicago Press, 1996), especially chap. 4. But the tradition of American pragmatism is also cru-cial in this regard.

5. Joas, *Do We Need Religion? On the Experience of Self-Transcendence*. Boulder, CO: Paradigm, 2008, 7–10.

6. William Schweiker, *Responsibility and Christian Ethics* (Cambridge, UK: Cambridge University Press, 1995), 176.

7. I will return to this key concept of David Tracy's theology later.

8. See David Tracy, *The Analogical Imagination: Christian Theology and the Culture of Pluralism* (New York: Crossroad, 1981). Tracy's argument in this book is fundamentally shaped, and even organized, by Ricœur's dialectic of mani-festation and proclamation. However, as Tracy underscores in fn. 26 in chap. 5 (221–222), he has some differences with Ricœur's account. My reading also differs from Ricœur's reading in certain aspects, drawing from Tracy and Joas instead, but like Tracy, I recognize the seminal role of Ricœur's essay and use it as a starting point.

9. Paul Ricœur, "Manifestation and Proclamation," in *Figuring the Sacred: Religion, Narrative, and Imagination*, ed. Mark I. Wallace, trans. David Pellauer (Minneapolis: Fortress Press, 1995), 48.

10. Ricœur, in fact, mentions five features, but the fifth one (which he calls the "logic of manifestation" or "logic of meaning") is simply a summary of the first four. This fifth feature operates through a "law of correspondences." He writes: "In the sacred universe the capacity for saying is founded on the capacity of the cosmos to signify something other than itself" (Ricœur, "Manifestation and Proclamation," 54).

11. Ricœur, "Manifestation and Proclamation," 49.

12. Émile Durkheim, *The Elementary Forms of the Religious Life* (New York: Free Press, 1965), 246–252. Although, as Joas notes, Durkheim overemphasizes *collective* effervescence, leaving little room for individual experiences of self-tran-scendence. For his critique of Durkheim and his own proposal, see Joas, *The Power of the Sacred*.

13. Johann Michel, *Homo Interpretans: Towards a Transformation of Hermeneu-tics*, trans. David Pellauer (London: Rowman and Littlefield, 2019), 16. Michel advances a three-level model to account for our interpretative processes. *Proto-interpretations* designate "in the ethological, psycho-biological sense . . . the pre-reflexive operations, valid for every living organism, including human beings, of selecting among the signs that constitute an Umwelt" (16). *Interpretation*, by con-trast, is human activity proper, and emerges as a form of "qualifying the ordinary

activity produced by human agents when they experience a breakdown in immediate understanding and bring into play reflexive procedures meant to remove a problem" (16). Lastly, *meta-interpretation*, as an epistemological endeavor, consists in "the deliberate activity of interpretation, as well as hermeneutic reflection on questions about interpretation that the sciences, beyond those that study texts, draw on" (16).

14. According to Michel (*Homo Interpretans*, 43–50), collectives develop "cultural schemes" that shape the way in which their members relate to their surroundings. Such schematism is not universally present in all human collectives. Rather, it expresses certain form of "seeing as" developed in time and place. Nevertheless, cultural schemes become second nature to the members of a given culture, allowing the production of relatively immediate meanings. Cultural variations in the way people greet each other provides a helpful example. These are not innate forms of conduct; they are learned. However, they do become "cultural schemes" because they are not the subject of repeated reflection every time we greet somebody. As Michel notes, "cultural schematism intervenes in ordinary non-problematic situations" (41). In this sense we are speaking of a pre-reflective, proto-interpretative, pre-propositional, habitual activity.

15. Thus described, the logic of manifestation very much resembles the phenomenology of givenness developed by Jean-Luc Marion. However, Marion's work often lacks the hermeneutical dimension that is so central to Ricœur, Tracy, and this book. On how the hermeneutical limitations of Marion's work can be overcome, in dialogue with Ricœur and liberation theology, see Raúl E. Zegarra, "Una fenomenología (hermenéutica) de la revelación para una teología de la liberación," in *Jean-Luc Marion: límites y posibilidades de la filosofía y de la teología*, ed. Jorge Roggero (Buenos Aires: Editorial SB, 2017).

16. Ricœur, "Manifestation and Proclamation," 50.

17. Here Ricœur has in mind Immanuel Kant's *Critique of Judgment*. Ricœur sees a parallel between the hierophanies he is describing and the surplus of experience given by the imagination that finds no correlate in the categories of understanding in Kant's aesthetic judgment.

18. Ricœur, "Manifestation and Proclamation," 51.

19. Ricœur, "Manifestation and Proclamation," 53, 54.

20. Joas, *Do We Need Religion?*, 98–101. For the text discussed by Joas, see Paul Ricœur, "Experience and Language in Religious Discourse," in *Phenomenology and the "Theological Turn": The French Debate*, ed. Dominique Janicaud (New York: Fordham University Press, 2000).

21. There is a variety of experiences of sacralization that are by no means restricted to the world of sacred texts or conventionally understood religious traditions. In this sense, as Joas does, we can speak compellingly of the "sacralization of the person" in the culture of human rights. See Hans Joas, *The Sacredness*

of the Person: A New Genealogy of Human Rights (Washington, DC: Georgetown University Press, 2013).

22. Ricœur, "Manifestation and Proclamation," 56.

23. Ricœur, "Manifestation and Proclamation," 57. See also Paul Ricœur, "Toward a Hermeneutic of the Idea of Revelation," in *Essays on Biblical Interpretation*, ed. Lewis Seymour Mudge (Philadelphia: Fortress Press, 1980).

24. Ricœur, "Manifestation and Proclamation," 56–57. Ricœur's reflections here overlap considerably with Taylor's characterization of the disembedding process that started taking place in the Axial Age. See Charles Taylor, "What Was the Axial Revolution?," in *The Axial Age and Its Consequences*, ed. Robert N. Bellah and Hans Joas (Cambridge, MA: Belknap Press of Harvard University Press, 2012).

25. Ricœur, "Manifestation and Proclamation," 59. On the role of paradoxes, see Jean-Luc Marion, *Being Given: Toward a Phenomenology of Givenness*, trans. Jeffrey Kosky (Stanford, CA: Stanford University Press, 2013), especially §§23–24. For his more recent account, see Jean-Luc Marion, *Givenness and Revelation*, trans. Stephen E. Lewis (Oxford, UK: Oxford University Press, 2016).

26. The Greek only says "brothers" (adelphoi), but there is no reason to believe that there is an explicit gender distinction here. In fact, it would not make any sense. Hence the New Revised Standard Version of the Bible correctly renders adelphoi as "these who are the members of my family."

27. I do not engage here with the theological problems related to the status of ta ethne in v. 32 and ton elachiston in v. 40 and v. 45. I have studied this problem in detail as well as the importance of this text for liberation theology in chap. 3 of Raúl E. Zegarra, *La subversión de la esperanza: diálogo contemporáneo entre teología de la liberación, filosofía y opción por los pobres* (Lima, Perú: PUCP; IBC; CEP, 2015).

28. Ricœur, "Manifestation and Proclamation," 61.

29. Ricœur, "Manifestation and Proclamation," 65. Similar considerations in relation to language and revelation can be found in Martin Buber, "Biblical Humanism," in *The Martin Buber Reader: Essential Writings*, ed. Asher Biemann (New York: Palgrave, 2002).

30. Even though I draw this basic typology mostly from Joas and Ricœur, it also fits with William James's own characterization of religion. For a summary of his findings, see William James, *The Varieties of Religious Experience: A Study in Human Nature* (New York: Longmans, Green, 1916), 485–486. It is important to underscore, though, that my account here pays great attention to the social dimensions of religious experience and its articulation in religious traditions, something significantly overlooked in James's work. For more on James, his contributions to the study of religion, and his affinities with liberation theology, see Raúl E. Zegarra, *Dos lenguajes teológicos: un*

ensayo sobre el carácter público de nuestras creencias religiosas (Bogotá: Editorial Bonaventuriana, 2015).

31. From a historical perspective, these are also the main contributions of the axial revolution or the Axial Age. On this, see Robert N. Bellah and Hans Joas, eds., *The Axial Age and Its Consequences* (Cambridge, MA: Harvard University Press, 2012); Robert N. Bellah, *Religion in Human Evolution: From the Paleolithic to the Axial Age* (Cambridge, MA: Harvard University Press, 2011).

32. On the limits of articulation, see Joas, *Do We Need Religion?*, 44ff.

33. Ricœur sees this pattern reiterated in the dialectic of sacraments and preaching. Sacraments replicate the intensity of the logic of manifestation whereas preaching performs the disembedding of the logic of proclamation, directing us to make the world sacred by bringing justice to it instead of taking its sacredness comfortably for granted (Ricœur, "Manifestation and Proclamation," 67).

34. However, some forms of institutionalized meaning can become a "cultural scheme" (see previous notes on J. Michel's definition of this concept) that now operates as the pre-reflective background from which new experiences can emerge. In this sense, the example of the Eucharist is helpful. The doctrine of the Eucharist is clearly a theological, rational, elaboration of an initial religious experience that, in turn, becomes the pre-condition of new religious experiences. In this sense, manifestation, proclamation, and institutionalization find an illuminating parallel in Michel's scheme for hermeneutics. Manifestation is the moment of fundamental givenness. Hence, here we only see proto-interpretations. Proclamation, by contrast, is the moment of interpretation proper. Institutionalization requires a higher level of reflection and matches with Michel's meta-interpretative level. But, as noted, these moments are fluid and somewhat circular: interpretations and meta-interpretations can become proto-interpretations, and proto-interpretations are the condition of possibility of any active interpretative act.

35. Joas, *Do We Need Religion?*, 45.

36. Joas, *Do We Need Religion?*, 46. "These levels" refer to Joas's four components in the process of articulation: "the situation experienced, our pre-reflective experience, our individual articulation, and the cultural repertoire of interpretative patterns" (46). Yet the point is equally valid for the articulation of religious experience in terms of the triad of manifestation-proclamation-institutionalization.

37. See James, *The Varieties of Religious Experience.*

38. Edward Shils, *Tradition* (Chicago: University of Chicago Press, 1981), 12.

39. As Shils notes, this often requires an external observer or at least some stepping back, since the immediate recipients of the tradition may lack the sufficient distance to see the patterns (*Tradition*, 14).

40. I develop this idea and its methodological implications in the introduction to Raúl E. Zegarra, "The Revolution of Tradition: Liberation Theology's

Contribution to the Formulation of a Comprehensive Theory of Social Justice" (PhD dissertation, University of Chicago, 2021). For a similar approach to tradition, see Jeffrey Stout, *Democracy and Tradition* (Princeton, NJ: Princeton University Press, 2004), 3–15. In the context of Catholic theology, this emphasis on practices is especially strong in Terrence W. Tilley, *Inventing Catholic Tradition* (Maryknoll, NY: Orbis Books, 2000). The pragmatic vein of Tilley's work is present in the entirety of the book, although, surprisingly, without any reference to the American pragmatists.

41. For one of the classic contributions to this turn in the context of Catholic theology, see Yves Congar, *Tradition and Traditions: An Historical and a Theological Essay* (New York: Macmillan, 1967). Congar's influence cannot be overstated and has been decisive in more contemporary appropriations of *traditio* that stress issues like inculturation and popular religion. On these issues, see Orlando Espín and Gary Macy, *Futuring Our Past: Explorations in the Theology of Tradition* (Maryknoll, NY: Orbis Books, 2006). Espín's essay in this volume as well as Nancy Pineda-Madrid's are especially important in this regard. For perhaps the most comprehensive account of the debates over tradition in the twentieth century in Christian, especially Catholic, theology, see Jean-Georges Boeglin, *La question de la tradition dans la théologie catholique contemporaine* (Paris: Editions du Cerf, 1998).

42. The classic study is still Ernst Troeltsch, *The Social Teaching of the Christian Churches*, trans. Olive Wyon, 2 vols. (New York: Harper Torchbooks, 1960).

43. On this issue, see Joas, *Do We Need Religion?*, 46. Here Joas builds on the classic formulation of these tension between ideal and actual self in Charles Taylor, *Sources of the Self: The Making of the Modern Identity* (Cambridge, MA: Harvard University Press, 1989).

44. See Paul Ricœur, *Freud and Philosophy: An Essay on Interpretation* (New Haven, CT: Yale University Press, 1970), 20–36.

45. On the "inevitable self-positioning of the historian," drawing from Troeltsch, see Joas, *The Sacredness of the Person*, 121–124.

46. I am not particularly concerned with a very strict determination of the historically verifiable content of Jesus's preaching and practice. The scholarship on this issue is voluminous, and beyond the interests of my sketch here. On this topic, I follow the remarkable work of John Meier's multivolume *A Marginal Jew*. My brief characterization, however, suffices for the present context. For a classic account of the key ideals present in Jesus's preaching, see Troeltsch, *The Social Teaching of the Christian Churches*, 1:51ff. For an account of the distinctiveness of Jesus's message vis-à-vis the Judaism of his time, with special emphasis on the question of radical forgiveness, see E. P. Sanders, *The Historical Figure of Jesus* (London: Allen Lane, 1993), esp. chap. 14, "Contention and Opposition in Galilee." For a feminist account of the key values of Jesus's preaching and the early

Jesus-movement that pays special attention to the prominent role of women in the movement, see Elisabeth Schüssler Fiorenza, *In Memory of Her: A Feminist Theological Reconstruction of Christian Origins*, 10th anniversary ed. (New York: Crossroad, 1994).

47. For some of the most drastic transformations of the early Jesus-movement due to the incorporation of wealthy and powerful figures, see Jef Van Gerwen, "Origins of Christian Ethics," in *The Blackwell Companion to Religious Ethics*, ed. William Schweiker (Malden, MA: Blackwell, 2005).

48. Of course, this does not have to undermine "the quest for the historical Jesus." It only shows that any attempt to find the most historically accurate facts about the person of Jesus of Nazareth depends on complex efforts of abstraction from the context of faith-based claims about him. On the differences between the "historical Jesus" and the "real Jesus," see John P. Meier, *A Marginal Jew: Rethinking the Historical Jesus*, vol. 1 (New Haven, CT: Yale University Press, 1991), 21–40.

49. As Shils notes, normativity is a key element of any tradition, although not all traditions aim to be explicitly normative. Yet regardless of the original intentions of the shapers of the tradition, the tradition must be taken as normative in some regard for its very existence. Otherwise, the tradition cannot be recognized as one and persist over time (*Tradition*, 23–25).

50. Shils, *Tradition*, 17.

51. See Shils, *Tradition*, 25–27.

52. For an excellent example of this, see Bowman, *Christian*.

53. Shils, *Tradition*, 45.

54. Shils, *Tradition*, 53. Selective appropriations of the past are not the sole prerogative of traditionalist groups. Progressive figures and groups can also use this selective recollection and emphasis on certain aspects of the tradition to advance their causes (*Tradition*, 209–212).

55. For a good study of the complex power dynamics of these selective emphases in the context of "fundamentalists" groups, see Gabriel Abraham Almond, R. Scott Appleby, and Emmanuel Sivan, *Strong Religion: The Rise of Fundamentalisms around the World* (Chicago: University of Chicago Press, 2003).

56. Shils, *Tradition*, 95.

57. Such is also the position of Sandra M. Schneiders, *The Revelatory Text: Interpreting the New Testament as Sacred Scripture*, 2nd ed. (Collegeville, MN: Liturgical Press, 1999), 53–59.

58. Shils, *Tradition*, 45.

59. Shils, *Tradition*, 95.

60. Shils, *Tradition*, 39.

61. Shils, *Tradition*, 96. On the complex relationship between orthodoxy and heterodoxy, see Lester R. Kurtz, *The Politics of Heresy: The Modernist Crisis in Roman Catholicism* (Berkeley: University of California Press, 1986).

62. Shils, *Tradition*, 97.

63. Shils, *Tradition*, 41.

64. Shils, *Tradition*, 27–31.

65. Shils, *Tradition*, 201–202.

66. An alternative tradition may be considered a *valuable* alternative. In such case, its values can be assimilated through adaptation without major conflict. It may also be seen less favorably, but adapted still for strategic reasons in order to avoid the risk of revolutionary confrontation. If the competing tradition appears to be a dangerous threat, it may be discredited on rational or moral grounds. The threatened tradition may even attempt to physically annihilate its competitor, as has often happened in the context of wars of religion.

67. Shils, *Tradition*, 98–99.

68. Shils, *Tradition*, 127.

69. Shils, *Tradition*, 167–169; 175ff. Hence, even outlier groups or figures (Shils has in mind the "sect" and "mystic" types in Ernst Troeltsch's famous typology) keep most of the tradition in their untraditional ways.

70. This dialectic is best identified and developed in Ernst Troeltsch, "What Does 'Essence of Christianity' Mean?," in *Writings on Theology and Religion* (Atlanta, GA: John Knox Press, 1977).

71. What better example than what we *now* call the Protestant Reformation, which very clearly started as a reformist movement *within* Latin/Roman Christianity and yet developed into a revolutionary new interpretation of the Christian tradition. On this issue, see Brad S. Gregory, *The Unintended Reformation: How a Religious Revolution Secularized Society* (Cambridge, MA: Belknap Press of Harvard University Press, 2012). For a less partisan approach that yet confirms the unintended outcome, see Susan E. Schreiner, *Are You Alone Wise? The Search for Certainty in the Early Modern Era*, Oxford Studies in Historical Theology (Oxford: UK: Oxford University Press, 2011).

72. The otherness-ownness dynamic is essential for what Ricœur describes as the dialectic of appropriation and distanciation. See Ricœur, *Interpretation Theory*, 43ff.

73. Tracy, *The Analogical Imagination*, 154.

74. Tracy, *The Analogical Imagination*, 108.

75. Tracy, *The Analogical Imagination*, 154.

76. Tracy, *The Analogical Imagination*, 203–218.

77. Tracy, *The Analogical Imagination*, 183, fn. 22.

78. Tracy, *The Analogical Imagination*, 159; 154–166, for his examination of the definitions of religion.

79. Tracy, *The Analogical Imagination*, 160–169.

80. Tracy, *The Analogical Imagination*, 233.

81. Tracy, *The Analogical Imagination*, 175.

82. Tracy, *The Analogical Imagination*, 175–178.

83. Tracy, *The Analogical Imagination*, 249. Implied in this dynamism is the disclosure-concealment dialectical nature of the Christ-event. Hence, the reference to the normative role of the Christian scriptures should not be understood as an example of the genetic fallacy. Neither Tracy nor I assume that the earliest expression of the event is by definition the best. Rather, this is simply an empirical claim: the early articulation of the Christ-event through the Christian scriptures is the condition of possibility of later ones, even if the latter express more fully the intention of the former (see *The Analogical Imagination*, 263–264).

84. Tracy, *The Analogical Imagination*, 249.

85. Tracy, *The Analogical Imagination*, 250.

86. Tracy, *The Analogical Imagination*, 233–241. Furthermore, we should always keep in mind that these methods of analysis work at the level of *explanation*, not at the *constitution* of meaning. From this follows that their role must be subordinated to the nature of the event they attempt to explain. *Criteria of appropriateness* to the event, then, is crucial. In Tracy's view these criteria have two key components: "an interpretation whose understanding honors in practice the kind of fundamental existential religious questions these texts address, and an interpretation which recognizes that the fundamental disclosure of the text . . . is the world of a religious event: an event of disclosure and concealment from and by the power of the whole" (259). Here Tracy builds on the understanding-explanation-understanding/comprehension hermeneutics developed in, among other texts, Ricœur's *Interpretation Theory*.

87. Among other reasons, this is because each theologian, even if they apply these critical methods, may come to different conclusions depending on their own hermeneutical situations and their own "working canon." On this issue, see the fine analysis in Tracy, *The Analogical Imagination*, 252–258.

88. Tracy, *The Analogical Imagination*, 252. On this issue, with special emphasis on dialogue with the Buddhist and Jewish traditions, see David Tracy, *Dialogue with the Other: The Inter-Religious Dialogue* (Louvain, Belgium: Peeters Press, 1990).

89. Tracy, *The Analogical Imagination*, 264–265. Moreover, for Tracy (196ff.) the correctives stand as an example of "critique" as a classic form of religious expression itself in the Christian tradition. So, it is not only that any classic must be examined through critical reflection as a matter of principle and intellectual honesty, but that such criticism itself is a fundamental component of the Bible as a classic expression of the Christian faith. We see this in the books of the prophets, wisdom literature, Job, and so on.

90. Tracy, *The Analogical Imagination*, 265, 266.

91. Tracy, *The Analogical Imagination*, 267.

92. Tracy, *The Analogical Imagination*, 268.

93. Tracy, *The Analogical Imagination*, 274.

94. Tracy, *The Analogical Imagination*, 269, 274.

95. I am not arguing here for the historicity of the resurrection since it is the faith-event par excellence. Yet neither am I arguing for the historicity of the incarnation and the death on the cross. Not because these events have no historical reality outside the context of faith, which does not seem to be the case, but because all three events are, above all, *faith-events* and, as such, from the value-formation point of view it is undeniable that they took place.

96. Tracy, *The Analogical Imagination*, 281–282.

97. This is not an isolated topic in Tracy's work but instead part of his great interest in moments of radical interruption/disruption in human history that allow us to reconsider the meaning of things and the trajectory of human life. On this issue, see Dario Balocco, *Dal cristocentrismo al cristomorfismo: in dialogo con David Tracy*, vol. 48, Dissertatio. Series Romana (Milan: Glossa, 2012), especially part II, for the importance of the Second Coming; see 188–193.

98. David Tracy, "The Christian Option for the Poor," in *The Option for the Poor in Christian Theology*, ed. Daniel G. Groody (Notre Dame, IN: University of Notre Dame Press, 2007), 130.

99. Tracy, "The Christian Option for the Poor," 129. Even though this "fragmenting" role of certain symbols and correctives has always been present in Tracy's career, it is true that Tracy has paid more attention to "fragments" in his later writings. On this issue, see Stephen Okey, *A Theology of Conversation: An Introduction to David Tracy* (Collegeville, MN: Liturgical Press Academic, 2018), especially chap. 3, "The Classic and the Fragment."

100. Tracy, "The Christian Option for the Poor," 128.

101. I draw here from chap. 4 of Zegarra, *La subversión de la esperanza*, where I expand on these issues in dialogue with the theologies of Joseph Ratzinger and Johann Baptist Metz.

102. However, less constructively, Tracy has been concerned with the situation of the marginalized since his first major publication *Blessed Rage for Order*. In this book, originally published in 1975, Tracy pays great attention to the "theologies of praxis," the term he uses to describe political and liberation theologies alike. Here, however, although he refers to liberation theology's key preoccupations approvingly (245ff.), the main concern is to analyze them in the context of his theological method. Hence, he stresses certain uncritical appropriations of theological doctrines and symbols by liberation theologians, suggesting further dialogue with what at that time seemed to be a natural ally, namely, the Frankfurt School of critical theory.

103. David Tracy, "On Naming the Present," in *On Naming the Present: God, Hermeneutics, and Church* (Maryknoll, NY: Orbis Books, 1994), 4.

104. Tracy, "On Naming the Present," 5.

105. Tracy, "On Naming the Present," 11.
106. Tracy, "On Naming the Present," 18.
107. Tracy, "The Christian Option for the Poor," 124.
108. Tracy, "The Christian Option for the Poor," 129.
109. Tracy, "The Christian Option for the Poor," 129.
110. For a response to the Tracy essay discussed here, with greater emphasis on how to materialize the interruptive nature of the symbol of the Second Coming, see J. Matthew Ashley, "The Turn to Apocalyptic and the Option for the Poor," in *The Option for the Poor in Christian Theology*, ed. Daniel G. Groody (Notre Dame, IN: University of Notre Dame Press, 2007). Ashley's emphasis on the Ignatian paradigm of contemplation *in* action and the role of contemporary martyrs is indeed very helpful, but Ashley overlooks at times that the symbol of the Second Coming is to be construed in tandem with the other three (incarnation, cross, and resurrection).

111. In his recent tribute to Gustavo Gutiérrez, Tracy expands on this issue, stressing that one of the key contributions of Gutiérrez is his balance between political and spiritual liberation. Tracy does so focusing on Gutiérrez's *On Job*, underscoring that the accomplishment of this book is to provide an account of "innocent suffering inflicted by any tragic misfortune." This opens a contemplative stream of his liberation theology that is often overlooked. See David Tracy, "Gustavo Gutiérrez, teólogo," in *Memoria, presencia, y futuro de la teología de la liberacion: A los 50 años de Teología de la liberación*, ed. Andrés Gallego, Carmen Lora, and Pedro De Guchteneere, trans. Raúl E. Zegarra (Lima: PUCP, IBC, and CEP, 2021).

112. Tracy, *The Analogical Imagination*, 174.

113. Tracy also considers the option of "dialectical language," which stresses negations and the impossibility of fully grasping the meaning of revelation. Nevertheless, he argues that all theologians that stress these negations, from Karl Barth to Jürgen Moltmann, Johann Baptist Metz, and some liberation theologians, *also* develop their own constructive projects, which are to some degree inevitably analogical (*The Analogical Imagination*, 414–421).

114. Tracy, *Blessed Rage for Order*, 43, 44. Tracy considers both "texts" *and* "expressions," since "texts" sometimes appear to receive more attention in the commentary on his work. Moreover, the emphasis on multiple forms of religious expression beyond the important canonical texts is clear in Tracy's later writings. For instance, in David Tracy, *Plurality and Ambiguity: Hermeneutics, Religion, Hope* (San Francisco: Harper and Row, 1987), 102ff., the author values the experiences of the poor in the process of interpretation of the Christian mystery. A similar approach is developed in the already cited piece, Tracy, "On Naming the Present." On Tracy's expansion of his initial emphasis on "the classic" to include

"fragments" and more ordinary experience, see Okey, *A Theology of Conversation*, 86–97.

115. Tracy, *The Analogical Imagination*, 25.

116. On the relationship between intramural and extramural questions, see Gene Outka, "Christian Ethics?," in *The Blackwell Companion to Religious Ethics*, ed. William Schweiker (Malden, MA: Blackwell, 2005).

117. Tracy, *Blessed Rage for Order*, 6, 44.

118. The *kind* of the publicness will vary depending on who is the theologian's principal addressee or public. For Tracy's account of the three main types of theologians (systematic, fundamental, and practical), their publics, and the different types of warrants needed in each case, see Tracy, *The Analogical Imagination*, 56–79.

119. Tracy, *Blessed Rage for Order*, 46.

120. For further criteria see Tracy, *The Analogical Imagination*, 422.

121. Tracy, *The Analogical Imagination*, 408, 410. For another philosophical-theological project that sees in analogy the best way to approach the God-self-society relationship, see John E. Smith, *The Analogy of Experience: An Approach to Understanding Religious Truth* (New York: Harper and Row, 1973). Smith's project, however, is significantly different from Tracy's in a couple of ways. First, Smith's main philosophical interlocutor is American Pragmatism, not the tradition of philosophical hermeneutics. One of the key advantages of this approach is greater focus on the category of experience. Yet Smith has very little to say about the interpretation of sacred texts in a way that renders some of his ways to describe God, Christ, and the Church unwarranted. Second, for similar reasons, Smith does not engage in any detail the tradition of interpretation of what we have called the Christ-event. His approach in this sense is rather abstract, dependent on the tradition, but without an account of his standing before it. That said, I believe Smith's work nicely complements Tracy's and further advocates for the complementarity of the pragmatist and hermeneutical traditions.

122. Tracy, *The Analogical Imagination*, 409–410.

123. Tracy, *The Analogical Imagination*, 410. Further, in the process of establishing correlations the very analogical concepts chosen can prove to be inadequate or, at least, in need of transformation (423).

124. Tracy, *The Analogical Imagination*, 409.

125. Here I draw freely from the following authors, among others: Gustavo Gutiérrez, *A Theology of Liberation: History, Politics, and Salvation*, 2nd ed. (Maryknoll, NY: Orbis Books, 1988); Ignacio Ellacuría, "The Crucified People," in *Ignacio Ellacuría: Essays on History, Liberation, and Salvation*, ed. Michael Edward Lee (Maryknoll, NY: Orbis Books, 2013); Jon Sobrino, *Jesus the Liberator: A Historical-Theological Reading of Jesus of Nazareth* (Maryknoll, NY: Orbis Books, 1993); María Pilar Aquino, *Our Cry for Life: Feminist Theology from Latin*

America (Maryknoll, NY: Orbis Books, 1993); James H. Cone, *A Black Theology of Liberation*, 20th anniversary ed. (Maryknoll, NY: Orbis Books, 1990); J. Deotis Roberts, *Liberation and Reconciliation: A Black Theology*, 2nd ed. (Louisville, KY: Westminster John Knox Press, 2005); Delores S. Williams, *Sisters in the Wilderness: The Challenge of Womanist God-Talk* (Maryknoll, NY: Orbis Books, 1993); Kelly Brown Douglas, *The Black Christ* (Maryknoll, NY: Orbis, 1994); Schüssler Fiorenza, *In Memory of Her.*

126. It is key to distinguish two types of criticisms here. On the one hand are those criticisms that come from conservative politicians, intellectuals, and theologians who argue for the strict separation of political and spiritual affairs. Such critique is unsustainable since politics and religion are constantly mixed. In reality, what this criticism often shows is the non-explicit politics-religion entanglements of the critic. On the other is the immanent critique coming from liberation theologians themselves or their allies, who try to keep the right balance between politics and religion. In the latter group we could count J. Deotis Roberts's, and to a lesser extent, also Cecile Cone's, critique of the identification of black theology with the "Black power" movement. Gustavo Gutiérrez's criticisms of the identification of liberation theology with "Christian socialism" have a similar role in the context of Latin American politics.

127. José Míguez Bonino, *Doing Theology in a Revolutionary Situation*, Confrontation Books (Philadelphia: Fortress Press, 1975), 2ff.

128. For a compelling critique of some of the problems of this identification and the lack of plurality in the understanding of blackness, see Victor Anderson, *Beyond Ontological Blackness: An Essay on African American Religious and Cultural Criticism* (New York: Continuum, 1995).

129. David J. O'Brien and Thomas A. Shannon, eds., *Catholic Social Thought: The Documentary Heritage*, expanded ed. (Maryknoll, NY: Orbis Books, 2010), 198.

130. Even though the concepts of "image of God" and "children of God" are related, they are not identical and have received different emphases in the Christian tradition, often depending on the denominational theological orientations. "Image of God" refers to the presence of the divine essence in every human being, which, in turn, makes every person sacred. "Children of God" stresses that our lives are a gift from God, which, in turn, inserts us in a relationship of reciprocity with the creator and creates certain limits and obligations in our disposal over our life. On this issue, see Joas, *The Sacredness of the Person*, chap. 5.

131. Some decisive work has been done in this regard comparing the work of theologian Gustavo Gutiérrez and economist Amartya Sen in Javier Iguíñiz, *Desarrollo, libertad y liberación en Amartya Sen y Gustavo Gutiérrez* (Lima, Perú: CEP, 2003).

Chapter 3

1. On the "lived religion" approach, see the Introduction to Hugo H. Rabbia et al., eds., *La religión como experiencia cotidiana: Creencias, prácticas y narrativas espirituales en Sudamérica* (Lima: PUCP, EDUCC, and Universidad Católica del Uruguay, 2019). See also Susan C. Sullivan, *Living Faith: Everyday Religion and Mothers in Poverty* (Chicago: University of Chicago Press, 2011).

2. "La corriente" ("current," "stream") is the shortened version for "La corriente de Iglesia" or "la corriente teológica" ("the church current" or "the theological current"). It refers to the theological current that liberation theology represents within the Catholic Church. This is the way most people who are consciously related to liberation theology in Perú refer to themselves; as members or part of la corriente.

3. Active political violence in Perú basically ended with the capture of Abimael Guzmán, the leader of Sendero Luminoso, on September 12, 1992, although some attacks continued after 1992, most notably the 1996 Japanese embassy hostage crisis led by the Túpac Amaru Revolutionary Movement (MRTA).

4. For two excellent monographs on Sendero Luminoso, see Carlos Iván Degregori, *Que difícil es ser Dios: ideología y violencia política en Sendero Luminoso* (Lima: El Zorro de Abajo Ediciones, 1989); Gonzalo Portocarrero, *Profetas del odio: raíces culturales y líderes de Sendero Luminoso* (Lima: PUCP, 2012). For a brief but informative account, see "Shining Path," Encyclopaedia Britannica, accessed November 28, 2021, https://www.britannica.com/topic/Shining-Path.

5. See Comisión de la Verdad y Reconciliación, *Hatun Willakuy: Versión abreviada del Informe Final de la Comisión de la Verdad y Reconciliación, Perú.* (Lima: Comisión de la Verdad y Reconciliación, 2004), 1–24.

6. Since Perú is a majority Catholic country and Catholics were the most active respondents to the time of political violence, I will focus on them. For more details on religious diversity in Perú, see Catalina Romero, "El Perú, país de diversidad religiosa," in *Diversidad religiosa en el Perú: Miradas múltiples,* ed. Catalina Romero (IBC, CEP, and PUCP, 2016).

7. Comisión de la Verdad y Reconciliación, *Hatun Willakuy,* 460. All translations in this chapter are mine, unless otherwise indicated. Here I translate with minor alterations to properly convey the intent of the authors. The CVR Report also notes the important work of Evangelical churches in the defense of human rights, especially at the level of national coordinating boards. But many pastors and farmers in peripheral areas committed to this defense as well (460).

8. Several other organizations deserve attention, but for the sake of brevity I focus only on the CPDH. For other emblematic cases, see the studies presented in Cecilia Tovar, ed., *Ser Iglesia en tiempos de violencia* (Lima: CEP and IBC, 2006). For a general history of the role of the church during the time of political

violence in Perú, see Jeffrey L. Klaiber, *Iglesia, dictaduras y democracia en América Latina* (Lima: PUCP, 1997), chap. 8. For the role of the Jesuits, see Emilio Martínez, *Los jesuitas en tiempos de violencia (1980–1992)* (Lima: Compañía de Jesús en el Perú; UARM, 2018). For the Centro de Estudios y Publicaciones and its newsletter *Signos*, a key source of information during this period, see Pablo Espinoza Espinoza, *Signos: Una voz de la iglesia de los pobres en el Perú, 1980–2008* (Lima: IBC and CEP, 2008).

9. Jeffrey L. Klaiber, *Historia contemporánea de la Iglesia Católica en el Perú* (Lima: Fondo Editorial de la Pontificia Universidad Católica del Perú, 2016), 140.

10. Pilar Coll, "Coordinación de Pastoral de Dignidad Humana," in *Ser Iglesia en tiempos de violencia*, ed. Cecilia Tovar (Lima: CEP and IBC, 2006), 40–43.

11. Coll, "Coordinación de Pastoral," 44, 45.

12. Coll, "Coordinación de Pastoral," 45, 46.

13. Coll, "Coordinación de Pastoral," 46, 47.

14. Coll, "Coordinación de Pastoral," 49.

15. Coll, "Coordinación de Pastoral," 50–51.

16. Coll, "Coordinación de Pastoral," 68–69.

17. Coll, "Coordinación de Pastoral," 52. In this sense, I take issue with the interpretation of liberation theologians' defense of human rights presented in Carlos David Castro-Gómez, "La opción por los pobres: Análisis crítico de sus posibilidades y limitaciones en un mundo globalizado," in *¿El reino de Dios es de este mundo? El papel ambiguo de las religiones en la lucha contra la pobreza*, ed. Genaro Zalpa and Hans Egil Offerdal (Bogotá: Siglo del Hombre, CLACSO, and CROP, 2008). In this otherwise fine study, Castro-Gómez suggests that the defense of human rights became the way through which the conservative-traditional wing of the Catholic Church strategically tamed the more radical discourse of liberation theology, thus reducing the influence of this theology incorporating its positive aspects into official Vatican teaching. My account in this chapter tells a different, less Machiavellian story: liberation theologians responded to the needs of their people in a new social situation. Gaining intra-ecclesial power or becoming a hegemonic theological school were never the driving forces of their work.

18. Coll, "Coordinación de Pastoral," 72.

19. Coll, "Coordinación de Pastoral," 72–73.

20. For the early response of the Vatican to liberation theology, see "Ten Observations on the Theology of Gustavo Gutiérrez" (1983), "Instruction on Certain Aspects of the 'Theology of Liberation'" (1984), and "Instruction on Christian Freedom and Liberation" (1986), all included in Alfred T. Hennelly, ed., *Liberation Theology: A Documentary History* (Maryknoll, NY: Orbis Books, 1990). For Gutiérrez's response to these documents, see *The Truth Shall Make You Free: Confrontations* (Maryknoll, NY: Orbis Books, 1990), especially the essay

"Theology and Social Sciences." For an excellent study of then-cardinal Ratzinger's disagreements with Gutiérrez, see James Corkery, "Joseph Ratzinger on Liberation Theology: What Did He Say? Why Did He Say It? What Can Be Said About It?," in *Movement or Moment? Assessing Liberation Theology Forty Years After Medellín*, ed. Patrick Claffey and Joe Egan, vol. 1, Studies in Theology, Society, and Culture (Oxford, UK: Peter Lang, 2009).

21. Alistair Kee, *Marx and the Failure of Liberation Theology* (London: SCM Press, 1990), confirms this assessment through a meticulous exegetical reading of the work of some of the key liberation theologians, including Gutiérrez. Kee does this, however, disapprovingly, which makes my point even stronger. For him, liberation theologians were too theological and Christian. Hence, they were not able to embrace the radical politics of Marx.

22. See Congregation for the Doctrine of the Faith, "Ten Observations," 350.

23. After the times of political violence, Human Dignity stopped working as such and instead became a permanent workshop at the Instituto Bartolomé de las Casas in Lima in 1993. Since then it has operated under the institute's umbrella as the Taller de Iglesia y Derechos Humanos (Church and Human Rights Workshop). The group still meets today.

24. For an excellent exception, see Sarah Brooks, "Catholic Activism in the 1990s: New Strategies for the Neoliberal Age," in *Latin American Religion in Motion*, ed. Christian Smith and Joshua Prokopy (New York: Routledge, 1999). Brooks's study and mine share the same basic argument regarding the continuity of the convictions of liberation theology despite its change of strategy in new social contexts. The advantage of my work, in addition to its theological contributions, is that it covers twenty more years of historical developments.

25. In terms of systematic approaches to this topic, the works of Ivan Petrella, *The Future of Liberation Theology: An Argument and Manifesto* (Aldershot, UK: Ashgate, 2004) and *Beyond Liberation Theology: A Polemic* (London: SCM Press, 2008), are perhaps the most notable exceptions. In fact, Petrella addresses some of the very same issues I am concerned with in these pages. However, I substantially disagree with his interpretation of liberation theology. I will engage his work in footnotes to show the contrasts between his interpretation and mine. Enrique D. Dussel, *Ethics of Liberation: In the Age of Globalization and Exclusion*, ed. Alejandro A. Vallega (Durham, NC: Duke University Press, 2013) is another exception, but it only addresses my questions indirectly. First, Dussel's *Ethics* was originally published in 1998, which means that it leaves over two decades of argument and events unexamined. Second, Dussel's *Ethics* is a philosophical treatise, not a theological piece. But even in its philosophical depth it leaves aside key issues like the role of tradition that I consider essential for my approach to liberation theology. Two compilations of essays are worth consulting as well: Patrick Claffey and Joe Egan, eds., *Movement or Moment? Assessing Liberation Theology Forty Years after*

Medellín, vol. 1, Studies in Theology, Society, and Culture (Oxford, UK: Peter Lang, 2009), and Christopher Rowland, ed., *The Cambridge Companion to Liberation Theology*, 2nd ed. (Cambridge, UK: Cambridge University Press, 2008).

26. On this issue, see Rolando Ames, "La realidad nacional desde el límite: Riesgos y horizontes," and Sinesio López, "Una modernización frustrada (1930–1991)," in *Desde el límite: Perú, reflexiones en el umbral de una nueva época* (Lima: Instituto Democracia y Socialismo, 1992); and Sinesio López, "La reinvención de la historia desde abajo: autoría y lectoría," in *Entre la tormenta y la brisa : homenaje a Gustavo Gutiérrez*, ed. Catalina Romero and Luis Peirano (Lima: PUCP, 2010).

27. Tom Powers, *The Call of God: Women Doing Theology in Peru* (Albany: State University of New York Press, 2003).

28. Powers, *The Call of God*, 35–36. For more on their projects and workshops, see 106–113.

29. Powers, *The Call of God*, 5–6.

30. Powers, *The Call of God*, 88.

31. Gustavo Gutiérrez, *On Job: God-Talk and the Suffering of the Innocent* (Maryknoll, NY: Orbis Books, 1987), xiv.

32. Powers, *The Call of God*, 89–101.

33. Powers, *The Call of God*, 94.

34. Powers, *The Call of God*, 95. "Comedor" is a popular dining hall that was organized by poor women, mostly in urban areas, as a survival strategy to provide meals in their neighborhoods. Comedores populares still exist today, but were especially important in the decades of greatest poverty in Perú. Carmen Lora, one of my interviewees, had a prominent role working with the poor women of these comedores.

35. On Landázuri and Vargas Alzamora, see Klaiber, *Historia contemporánea*, 98–99, 221–223, respectively.

36. For more context on Cipriani's tenure, see Luis Pásara and Carlos Indacochea, *Cipriani como actor político*, (Lima: IEP, 2014).

37. All citations and references come from Gustavo Gutiérrez, interview by Raúl E. Zegarra, December 20, 2019. This and all the interviews were conducted in Spanish. The translations are mine.

38. The "Curso de teología," initially sponsored by the Pontifical Catholic University of Perú under the name "Jornadas de reflexión teológica," began in 1971 and has continued to this day with only occasional interruptions. Klaiber notes that up until 1995 over eighteen thousand people attended the course (*Historia contemporánea*, 174–175). The curso was and still is one of the most important ways to share some of the key theological insights of liberation theology among pastoral agents and laypeople in Perú and Latin America. For a careful study of the cursos, see Juan Miguel Espinoza Portocarrero, "Las 'Jornadas de

Reflexión Teológica' y el desarrollo de un proyecto eclesial posconciliar asociado a la teología de la liberación en el Perú: Discurso teológico, redes sociales y cultura eclesial (1969–2000)" (Master's thesis, Lima, Perú, Pontificia Universidad Católica del Perú, 2015).

39. On the institute, its history, and its mission, see Eddy José Muskus, *The Origins and Early Development of Liberation Theology in Latin America: With Particular Reference to Gustavo Gutiérrez* (Carlisle, UK: Paternoster Press, 2002), appendixes A and B.

40. For an excellent study on the contributions of *Signos* to the option for the poor in Perú, see Espinoza Espinoza, *Signos*.

41. For a transcript of his dissertation defense, see Gutiérrez, *The Truth Shall Make You Free*, chap. 1.

42. See Petrella, *Beyond Liberation Theology*, 113–117.

43. See Kee, *Marx and the Failure of Liberation Theology*. The difference is that Kee believes that such concern and attentiveness are a mistake. True transformation requires a full embrace of Marx's ideological critique and giving up on theological commitments. That said, Kee defends a nonreductionist interpretation of "historical materialism" (278–283) that is open to religious experience, rendering his view more compatible with liberation theology than it may seem at first.

44. Most citations and references in the three following subsections come from my interviews, unless otherwise indicated. Therefore, for the sake of avoiding excessive footnotes, I will cite them fully only the first time. Then I will indicate the name of the respondent and quote them without adding a footnote.

45. Gallego is a diocesan priest, a professor of theology at the Pontifical Catholic University of Perú (PUCP), a key figure of the pastoral work done in the Sur Andino, and one of Gutiérrez's closest collaborators since the mid-1970s. All citations and references come from Andrés Gallego, interview by Raúl E. Zegarra, January 7, 2020. The Sur Andino (the South of the Andes, covering the prelatures of Juli and Ayaviri, Puno, and Sicuani, Cusco) was one of the areas of greater development and creativity for the option for the poor for several years due to the presence of great missionary activity (Fr. Gallego is himself a Spanish missioner) and support of the bishops in the area. For more on the experience of the Sur Andino, see Lupe Jara, "El Sur Andino: Una iglesia que responde a los signos de los tiempos," in *Ser Iglesia en tiempos de violencia*, ed. Cecilia Tovar (Lima: CEP and IBC, 2006).

46. Romero is a professor of sociology at the PUCP, former dean of the Social Sciences division, a former member of UNEC, a current member of the MPC, and a former president of the IBC. All citations and references come from Catalina Romero, interview by Raúl E. Zegarra, January 8, 2020.

47. In 1968, General Juan Velasco Alvarado overthrew the democratically elected government of President Fernando Belaúnde Terry. However, Velasco's

was an atypical military coup. His "revolutionary government of the armed forces" developed key social reforms not unlike those of left-wing revolutionary movements, including massive land reform. For this reason, the relationship with the progressive, left-wing groups was somewhat friendly. Yet, as Iguíñiz notes, people in la corriente were suspicious of this top-down revolution and very critical of its authoritarianism. For more on the Velasco regime, see Carlos Aguirre and Paulo Drinot, eds., *The Peculiar Revolution: Rethinking the Peruvian Experiment Under Military Rule* (Austin: University of Texas Press, 2017).

48. Iguíñiz is a professor of economics at the PUCP, a former member of UNEC, and a current member of the MPC. He has been active in politics for many decades, and most recently was the chair of the Acuerdo Nacional (National Agreement), a multi-party, multi-institution board in which most Peruvian political parties, institutions of civil society, and the three branches of government gather to build consensus over policy. All citations and references come from Javier Iguíñiz, interview by Raúl E. Zegarra, January 9, 2020.

49. Lora is a social psychologist, a former member of UNEC, and a current member of the MPC. She is the current director of the CEP, a longtime editor of Gutiérrez's publications in Spanish, and a religious journalist who attended the Episcopal Conferences of Puebla (1979), Santo Domingo (1992), and Aparecida (2007). All citations and references come from Carmen Lora, interview by Raúl E. Zegarra, January 13, 2020.

50. Ames is a lawyer and political scientist, a professor of political science at the PUCP, a member of the MPC, a former senator of Lima, and a former commissioner of the CVR. All citations and references come from Rolando Ames, interview by Raúl E. Zegarra, February 16, 2020.

51. Gutiérrez, interview.

52. All these observations on the greater horizon of liberation theology should also operate as a rebuke of Petrella's interpretation. People committed to the option for the poor understood the formation of "historical projects" within the complex fabric of their own faith in God's project. In this sense, Petrella might invite liberation theologians to go "beyond theology" in order to accomplish its promises (*Beyond Liberation Theology*, 148). But in doing so, he shows his selective interpretation of liberation theology, dismissing it as a theological, faith-based project.

53. Gustavo Gutiérrez, "Theology: An Ecclesial Function," in *The Density of the Present: Selected Writings* (Maryknoll, NY: Orbis Books, 1999).

54. She mentions the Instituto de Pastoral Andina (Institute for Andean Pastoral Work) and the work of the Maryknoll Order, both in the Sur Andino, as two examples of major spaces for the embodiment and development of the option for the poor. These and other initiatives were either progressively deactivated or undermined by the presence of more conservative bishops in the country.

55. On this, see Catalina Romero, "Religión y política en el Perú, 2000–2010," in *Cruces, intersecciones, conflictos: Relaciones político religiosas en Lationamérica*, ed. Aldo Rubén Ameigeiras (Buenos Aires: CLACSO, 2012), 125.

56. On the question of sacralization, with direct focus on human rights, see Hans Joas, *The Sacredness of the Person: A New Genealogy of Human Rights* (Washington, DC: Georgetown University Press, 2013).

57. Joas, *The Sacredness of the Person*, 91.

58. Of course, many members of la corriente were part of political parties which, *as political parties*, did not subscribe to religious interpretations of liberation. However, as noted before, this was not, in principle, a problem. Many atheist members of those parties even saw with admiration the commitment of the Christians in the Left. For helpful analytical distinctions about the secular and religious Left, and the role of religious people in the secular Left, see Steven H. Shiffrin, *The Religious Left and Church-State Relations* (Princeton, NJ: Princeton University Press, 2009), 100–109.

59. Lora points to the work of the Jesuit Francisco Chamberlain as one of the most important figures attempting to find theological answers to this moment. See, for instance, his "¿Qué queda por hacer en la perspectiva de la teología de la liberación?," in *Francisco Chamberlain, testigo del evangelio*, ed. Carmen de los Ríos and Santiago Paz (Lima: CEP, IBC, and Centro Loyola Ayacucho, 2019).

60. On Fe y Alegría, see Klaiber, *Historia contemporánea*, 230–232. The model of these schools is based on a sui generis state-church collaboration. The Jesuits build the schools and select the staff and the teachers, but the state pays them. The schools are Catholic and shaped by the ideals of the preferential option for the poor, but they are also ecumenical and focused on serving their communities.

61. See Romero, "El Perú, país de diversidad religiosa."

62. For a global history of Evangelical Christianity and Pentecostalism, see David Martin, *Tongues of Fire: The Explosion of Protestantism in Latin America* (Oxford, UK: Blackwell, 1993) and David Martin, *Pentecostalism: The World Their Parish* (Oxford, UK: Blackwell, 2002). For their role in the Peruvian context, see Véronique Lecaros, *La conversión al evangelismo*, trans. Gustavo Martínez Sánquiz (Lima: PUCP, 2016). See also the essays of Rolando Pérez Vela, José Sánchez Paredes, and Uta Ihrke-Buchroth in Catalina Romero, ed., *Diversidad religiosa en el Perú: Miradas múltiples* (Lima: IBC, CEP, and PUCP, 2016).

63. See José Casanova, "Parallel Reformations in Latin America: A Critical Review of David Martin's Interpretation of the Pentecostal Revolution," in *David Martin and the Sociology of Religion*, ed. Hans Joas (New York: Routledge, 2018).

64. On the influence of Methodism on Evangelical Christianity, see Martin, *Tongues of Fire*.

65. Since my focus here is on liberation theology and not on Pentecostalism, I cannot go beyond some rather succinct observations on the latter. For more

substantial remarks on the relationship between Pentecostalism and liberation theology, see Raúl E. Zegarra, "The Preferential Option of the Poor: Liberation Theology, Pentecostalism, and the New Forms of Sacralization," *European Journal of Sociology/Archives Européennes de Sociologie*, forthcoming 2023. For the question of Pentecostalism and its transnational nature, in addition to the texts of David Martin already, see the insightful account provided by José Casanova, "Public Religions Revisited," in *Religion: Beyond a Concept*, ed. Hent de Vries (New York: Fordham University Press, 2008), 115–119.

66. See Philip Wingeier-Rayo, *Where Are the Poor? A Comparison of the Ecclesial Base Communities and Pentecostalism, a Case Study in Cuernavaca, Mexico* (Eugene, OR: Pickwick, 2011), 76; Ihrke-Buchroth, "Movilidad religiosa y aspiración social en iglesias neopentecostales de Lima"; Sánchez Paredes, "Cambios y modernización en el pentecostalismo peruano."

67. See Pérez Vela, "Las apropiaciones religiosas de lo público," 206.

68. Such is the argument of Carlos Castillo, "Ser cristiano entre dos milenios: Hacia una teología de la regeneración," *Debates en Sociología* 25–26 (2001).

69. See Chamberlain, "¿Qué queda por hacer?"

70. Indeed, the migration of Pentecostalism from the more democratic culture of the United States to the more vertical culture of Latin America has created some tensions, among them the monopolistic tendencies noted earlier. On this, with emphasis on the Chilean and Guatemalan cases and the relationship between dictators and Pentecostals, see Martin, *Tongues of Fire*, 240ff., 253–255. Martin also points out (254) that despite the generally favorable situation of Pentecostals during General Ríos Montt's tenure, thirty members of a Pentecostal church in El Quiché were killed, suspected of radicalism. On Pinochet's and Ríos Montt's complex relationship with Pentecostals, see also Hartch, *The Rebirth of Latin American Christianity*, 82–87, 60–61. On the Peruvian case and the support of Evangelical leaders for Keiko Fujimori despite their prosecution against her for major corruption charges, see Pérez Vela, "Las apropiaciones religiosas de lo público." Some of these antidemocratic tendencies are becoming increasingly present among white Evangelicals in the United States. But the rationale is somewhat similar to that of Latin American Evangelicals: the perception of becoming a minority and losing social privileges is increasingly persuading Evangelicals of the need of alliances with authoritarian figures who promise to restate former (white) privileges. On this, see Philip S. Gorski and Samuel L. Perry, *The Flag and the Cross: White Christian Nationalism and the Threat to American Democracy* (Oxford, UK: Oxford University Press, 2022).

71. This notion of an integral mission (*misión integral*) that combines faith and active struggle for social justice has existed in the Evangelical, especially Latin American, milieu for several decades. In fact, this is the Evangelical theological development that parallels that of liberation theology in the Catholic

Church. However, because of the different institutional strengths of each—with the Catholic Church having a stronger and more unified transnational network—liberation theology became more globally widespread. Plus, despite the progressive globalization of misión integral, this remained a project of *some* of the Evangelical denominations. The Pentecostal churches, for instance, were not very much influenced by this movement, and their greater focus on structural issues of social justice is rather recent. On misión integral, see Robert Chao Romero, *Brown Church: Five Centuries of Latina/o Social Justice, Theology, and Identity* (Downers Grove, IL: InterVarsity Press, 2020), chap. 6.

72. Kevin Lewis O'Neill, *City of God: Christian Citizenship in Postwar Guatemala* (Berkeley: University of California Press, 2010), 204.

73. See O'Neill, *City of God*, 205.

74. For the Peruvian context, see Pérez Vela, "Las apropiaciones religiosas de lo público," where he notes that many Evangelicals and Pentecostals have been active in the defense of human rights and other forms of political activism from civil society. On Pentecostalsism and its liberationist activism, see Carmelo Alvarez, ed., *Pentecostalismo y liberación: una experiencia latinoamericana* (San José, Costa Rica: Editorial Departamento Ecuménico de Investigaciones, 1992).

75. On this, see Gustavo Gutiérrez, "La opción preferencial por el pobre en Aparecida," in *De Medellín a Aparecida: Artículos reunidos* (Lima: IBC, PUCP, and CEP, 2018).

76. On the affinities of Pope Francis's teachings and liberation theology, see Raúl E. Zegarra, *La subversión de la esperanza: diálogo contemporáneo entre teología de la liberación, filosofía y opción por los pobres* (Lima: PUCP, IBC, and CEP, 2015), chap. 8. For a more detailed account of Francis's pastoral concerns and theological background, see Rafael Luciani, *El Papa Francisco y la teología del pueblo* (Madrid: PPC, 2016).

77. My focus in this book has been the Latin American, mostly Peruvian, *Catholic* milieu. Hence, my comments here apply more accurately to that context. However, since parallel processes of radicalization took place in the Protestant milieu through the efforts of Black liberation theology, and in both milieus through feminist theology, it is not implausible to extend some of my conclusions beyond Latin American Catholic theology. For the African American context, see Gayraud S. Wilmore, *Black Religion and Black Radicalism: An Interpretation of the Religious History of African Americans*, 3rd ed. (Maryknoll, NY: Orbis Books, 1998). For the intersections of these three processes of radicalization, see Lilian Calles Barger, *The World Come of Age: An Intellectual History of Liberation Theology* (New York: Oxford University Press, 2018).

78. Hans Joas, *Faith as an Option: Possible Futures for Christianity* (Stanford, CA: Stanford University Press, 2014), 118.

79. Joas, *Faith as an Option*, 119.

80. Joas, *Faith as an Option*, 120.

81. See Rabbia et al., *La religión como experiencia cotidiana*.

82. For Troeltsch's presentation of some of these issues, other than the *Logos* article referred to by Joas, see *The Social Teaching of the Christian Churches*, trans. Olive Wyon, vol. 2 (New York: Harper Torchbooks, 1960), 993–1013.

83. Joas, *Faith as an Option*, 127–28.

84. See Robert N. Bellah, Richard Madsen, William M. Sullivan, Ann Swidler, and Steven M. Tipton, *Habits of the Heart: Individualism and Commitment in American Life: With a New Preface* (Berkeley: University of California Press, 2008).

85. Joas, *Faith as an Option*, 129.

86. Ignacio Ellacuría, "Fe y justicia," in *Escritos teológicos*, vol. 3 (San Salvador, El Salvador: UCA Editores, 2002), 315.

87. Ellacuría, "Fe y justicia," 316, my translation.

88. On this, see Hans Joas, *The Genesis of Values* (Chicago: University of Chicago Press, 2000), 172–173.

89. The relationship between love and justice is one of the most discussed topics in the Christian tradition. It is not my intention here to address those discussions but to restrict the scope of my inquiry to liberation theology's articulation of these values. For two important studies of the love-justice relationship that also address some of the historical figures and debates, see Nicholas Wolterstorff, *Justice: Rights and Wrongs* (Princeton, NJ: Princeton University Press, 2008), and *Justice in Love* (Grand Rapids, MI: Eerdmans, 2011). My main difference with Wolterstorff is that I find his argument against the secular foundation of human rights implausible, especially when the solution proposed is a theistic foundation. One of the goals of this dissertation is to show than neither foundation is solid and that secular and theological approaches need each other in order to advance the cause of human rights and democracy.

90. Joas, *Faith as an Option*, 132–133.

91. Charles Taylor, *A Secular Age* (Cambridge, MA: Belknap Press of Harvard University Press, 2007), 282.

92. In fact, this is already happening both in the European and Latin American context. On the Peruvian case, see Catalina Romero, "Católicos en Lima: Viviendo encuentros interreligiosos," in *La religión como experiencia cotidiana: Creencias, prácticas y narrativas espirituales en Sudamérica*, ed. Hugo H. Rabbia et al. (Lima: PUCP, EDUCC, and Universidad Católica del Uruguay, 2019). But this volume samples a significant number of cases that point in a similar direction in the rest of Latin America.

93. Joas, *Faith as an Option*, 132.

94. For the globalization of these forms of solidarity, see Dussel, *Ethics of Liberation*. See also Eduardo Mendieta, *Global Fragments: Globalizations,*

Latinamericanisms, and Critical Theory (Albany: State University of New York Press, 2007).

95. Joas, *Faith as an Option*, 133.

Chapter 4

1. José Casanova, *Public Religions in the Modern World* (Chicago: University of Chicago Press, 1994), 6.

2. Casanova, *Public Religions in the Modern World*, 234.

3. Casanova has revised his argument about public religions, especially after some of the criticisms provided by Talal Asad, *Formations of the Secular: Christianity, Islam, Modernity* (Stanford, CA: Stanford University Press, 2003). However, there has been no major revision in terms of what matters for my argument in this chapter. The main areas of reformulation are as follows. First is the stress on the Western trajectory of secularization. In his revision of the argument, Casanova takes a more global approach, stressing the concept of "multiple modernities" and hence the diverse patterns of the process of secularization. Second, he also acknowledges that the differentiation of the religious sphere from the political sphere is quite different in non-Christian societies. In turn, this affects what public religions look like in places where Islam, for instance, is the dominant religion. Lastly, and perhaps the only issue relevant for the argument in this chapter, Casanova recognizes that restricting the realm of action of public religions to civil society was probably too normative and unrealistic. Clearly, even in Western societies, public religions have actively gone beyond civil society to gain political power through the executive, legislative, and judicial branches of government. For these revisions, see José Casanova, "Public Religions Revisited," in *Religion: Beyond a Concept*, ed. Hent de Vries (New York: Fordham University Press, 2008). On the Peruvian case and the limits of the civil society emphasis, see Rolando Pérez Vela, "Las apropiaciones religiosas de lo público: El caso de los evangélicos en el Perú," in *Diversidad religiosa en el Perú: Miradas múltiples*, ed. Catalina Romero (Lima: IBC, CEP, and PUCP, 2016).

4. Casanova, *Public Religions in the Modern World*, 233.

5. Such an inclusive account of justice is, of course, not a new project. Important and relatively recent projects dealing with this issue are Jeffrey Stout, *Democracy and Tradition* (Princeton, NJ: Princeton University Press, 2004); David Hollenbach, *The Common Good and Christian Ethics* (New York: Cambridge University Press, 2002); Cathleen Kaveny, *Prophecy Without Contempt: Religious Discourse in the Public Square* (Cambridge, MA: Harvard University Press, 2016); and Nichole M. Flores, *The Aesthetics of Solidarity: Our Lady of Guadalupe and American Democracy* (Washington, DC: Georgetown University Press, 2021), among others. I share the general thrust of these projects, and feel especially

close to the goals of Flores's work because of her focus on the Latinx community. However, I have some important disagreements regarding how to read the work of John Rawls—a task that these four books also pursue—that will progressively show the distinctiveness of my approach.

6. Some form of this argument is defended by scholars as diverse as Nicholas Wolterstorff, Jeffrey Stout, Cathleen Kaveny, and Nichole Flores, among others. I will engage the work of some of these authors in footnotes but will mainly focus on Rawls's own account of public reason. Since, in my view, Stout's position is the most carefully developed—among the authors just cited—analysis and critique of Rawls's position on public reason, I will engage his critique in the body of the text.

7. The notion of "comprehensive doctrine" is anticipated in *Theory* in speaking of "complete conceptions" (Rawls, *A Theory of Justice* [Cambridge, MA: Harvard University Press, 1971], §2, 9), but it only becomes a key element of Rawls's project in *Political Liberalism*, expanded ed. (New York: Columbia University Press, 2005). He writes that a conception is comprehensive "when it includes conceptions of what is of value in human life, and ideals of personal character, as well as ideas of friendship and of familial and associational relationships, and much else that is to inform our conduct, and in the limit to our life as a whole. A conception is fully comprehensive if it covers all recognized values and virtues within one rather precisely articulated system" (Rawls, *Political Liberalism*, 13). In contrast, *justice as fairness* is only a *political* conception that applies to the basic structure of society (11ff.). Now, the overlapping consensus requires "*reasonable* comprehensive doctrines," that is, doctrines which respect and tolerate other comprehensive doctrines according to the principles of justice (58–66).

8. Raúl E. Zegarra, "The Revolution of Tradition: Liberation Theology's Contribution to the Formulation of a Comprehensive Theory of Social Justice" (PhD dissertation, University of Chicago, 2021).

9. Rawls, *A Theory of Justice*, §3, 12.

10. Rawls, *A Theory of Justice*, §3, 12, my emphasis; see also §20, 120ff. He stresses the same thing in Rawls, *Political Liberalism*, 24: the original position is only a "device of representation."

11. Indeed, Rawls explicitly acknowledges that his ideal of a well-ordered society does not resemble what he calls a "private society." In a private society, Rawls argues, (a) persons or associations have their own private ends, which may be independent of or competing against each other, but not complementary; and (b) institutions are not goods in themselves but are considered a burden. From this follows that "each person assesses social arrangements solely as means to his private ends." (*A Theory of Justice*, §79, 521). But for Rawls, human beings are not mere means to their private ends: "human beings have in fact shared final ends and they value their common institutions and activities as good in themselves.

We need one another as partners in ways of life that are engaged in for their own sake, and the successes and enjoyments of others are necessary for and complimentary to our own good." (§79, 522). Part III of *A Theory of Justice* is a compelling development of this community-oriented perspective by advancing the ideal of social union as essential for *justice as fairness*.

12. Rawls, *A Theory of Justice*, §3, 12.

13. See Rawls, *A Theory of Justice*, §3, 13. Note that this mutual lack of interest is the correlative to the free desire to enter the contract for mutual advantage (14). That is, not having a prior interest in the other person is for Rawls the most uncontroversial starting point. Assuming that we always have a tendency to solidarity or benevolence, for instance (see §22, 129), appears to him as extremely high moral expectation and, hence, as an inadequate starting point to conceive terms of fair cooperation. However, his minimalistic stipulations lead to the acknowledgment that we do depend on one another, even if it is only to further our personal interests. *But* when we realize that and enter the system of social cooperation, the notion of reciprocity or mutual responsibility arises (§17, 102ff.). Plus, we should note that even at the level of mutual disinterest of the original position stipulations, the representative parties care at least for their close ones. So we are not describing here solipsistic, only self-centered individuals.

14. Rawls, *A Theory of Justice*, §22, 126; also §16, 95ff., where Rawls discusses the "circumstances of justice" in terms of the "relevant social positions" that the theory of justice must consider. Typically, people know what Rawls calls the "general facts of human society" (§24, 137), a key stipulation given how much these could affect the choice of the principles of justice.

15. Rawls, *A Theory of Justice*, §24, 136.

16. Rawls later offers a richer conception of reasonableness that includes the following features: (a) people have the two moral powers of the capacity for a sense of justice and for a conception of the good; (b) intellectual powers of judgment, thought, and inference; (c) a conception of the good interpreted in light of a reasonable comprehensive view; and (d) the basic capacities and abilities to be cooperating members of society. To this, Rawls adds (e) readiness to propose fair terms of cooperation; (f) recognition of the burdens of judgment; (g) not only being cooperating members of society, but wanting to be so; and (h) a reasonable moral psychology (Rawls, *Political Liberalism*, 81ff.).

17. Rawls, *A Theory of Justice*, §4, 21.

18. Hence, the original position as a device of representation can have educational value as well. Appealing to it may help people who have doubts about how just our current arrangements are; considering the principles of justice as a threshold may allow the affirmation or the criticism of current arrangements (Rawls, *A Theory of Justice*, §78, 514–515).

19. Rawls, *A Theory of Justice*, §24, 138.

20. I have skipped several important considerations that Rawls adds prior to the formulation of the two principles of justice, as I will skip several reformulations of the principles themselves. However, my brief presentations should suffice both for the purposes of my argument and to do justice to Rawls's approach. For a more detailed account, see Zegarra, "The Revolution of Tradition," chaps. 1 and 2.

21. Given the proposed stipulations, Rawls believes that people would choose these principles even if our enemies would assign us our place in society, for the principles would protect the most basic rights of all. In his view, that such extreme possibility does not undermine the type of principles to be chosen is proof of their strength (Rawls, *A Theory of Justice*, §26, 152–53).

22. Rawls, *A Theory of Justice*, §3, 14–15.

23. Rawls, *A Theory of Justice*, §26, 151; §11, 62.

24. Such is the position of Michael J. Sandel, *Liberalism and the Limits of Justice*, 2nd ed. (Cambridge, UK: Cambridge University Press, 1998).

25. I draw here from William Schweiker, "On Religious Ethics," in *The Blackwell Companion to Religious Ethics*, ed. William Schweiker (Malden, MA: Blackwell, 2005), 3, where the author discusses similar ideas in regards to the critical, constructive, and comparative tasks of religious ethics.

26. Nichole M. Flores, *The Aesthetics of Solidarity*, 10 and chap. 2, has recently highlighted the importance of the role of imagination in Rawls's conception of justice and public reason. However, Flores interprets Rawls as implicitly defending an exclusionary conception of the imagination and public reason. She writes: "Specifically, the Rawlsian aesthetic has shaped the aesthetics of public life to exclude the histories, experiences, and concerns of Black and Brown people who have been subjected to profound communal and personal injury by the same basic structures—including law enforcement agencies such as local police departments and federal immigrations authorities—that Rawls's philosophies seek to construct and protect" (10). As I have shown so far, I disagree with this reading and provide textual evidence in the following pages to stress why Flores's position regarding Rawls's account of public reason and justice is untenable. In addition, this citation suggests some confusion about the meaning of the "basic structure" in Rawls's thought, which does not apply to the discretionary choices of police officers and immigration authorities but to constitutional essentials. Otherwise, any conception of justice will be liable for people's unwillingness to act justly. Hollenbach, *The Common Good and Christian Ethics*, clearly sees the contribution of Rawls's focus on the basic structure, and thus supports an account of social justice very similar to Rawls *in this regard*, but in dialogue with the Catholic tradition.

27. For a systematic study of Rawls's approach to religion, see Daniel A. Dombrowski, *Rawls and Religion: The Case for Political Liberalism* (Albany: State

University of New York Press, 2001). For a more recent account, in the form of constructive essays engaging Rawls's take on religion or developing some of his key ideas, see Tom Bailey and Valentina Gentile, eds., *Rawls and Religion* (New York: Columbia University Press, 2015).

28. Rawls, *A Theory of Justice*, §33, 206, 207. Note that the deliberating parties in the original position *do* have religious, moral beliefs and so forth, which is obviously implied in the stipulation according to which all parties have a conception of the good.

29. Rawls, *A Theory of Justice*, §33, 208. More on this can be found in §35, "Toleration of the Intolerant." Similarly, Rawls claims that we are not literally obliged to respect all forms of conscientious disagreement. Therefore, limiting actions that would follow conscience but could harm others is a form of showing respect to the very conscientious objector (§78, 519).

30. Rawls, *A Theory of Justice*, §34, 212.

31. Rawls, *A Theory of Justice*, §34, 213, 215.

32. For a critical discussion of Lincoln's speech, see Stout, *Democracy and Tradition*, 69–77.

33. See Rawls, *A Theory of Justice*, §1, 5.

34. "Publicity" is a central feature of his conception of justice. Yet other formal requirements must be present too. Thus, the principles of justice should be (1) general (no proper names or definite descriptions), (2) universal in application, (3) capable of ordering conflicting claims, and (4) the final court of appeal in practical reasoning (see Rawls, *A Theory of Justice*, §23, 130–135). Rawls provides his own summary: "A conception of right is a set of principles, general in form and universal in application, that is to be publicly recognized as a final court of appeal for ordering conflicting claims of moral persons" (135). But, of course, these are general criteria that apply to *justice as fairness* as well as to other approaches to social cooperation. They do, however, get rid of egoism as a legitimate social arrangement (135–136).

35. Rawls, *Political Liberalism*, 213.

36. The notion of "public reason" is developed at greater length in *Political Liberalism*, Lecture VI. However, its key elements are already present in *A Theory of Justice* through the discussion of the publicity of *justice as fairness*. Also, public reason as "the reason of the public" is not subject to mere majority rule (*Political Liberalism*, 234). Rawls's premise is that the Constitution and the Bill of Rights represent a "higher law" that "fixes once and for all certain constitutional essentials" that are then, in principle, not subject to change (232). Hence "ordinary laws" can only be put forward within certain parameters that warrant that all citizens can express themselves and act as free and independent.

37. See Rawls, *Political Liberalism*, 249ff. We have seen a similar rationale in Rawls, *A Theory of Justice*, §26, 152; §39, 250, regarding possible restrictions

on people's freedom: they are only allowed *if* they are needed to achieve greater freedom.

38. Rawls, *Political Liberalism*, 254.

39. Rawls, *Political Liberalism*, xlix.

40. This key concept of Rawls's theory is defined as follows: "In such a consensus, the reasonable [comprehensive] doctrines endorse the political conception, each from its own point of view. Social unity is based on a consensus on the political conception; and stability is possible when the doctrines making up the consensus are affirmed by society's politically active citizens and the requirements of justice are not too much in conflict with citizens' essential interest as formed and encouraged by their social arrangements" (Rawls, *Political Liberalism*, 134).

41. Rawls, *Political Liberalism*, xlix–l.

42. John Rawls, "The Idea of Public Reason Revisited," in *Political Liberalism*, expanded ed. (New York: Columbia University Press, 2005), 463.

43. For a more general critique of the room for religious expression that Rawls allows in the public sphere, see Nicholas Wolterstorff, "Why We Should Reject What Liberalism Tells Us About Speaking and Acting in Public for Religious Reasons," in *Religion and Contemporary Liberalism*, ed. Paul Weithman (Notre Dame, IN: University of Notre Dame Press, 1997). In this piece, however, Wolterstorff inaccurately attributes to Rawls's principles of justice the status of mere consensus populi. Even though this reading is possible if one isolates some of the statements presented in *Political Liberalism*, a more comprehensive reading of Rawls's corpus would recognize this position as not tenable.

44. Stout, *Democracy and Tradition*, 70. For similar critiques of Rawls and public reason—for which my arguments in this section are also a response—see Steven H. Shiffrin, *The Religious Left and Church-State Relations* (Princeton, NJ: Princeton University Press, 2009), chap. 8; and Cathleen Kaveny, *Prophecy Without Contempt*, chap. 2.

45. For more on our capacity to express our fundamental commitments through nonpartisan or non-tradition-specific means, see Hans Joas, *The Sacredness of the Person: A New Genealogy of Human Rights* (Washington, DC: Georgetown University Press, 2013), chap. 6.

46. Wolterstorff, "Why We Should Reject What Liberalism Tells Us," 177.

47. On "role taking" and its essential value in human sociability, see Hans Joas, *The Creativity of Action* (Cambridge, UK: Polity Press, 1996), 187ff. See also Martha C. Nussbaum, *Political Emotions: Why Love Matters for Justice* (Cambridge, MA: Harvard University Press, 2013), 250–255; and *The Monarchy of Fear: A Philosopher Looks at Our Political Crisis* (New York: Simon and Schuster, 2018), 60–62, for the importance of "role taking" in democracy.

48. Rawls, "The Idea of Public Reason Revisited," 464.

49. Rawls, "The Idea of Public Reason Revisited," 465.

50. Rawls, "The Idea of Public Reason Revisited," 465, fn. 55.

51. For a similar view, under the label of "immanent criticism," see Stout, *Democracy and Tradition*, 72–73.

52. See Rawls, "The Idea of Public Reason Revisited," 466, fn. 57.

53. Among the critics of Rawls mentioned before (Wolterstorff, Stout, Hollenbach, Kaveny, and Flores), Hollenbach is certainly the most perceptive reader of Rawls's account of the role of religious discourse in public reason. Indeed, despite other criticisms about Rawls's larger project, Hollenbach writes: "Rawls's recent [in the newer edition of *Political Liberalism*] approach to the social role of religion is generally compatible with the position being taken here." Hollenbach continues: "Rawls is ready to accept this influence of religion and culture on the political sphere, but only under the proviso that it be influence under the constraint of reciprocity. If this means that such influence must be exercised with due respect for the religious freedom of all citizens, it is fully compatible with the idea of a community of freedom for which we have been arguing. But if it means that we should presume that existing constitutional democracies and Rawls's own theory of democracy already know the best way for us to live our common life together, it must be judged shortsighted" (*The Common Good and Christian Ethics*, 167, 168). As I have argued all along, the first option given by Hollenbach is the most accurate and productive reading of Rawls's position.

54. Jeffrey Stout, "Public Reason and Dialectical Pragmatism," in *Pragmatism and Naturalism: Scientific and Social Inquiry After Representationalism*, ed. Matthew C. Bagger (New York: Columbia University Press, 2018).

55. The more flexible and dialectical type would be represented by Rawls's understanding of "reflective equilibrium" in *A Theory of Justice*. The more restrictive type, that Stout calls "public reason restriction" (PRR) would appear in "The Idea of Public Reason"; see Stout, "Public Reason and Dialectical Pragmatism," 175–178.

56. Stout, "Public Reason and Dialectical Pragmatism," 195–99.

57. In fact, Stout makes a very similar point in *Democracy and Tradition*, 195–196, while discussing "unconditional obligations." For Stout, these are moral obligations (the repudiation of torture or slavery, for instance) that people must follow unconditionally. This does not imply that everybody embraces them or that they are unconditional sub specie aeternitatis. It only means that they are attributed to everyone by those committed to the values of the democratic tradition. They are the expression of the practice of democracy. Hence Stout's name for his approach: pragmatic expressivism. The difference with Rawls is that he reaches his principles of justice (the unconditional obligations) via theoretical speculation. Stout focuses on practices and inductively identifies the principles. In my view, these approaches complement each other.

58. Stout, "Public Reason and Dialectical Pragmatism," 206–209.

59. Rawls, *Political Liberalism*, xxix.

60. Gutiérrez, *A Theology of Liberation: History, Politics, and Salvation*, 2nd ed. (Maryknoll, NY: Orbis Books, 1988), 24–25.

61. Rawls, "The Idea of Public Reason Revisited," 465, fn. 55.

62. Gutiérrez, *A Theology of Liberation*, 24.

63. For the lexical order of the principles of justice, see Rawls, *A Theory of Justice*, §8, 43.

64. In this sense, Enrique Dussel, *Para una política de la liberación* (Buenos Aires: Editorial Gorla, 2013), argues for the transformation of the ideals of "equality, fraternity, and liberty" into a new triad: "alterity, solidarity, liberation" (203).

65. Gutiérrez, *A Theology of Liberation*, 25.

66. The following argument operates also as a response to the concerns raised by Joas, *Faith as an Option: Possible Futures for Christianity* (Stanford, CA: Stanford University Press, 2014), 129: "Yet it remains unresolved in these impressive intellectual edifices [Kant's, Rawls's, Habermas's] why people should, in fact, be motivated to enter into such processes of reflection when it comes to leading their own lives in a moral way. It is also unclear how sensitization to the suffering of others, which is not after all, the result of rational argument, is achieved."

67. See Joas, *The Sacredness of the Person*, 124–30. For a detailed account of my affirmative genealogy of liberation theology, in dialogue with the history of democracy and the work of Martha Nussbaum on political emotions, see Zegarra, "The Revolution of Tradition," chap. 3.

68. See Wolterstorff, "Why We Should Reject What Liberalism Tells Us," for a similar point. However, Wolterstorff sees incompatibility between a "religiously integrated existence" and liberalism. My argument is the opposite.

69. On self-transcendence and the genesis of value-commitments, see Chapter 2 of this book and the multiple references to the work of Hans Joas.

70. Charles Taylor, "A Catholic Modernity?," in *Dilemmas and Connections: Selected Essays* (Cambridge, MA: Belknap Press of Harvard University Press, 2011), 183–187. For a very similar point, see Joas, *Faith as an Option*, 129.

71. Taylor insightfully writes about the "tragic irony" of exclusive-humanist philanthropy: "faced with the immense disappointments of actual human performance and with the myriad ways in which real, concrete human beings fall short, ignore, parody, and betray this magnificent [human] potential, one experiences a growing sense of anger and futility. Are these people really worthy objects of all these efforts? Perhaps in the face of all this stupid recalcitrance it would not be a betrayal of human worth, or one's worth, to abandon them—or perhaps the best that can be done for them is to force them to shape up" (Taylor, "A Catholic Modernity?," 183).

72. For a historical and theological account of the "Jesuit martyrs," see Robert Lassalle-Klein, *Blood and Ink: Ignacio Ellacuría, Jon Sobrino, and the Jesuit Martyrs of the University of Central America* (Maryknoll, NY: Orbis Books, 2014).

73. Gutiérrez, *A Theology of Liberation*, xxvii.

74. Stephen J. Pope, "Proper and Improper Partiality and The Preferential Option for the Poor," *Theological Studies* 54 (1993): 256.

75. Gustavo Gutiérrez, "No hay nada más práctico que una buena teoría" (presented at the Universidad Ricardo Palma, Doctor Honoris Causa Awards Ceremony, Lima, Perú, December 11, 2019).

76. See, among other texts, the programmatic approach presented in Gustavo Gutiérrez, "Situación y tareas de la teología de la liberación," in *Acordarse de los pobres: Gustavo Gutiérrez, textos esenciales*, ed. Rolando Ames and Andrés Gallego (Lima: Fondo Editorial del Congreso del Perú, 2004).

77. See, for instance, Juan Luis Segundo, *Liberation of Theology* (Eugene, OR: Wipf and Stock, 2002), where the author has a complex relation with the institution of academic theology. On the one hand, he advocates for the liberation of theology from the ideological constraints of academic theology. On the other, he develops his own academic account of liberation theology and further complicates the issue by giving certain priority in the process of liberation to the reflective theological elites.

78. Javier Iguíñiz, *Desarrollo, libertad y liberación en Amartya Sen y Gustavo Gutiérrez* (Lima: CEP, 2003).

79. See Iguíñiz, 146–147.

80. Dussel, *Para una política de la liberación*, 199. For a summary of Dussel's proposal regarding the transformation of the institutions of the state, see "Proposición 20" in *Para una política de la liberación*. For another approach to the reformation of democratic institutions in terms of human liberation, see Cornel West, *Democracy Matters: Winning the Fight Against Imperialism* (New York: Penguin Press, 2004).

81. Ismael García, "The Concept of Justice in Latin American Theology of Liberation" (PhD dissertation, University of Chicago, 1982), 2.

82. García, "The Concept of Justice," 147, 274–278, 368.

83. García, "The Concept of Justice," 315, my emphasis.

84. Rawls's point is that being, say, smarter does not confer more political rights on someone, which is quite different from saying that greater intelligence does not define who we are or that we cannot take advantage of it for our own good, within certain parameters. This latter confusion is present in both Sandel, *Liberalism and the Limits of Justice*, and Alasdair C. MacIntyre, *After Virtue: A Study in Moral Theory*, 3rd ed. (Notre Dame, IN: University of Notre Dame Press, 2007). The same applies to greater moral goodness: it does not make us worthy, in principle, of different treatment at the level of constitutional essentials. Pogge has followed this thread carefully and provided a powerful critique of Sandel's reading of Rawls on endowments and desert. See Thomas Pogge, *Realizing Rawls* (Ithaca, NY: Cornell University Press, 1989), 73ff.

85. See García, "The Concept of Justice," 269–282, 311–315.
86. See García, "The Concept of Justice," 322.
87. See García, "The Concept of Justice," 333–337, 366.
88. Systematicity here is essential. Despite the overlap between Rawls's theory and the concerns of liberation theologians, these concerns are not articulated systematically in a theory of justice by the latter. García's archaeological work (and Pope's, to a lesser extent) is important but also shows some issues that must be worked out. For instance, there seems to be a naïve or, at least, undertheorized understanding of social equality among liberation theologians that has difficulties accounting for *just* social and economic differences (García, "The Concept of Justice," 280). Similarly, there are issues regarding the adjudication of competing claims and too much trust in our capacity to care for others in that process (365–367).

89. Ignacio Ellacuría, "Fe y justicia," in *Escritos teológicos*, vol. 3 (San Salvador, El Salvador: UCA Editores, 2002), 315.

90. Joas, *Faith as an Option*, 129.

91. But Amartya Sen, *Development as Freedom* (New York: Anchor Books, 2000), and Thomas Pogge, *World Poverty and Human Rights: Cosmopolitan Responsibilities and Reforms*, 2nd ed. (Cambridge, UK: Polity Press, 2008), among others, also offer important and complementary perspectives. Further, from a Catholic perspective, Hollenbach, *The Common Good and Christian Ethics*, is one of the most sophisticated approaches to social justice that is not only compatible with mine—hence, with Rawls's and Nussbaum's—in most regards, but also advances an institutional framework in dialogue with Catholic Social Teaching absent in Gutiérrez's work. It is not surprising, returning to the question of analogy, that Nussbaum considers Catholic social teaching as deeply compatible with her Capabilities Approach. On this, see Martha C. Nussbaum, *Creating Capabilities: The Human Development Approach* (Cambridge, MA: Harvard University Press, 2011), 93.

92. For Nussbaum's account of her similarities and differences with Rawls, see Martha C. Nussbaum, *Frontiers of Justice Disability, Nationality, Species Membership* (Cambridge, MA: Harvard University Press, 2006). In this book, Nussbaum argues that benevolence should have a foundational role in a liberal theory of justice—something Rawls opposes. Yet Nussbaum has some trouble justifying her choice. For she admits that "benevolent sentiments are ubiquitous in the lives of real people; the problem is that we simply do not extend them consistently or wisely" (91). Rawls avoids this problem by proposing a less demanding way to formulate the principles of justice, which I think makes his theory stronger. In practice, however, as Nussbaum admits, this represents a "very subtle difference" with Rawls (91). Further, Nussbaum maintains that "because [her Capabilities Approach] shares some intuitive ideas with the Rawlsian version of

contractualism, and because the principles it generates have a close family resemblance to the principles of justice, we may view it as an extension of or complement to Rawls' theory" (69).

93. In *A Theory of Justice*, Rawls speaks rather vaguely about an "index of primary goods" that should include "rights and liberties, opportunities and powers, income and wealth" (§15, 92). Moreover, this is further complicated by the fact that average income tends to be taken by Rawls as a proxy for other social goods, an idea widely considered insufficient to analyze human development. Hence, Nussbaum's expansions here are quite needed.

94. On this, see Martha C. Nussbaum, *Political Emotions: Why Love Matters for Justice* (Cambridge, MA: Harvard University Press, 2013); Nussbaum, *The Monarchy of Fear*. Flores's reading of Nussbaum's account of political emotions and public discourse (see Flores, *The Aesthetics of Solidarity*, chap. 3) is another area of disagreement with my work. In her otherwise excellent book, Flores suggests that Nussbaum has no real place for religion in public discourse and that she also excludes anger from democratic engagement, solely considering it a negative force. Even though this reading is possible taking certain texts in isolation, Flores does not engage *Women and Human Development: The Capabilities Approach* (New York: Cambridge University Press, 2000), Nussbaum's most systematic treatment of religion. There, Nussbaum clearly defends the role of religious argument in public discourse in a way that resembles Rawls's position, studied earlier. Plus, Nussbaum encourages alliances with religious activists and heavily criticizes secularist feminists who dismiss religion altogether. On anger, Flores overlooks key ideas of Martha C. Nussbaum, *Anger and Forgiveness: Resentment, Generosity, Justice* (New York: Oxford University Press, 2016). In this book, Nussbaum distinguishes between types of anger and highlights the importance of "transition-anger" as a form of anger that is not destructive and can produce justice. Despite the fact that Flores mentions this form of anger in passing, she does not engage it. In this sense, and for the contributions of the Capabilities Approach, I have a significantly more favorable interpretation of the role of Nussbaum's work and how it can help to produce an inclusive theory of social justice.

95. Nussbaum, *Creating Capabilities*, 20.

96. Nussbaum, *Creating Capabilities*, 33–34.

97. Rather, Nussbaum's approach is "pluralistic about value," although that does not mean it lacks a normative core. Rawls makes a similar argument. Just societies must respect the freedom of all their members to pursue the life they want, but there must be restrictions. Therefore, Rawls's principles of justice and Nussbaum's central capabilities operate as a threshold for justice. In this sense, Nussbaum is critical of the work of Sen because he excessively stresses the importance of freedom without sufficiently discussing how to limit it (Nussbaum, *Creating Capabilities*, 70ff.).

98. In this sense, I agree with Kaveny (*Prophecy Without Contempt*, chap. 6), and her warnings regarding prophetic discourse: it can be a cure for some of our political maladies, but it is also risky if attempts to replace democratic deliberation.

99. On this issue, Pope writes: "Other things being equal, Christians should assign priority to addressing the needs of the poor and otherwise powerless rather than to the needs of others because the former are by definition less capable of providing for themselves than are the latter. As a principle of justice rather than simple charity, this preference is not only morally justifiable, it is morally required" ("Proper and Improper Partiality," 252).

100. On this two-fold sense of responsibility, see Paul Ricœur, *The Course of Recognition* (Cambridge, MA: Harvard University Press, 2005), 108–109; and Michael Le Chevallier, "The Stain of Association and the Burden of Membership: Institutional Ethics in Paul Ricœur and Catholic Social Thought" (PhD dissertation, University of Chicago, 2019).

101. The relationship between love and justice at the political level is compellingly articulated in Nussbaum, *Political Emotions*, whose subtitle is "Why Loves Matters for Justice."

102. For a recent and compelling sociological study of the motivations of some of the groups opposing equality and attention to the most vulnerable on "religious" grounds, see Philip S. Gorski and Samuel L. Perry, *The Flag and the Cross: White Christian Nationalism and the Threat to American Democracy* (Oxford, UK: Oxford University Press, 2022).

103. For similar arguments, see Steven H. Shiffrin, *The Religious Left and Church-State Relations* (Princeton, NJ: Princeton University Press, 2009), chap. 8, and Nussbaum, *Women and Human Development*, chap. 3.

Bibliography

Aguirre, Carlos, and Paulo Drinot, eds. *The Peculiar Revolution: Rethinking the Peruvian Experiment Under Military Rule.* Austin: University of Texas Press, 2017.

Almond, Gabriel Abraham, R. Scott Appleby, and Emmanuel Sivan. *Strong Religion: The Rise of Fundamentalisms Around the World.* Chicago: University of Chicago Press, 2003.

Alvarez, Carmelo, ed. *Pentecostalismo y liberación: una experiencia latinoamericana.* San José, Costa Rica: Editorial Departamento Ecuménico de Investigaciones, 1992.

Ames, Rolando. "La realidad nacional desde el límite: Riesgos y horizontes." In *Desde el límite: Perú, reflexiones en el umbral de una nueva época.* Lima: Instituto Democracia y Socialismo, 1992.

———. Interview by Raúl E. Zegarra, February 16, 2020.

Anderson, Victor. *Beyond Ontological Blackness: An Essay on African American Religious and Cultural Criticism.* New York: Continuum, 1995.

Aquinas, Thomas. *Summa theologiae: Latin Text and English Translation, Introductions, Notes, Appendices, and Glossaries*, vol. 30. Cambridge, UK: Blackfriars, 1964.

Aquino, María Pilar. *Our Cry for Life: Feminist Theology from Latin America.* Maryknoll, NY: Orbis Books, 1993.

Asad, Talal. *Formations of the Secular: Christianity, Islam, Modernity.* Stanford, CA: Stanford University Press, 2003.

———. *Genealogies of Religion: Discipline and Reasons of Power in Christianity and Islam.* Baltimore: Johns Hopkins University Press, 1993.

Ashley, J. Matthew. "To Change the World: An Intellectual History of Liberation Theology." *Commonweal*, January 31, 2019. https://www.commonweal-magazine.org/change-world.

———. "The Turn to Apocalyptic and the Option for the Poor." In *The Option for the Poor in Christian Theology*, edited by Daniel G. Groody. Notre Dame, IN: University of Notre Dame Press, 2007.

Bailey, Tom, and Valentina Gentile, eds. *Rawls and Religion*. New York: Columbia University Press, 2015.

Balocco, Dario. *Dal cristocentrismo al cristomorfismo: in dialogo con David Tracy*, vol. 48. Dissertatio. Series Romana. Milan: Glossa, 2012.

Barger, Lilian Calles. *The World Come of Age: An Intellectual History of Liberation Theology*. New York: Oxford University Press, 2018.

Bellah, Robert N. *Religion in Human Evolution: From the Paleolithic to the Axial Age*. Cambridge, MA: Harvard University Press, 2011.

Bellah, Robert N., and Hans Joas, eds. *The Axial Age and Its Consequences*. Cambridge: Harvard University Press, 2012.

Bellah, Robert N., Richard Madsen, William M. Sullivan, Ann Swidler, and Steven M. Tipton. *Habits of the Heart: Individualism and Commitment in American Life: With a New Preface*. Berkeley: University of California Press, 2008.

Benedict XVI. *Values in a Time of Upheaval*. New York: Crossroad, 2006.

Berryman, Phillip. *The Religious Roots of Rebellion: Christians in Central American Revolutions*. Maryknoll, NY: Orbis Books, 1984.

Bingemer, Maria Clara. *Latin American Theology: Roots and Branches*. Maryknoll, NY: Orbis Books, 2016.

Boeglin, Jean-Georges. *La question de la tradition dans la théologie catholique contemporaine*. Paris: Editions du Cerf, 1998.

Boff, Leonardo. "Libération." In *Dictionnaire historique de la théologie de la libération: les thèmes, les lieux, les acteurs*, edited by Pierre Sauvage, Luis Martínez Saavedra, and Maurice Cheza. Brussels: Lessius, 2017.

Bowman, Matthew. *Christian: The Politics of a Word in America*. Cambridge, MA: Harvard University Press, 2018.

Brackley, J. Dean. "Salvation and the Social Good in the Thought of Jacques Maritain and Gustavo Gutierrez." PhD dissertation, University of Chicago, 1980.

Brooks, Sarah. "Catholic Activism in the 1990s: New Strategies for the Neoliberal Age." In *Latin American Religion in Motion*, edited by Christian Smith and Joshua Prokopy. New York: Routledge, 1999.

Brown, Peter. *Through the Eye of a Needle: Wealth, the Fall of Rome, and the Making of Christianity in the West, 350–550 AD*. Princeton, NJ: Princeton University Press, 2012.

Buber, Martin. "Biblical Humanism." In *The Martin Buber Reader: Essential Writings*, edited by Asher Biemann. New York: Palgrave, 2002.

Casanova, José. "Parallel Reformations in Latin America: A Critical Review of David Martin's Interpretation of the Pentecostal Revolution." In *David Martin and the Sociology of Religion*, edited by Hans Joas. New York: Routledge, 2018.

————. *Public Religions in the Modern World.* Chicago: University of Chicago Press, 1994.

————. "Public Religions Revisited." In *Religion: Beyond a Concept,* edited by Hent de Vries. New York: Fordham University Press, 2008.

Castillo, Carlos. "Ser cristiano entre dos milenios: Hacia una teología de la regeneración." *Debates en Sociología* 25–26 (2001).

Castillo, Daniel P. *An Ecological Theology of Liberation: Salvation and Political Ecology.* Maryknoll, NY: Orbis Books, 2019.

Castro-Gómez, Carlos David. "La opción por los pobres: Análisis crítico de sus posibilidades y limitaciones en un mundo globalizado." In *¿El reino de Dios es de este mundo? El papel ambiguo de las religiones en la lucha contra la pobreza,* edited by Genaro Zalpa and Hans Egil Offerdal. Bogotá: Siglo del Hombre, CLACSO, and CROP, 2008.

Chamberlain, Francisco. "¿Qué queda por hacer en la perspectiva de la teología de la liberación?" In *Francisco Chamberlain, testigo del evangelio,* edited by Carmen de los Ríos and Santiago Paz. Lima: CEP, IBC, and Centro Loyola Ayacucho, 2019.

Chao Romero, Robert. *Brown Church: Five Centuries of Latina/o Social Justice, Theology, and Identity.* Downers Grove, IL: InterVarsity Press, 2020.

Claffey, Patrick, and Joe Egan, eds. *Movement or Moment? Assessing Liberation Theology Forty Years After Medellín.* vol. 1. Studies in Theology, Society, and Culture. Oxford, UK: Peter Lang, 2009.

Coll, Pilar. "Coordinación de Pastoral de Dignidad Humana." In *Ser Iglesia en tiempos de violencia,* edited by Cecilia Tovar. Lima: CEP and IBC, 2006.

Comisión de la Verdad y Reconciliación. *Hatun Willakuy: versión abreviada del Informe Final de la Comisión de la Verdad y Reconciliación, Perú.* Lima: Comisión de la Verdad y Reconciliación, 2004.

Cone, James H. *Black Theology and Black Power.* Maryknoll, NY: Orbis Books, 1997.

————. *A Black Theology of Liberation,* 20th anniversary ed. Maryknoll, NY: Orbis Books, 1990.

————. *God of the Oppressed,* rev. ed. Maryknoll, NY: Orbis Books, 1997.

Cone, James H., and Gayraud S. Wilmore, eds. *Black Theology: A Documentary History,* 2nd rev. ed. 2 vols. Maryknoll, NY: Orbis Books, 1993.

Congar, Yves. *Tradition and Traditions: An Historical and a Theological Essay.* New York: Macmillan, 1967.

Congregation for the Doctrine of the Faith. "Instruction on Certain Aspects of the 'Theology of Liberation'," In *Liberation Theology: A Documentary History,* edited by Alfred T. Hennelly. Maryknoll, NY: Orbis Books, 1990.

————. "Instruction on Christian Freedom and Liberation," In *Liberation*

Theology: A Documentary History, edited by Alfred T. Hennelly. Maryknoll, NY: Orbis Books, 1990.

―――. "Ten Observations on the Theology of Gustavo Gutiérrez." In *Liberation Theology: A Documentary History*, edited by Alfred T. Hennelly. Maryknoll, NY: Orbis Books, 1990.

Corkery, James. "Joseph Ratzinger on Liberation Theology: What Did He Say? Why Did He Say It? What Can Be Said About It?" In *Movement or Moment? Assessing Liberation Theology Forty Years After Medellín*, edited by Patrick Claffey and Joe Egan, vol. 1. Studies in Theology, Society, and Culture. Oxford, UK: Peter Lang, 2009.

Cox, Harvey. *The Market as God*. Cambridge, MA: Harvard University Press, 2016.

Degregori, Carlos Iván. *Que difícil es ser Dios: ideología y violencia política en Sendero Luminoso*. Lima: El Zorro de Abajo Ediciones, 1989.

De La Torre, Miguel A., ed. *The Hope of Liberation in World Religions*. Waco, TX: Baylor University Press, 2008.

Dombrowski, Daniel A. *Rawls and Religion: The Case for Political Liberalism*. Albany: State University of New York Press, 2001.

Dorrien, Gary J. *Breaking White Supremacy: Martin Luther King Jr. and the Black Social Gospel*. New Haven, CT: Yale University Press, 2018.

―――. *The New Abolition: W. E. B. Du Bois and the Black Social Gospel*. New Haven, CT: Yale University Press, 2015.

―――. *Social Democracy in the Making: Political and Religious Roots of European Socialism*. New Haven, CT: Yale University Press, 2019.

Douglas, Kelly Brown. *The Black Christ*. Maryknoll, NY: Orbis Books, 1994.

Durkheim, Émile. *The Elementary Forms of the Religious Life*. New York: Free Press, 1965.

Dussel, Enrique. *Para una política de la liberación*. Buenos Aires: Editorial Gorla, 2013.

Dussel, Enrique D. *Ethics of Liberation: In the Age of Globalization and Exclusion*, edited by Alejandro A. Vallega. Durham, NC: Duke University Press, 2013.

Ellacuría, Ignacio. "The Crucified People." In *Ignacio Ellacuría: Essays on History, Liberation, and Salvation*, edited by Michael Edward Lee. Maryknoll, NY: Orbis Books, 2013.

―――. "Fe y justicia." In *Escritos teológicos*, vol. 3. San Salvador, El Salvador: UCA Editores, 2000.

Encyclopaedia Britannica. "Shining Path." Accessed November 28, 2021. https://www.britannica.com/topic/Shining-Path.

Espín, Orlando, and Gary Macy. *Futuring Our Past: Explorations in the Theology of Tradition*. Maryknoll, NY: Orbis Books, 2006.

Espinoza Espinoza, Pablo. *Signos: una voz de la iglesia de los pobres en el Perú. 1980–2008.* Lima: IBC and CEP, 2008.

Espinoza Portocarrero, Juan Miguel. "Las 'Jornadas de Reflexión Teológica' y el desarrollo de un proyecto eclesial posconciliar asociado a la teología de la liberación en el Perú: Discurso teológico, redes sociales y cultura eclesial (1969–2000)." Master's thesis, Pontificia Universidad Católica del Perú, 2015.

Faggioli, Massimo. "A Church Within the Church: Behind the New Integralism Is the Old Intransigentism." *Commonweal*, January 8, 2019. https://www.commonwealmagazine.org/church-within-church.

Ferguson, Catherine. "The Poor in Politics: Social Change and Basic Church Communities in Santiago, Lima and Mexico City." PhD dissertation, University of Denver, 1990.

Flores, Nichole M. *The Aesthetics of Solidarity: Our Lady of Guadalupe and American Democracy.* Washington, DC: Georgetown University Press, 2021.

Gallego, Andrés. Interview by Raúl E. Zegarra, January 7, 2020.

García, Ismael. "The Concept of Justice in Latin American Theology of Liberation." PhD dissertation, University of Chicago, 1982.

Gibellini, Rosino. *La teologia del XX secolo.* Brescia, Italy: Queriniana, 1992.

Gorski, Philip S., and Samuel L. Perry. *The Flag and the Cross: White Christian Nationalism and the Threat to American Democracy.* Oxford, UK: Oxford University Press, 2022.

Gregory, Brad S. *The Unintended Reformation: How a Religious Revolution Secularized Society.* Cambridge, MA: Belknap Press of Harvard University Press, 2012.

Gutiérrez, Gustavo. *The God of Life.* Maryknoll, NY: Orbis Books, 1991.

———. "La opción preferencial por el pobre en Aparecida." In *De Medellín a Aparecida: Artículos reunidos.* Lima: IBC, PUCP, and CEP, 2018.

———. *Las Casas in Search of the Poor of Jesus Christ.* Maryknoll, NY: Orbis Books, 1993.

———. "No hay nada más práctico que una buena teoría." Presented at the Universidad Ricardo Palma, Doctor Honoris Causa Awards Ceremony, Lima, Perú, December 11, 2019.

———. *On Job: God-Talk and the Suffering of the Innocent.* Maryknoll, NY: Orbis Books, 1987.

———. "The Option for the Poor and Christian Theology." Presented at the Catholic Social Tradition Conference, Center for Social Concerns, University of Notre Dame, March 23, 2019. https://youtu.be/6G8xBPN-8oo.

———. "Situación y tareas de la teología de la liberación." In *Acordarse de los pobres: Gustavo Gutiérrez, textos esenciales*, edited by Rolando Ames and Andrés Gallego. Lima: Fondo Editorial del Congreso del Perú, 2004.

———. "Theology: An Ecclesial Function." In *The Density of the Present: Selected Writings*. Maryknoll, NY: Orbis Books, 1999.

———. *A Theology of Liberation: History, Politics, and Salvation*, 2nd ed. Maryknoll, NY: Orbis Books, 1988.

———. *The Truth Shall Make You Free: Confrontations*. Maryknoll, NY: Orbis Books, 1990.

———. *We Drink from Our Own Wells: The Spiritual Journey of a People*. Maryknoll, NY: Orbis Books, 1984.

———. Interview by Raúl E. Zegarra, December 20, 2019.

Hart, David Bentley. *That All Shall Be Saved: Heaven, Hell, and Universal Salvation*. New Haven, CT: Yale University Press, 2019.

Hartch, Todd. *The Rebirth of Latin American Christianity*. Oxford Studies in World Christianity. Oxford, UK: Oxford University Press, 2014.

Hauerwas, Stanley. *A Community of Character: Toward a Constructive Christian Social Ethic*. Notre Dame, IN: University of Notre Dame Press, 1981.

Hinojosa, Felipe. *Apostles of Change: Latino Radical Politics, Church Occupations, and the Fight to Save the Barrio*. Austin: University of Texas Press, 2021.

Hinson-Hasty, Elizabeth L. *The Problem of Wealth: A Christian Response to a Culture of Affluence*. Maryknoll, NY: Orbis Books, 2017.

Hollenbach, David. *The Common Good and Christian Ethics*. New York: Cambridge University Press, 2002.

Hunter-Bowman, Janna. "The Opportunity Stanley Hauerwas Missed." *Christian Century*. Accessed November 11, 2017. https://www.christiancentury.org/blog-post/guest-post/opportunity-stanley-hauerwas-missed.

Iguíñiz, Javier. *Desarrollo, libertad y liberación en Amartya Sen y Gustavo Gutiérrez*. Lima: CEP, 2003.

———. Interview by Raúl E. Zegarra, January 9, 2020.

Ihrke-Buchroth, Uta. "Movilidad religiosa y aspiración social en iglesias neopentecostales de Lima." In *Diversidad religiosa en el Perú: Miradas múltiples*, edited by Catalina Romero. Lima: IBC, CEP, and PUCP, 2016.

James, William. *The Varieties of Religious Experience: A Study in Human Nature*. New York: Longmans, Green, 1916.

Jara, Lupe. "El Sur Andino: Una iglesia que responde a los signos de los tiempos." In *Ser Iglesia en tiempos de violencia*, edited by Cecilia Tovar. Lima: CEP and IBC, 2006.

Joas, Hans. *The Creativity of Action*. Cambridge, UK: Polity Press, 1996.

———. *Do We Need Religion? On the Experience of Self-Transcendence*. Boulder, CO: Paradigm, 2008.

———. *Faith as an Option: Possible Futures for Christianity*. Stanford, CA: Stanford University Press, 2014.

———. *The Genesis of Values*. Chicago: University of Chicago Press, 2000.

———. *The Power of the Sacred: An Alternative to the Narrative of Disenchantment.* Oxford, UK: Oxford University Press, 2021.

———. *The Sacredness of the Person: A New Genealogy of Human Rights.* Washington, DC: Georgetown University Press, 2013.

Johnson, Karen J. *One in Christ: Chicago Catholics and the Quest for Interracial Justice.* New York: Oxford University Press, 2018.

Kaveny, Cathleen. *Prophecy Without Contempt: Religious Discourse in the Public Square.* Cambridge, MA: Harvard University Press, 2016.

Kee, Alistair. *Marx and the Failure of Liberation Theology.* London: SCM Press, 1990.

Klaiber, Jeffrey L. *Historia contemporánea de la Iglesia Católica en el Perú.* Lima: Fondo Editorial de la Pontificia Universidad Católica del Perú, 2016.

———. *Iglesia, dictaduras y democracia en América Latina.* Lima: PUCP, 1997.

Kurtz, Lester R. *The Politics of Heresy: The Modernist Crisis in Roman Catholicism.* Berkeley: University of California Press, 1986.

Lassalle-Klein, Robert. *Blood and Ink: Ignacio Ellacuría, Jon Sobrino, and the Jesuit Martyrs of the University of Central America.* Maryknoll, NY: Orbis Books, 2014.

Lecaros, Véronique. *La conversión al evangelismo,* translated by Gustavo Martínez Sánquiz. Lima: PUCP, 2016.

Le Chevallier, Michael. "The Stain of Association and the Burden of Membership: Institutional Ethics in Paul Ricœur and Catholic Social Thought." PhD dissertation, University of Chicago, 2019.

Lloyd, Vincent W., and Andrew L. Prevot, eds. *Anti-Blackness and Christian Ethics.* Maryknoll, NY: Orbis Books, 2017.

López, Sinesio. "La reinvención de la historia desde abajo: autoría y lectoría." In *Entre la tormenta y la brisa: homenaje a Gustavo Gutiérrez,* edited by Catalina Romero and Luis Peirano. Lima: PUCP, 2010.

———. "Una modernización frustrada (1930–1991)." In *Desde el límite: Perú, reflexiones en el umbral de una nueva época.* Lima: Instituto Democracia y Socialismo, 1992.

Lora, Carmen. Interview by Raúl E. Zegarra, January 13, 2020.

Luciani, Rafael. *El Papa Francisco y la teología del pueblo.* Madrid: PPC, 2016.

MacIntyre, Alasdair C. *After Virtue: A Study in Moral Theory,* 3rd ed. Notre Dame, IN: University of Notre Dame Press, 2007.

Mahmood, Saba. *Politics of Piety: The Islamic Revival and the Feminist Subject.* Princeton, NJ: Princeton University Press, 2005.

Marion, Jean-Luc. *Being Given: Toward a Phenomenology of Givenness,* translated by Jeffrey Kosky. Stanford, CA: Stanford University Press, 2013.

———. *Givenness and Revelation,* translated by Stephen E. Lewis. Oxford, UK: Oxford University Press, 2016.

Maritain, Jacques. *Man and the State*. Chicago: University of Chicago Press, 1951.
————. *True Humanism*. New York: Scribner, 1938.
Martin, David. *A General Theory of Secularization*. Oxford, UK: Blackwell, 1978.
————. "Has Secularization Gone into Reverse?" In *Sociology of Religion: A David Martin Reader*, edited by Dedong Wei and Zhifeng Zhong. Waco, TX: Baylor University Press, 2015.
————. *Pentecostalism: The World Their Parish*. Oxford, UK: Blackwell, 2002.
————. "Thinking with Your Life." In *David Martin and the Sociology of Religion*, edited by Hans Joas. New York: Routledge, 2018.
————. *Tongues of Fire: The Explosion of Protestantism in Latin America*. Oxford, UK: Blackwell, 1993.
————. "What I Really Said About Secularization." In *Sociology of Religion: A David Martin Reader*, edited by Dedong Wei and Zhifeng Zhong. Waco, TX: Baylor University Press, 2015.
Martínez, Emilio. *Los jesuitas en tiempos de violencia (1980–1992)*. Lima: Compañía de Jesús en el Perú; UARM, 2018.
Marx, Karl. "Contribution to the Critique of Hegel's Philosophy of Right: Introduction." In *The Marx-Engels Reader*, 2nd ed., edited by Robert C. Tucker. New York: Norton, 1978.
McRoberts, Omar M. *Streets of Glory: Church and Community in a Black Urban Neighborhood*. Chicago: University of Chicago Press, 2003.
Meier, John P. *A Marginal Jew: Rethinking the Historical Jesus*, vol. 1. New Haven, CT: Yale University Press, 1991.
Mendieta, Eduardo. *Global Fragments: Globalizations, Latinamericanisms, and Critical Theory*. Albany: State University of New York Press, 2007.
Michel, Johann. *Homo Interpretans: Towards a Transformation of Hermeneutics*, translated by David Pellauer. London: Rowman and Littlefield, 2019.
Míguez Bonino, José. *Doing Theology in a Revolutionary Situation*. Confrontation Books. Philadelphia: Fortress Press, 1975.
Molle, Leen van. *Charity and Social Welfare*, vol. 4. The Dynamics of Religious Reform in Northern Europe, 1780–1920. Leuven, Belgium: Leuven University Press, 2017.
Mulhern, Philip F. *Dedicated Poverty: Its History and Theology*. Staten Island, NY: Alba House, 1973.
Muskus, Eddy José. *The Origins and Early Development of Liberation Theology in Latin America: With Particular Reference to Gustavo Gutiérrez*. Carlisle, UK: Paternoster Press, 2002.
Niebuhr, H. Richard. *Christ and Culture*. New York: Harper, 1951.
————. *The Meaning of Revelation*. New York: Macmillan, 1941.
Nussbaum, Martha C. *Anger and Forgiveness: Resentment, Generosity, Justice*. New York: Oxford University Press, 2016.

———. *Creating Capabilities: The Human Development Approach*. Cambridge, MA: Harvard University Press, 2011.

———. *From Disgust to Humanity: Sexual Orientation and Constitutional Law*. Inalienable Rights Series. Oxford, UK: Oxford University Press, 2010.

———. *Frontiers of Justice Disability, Nationality, Species Membership*. Cambridge, MA: Harvard University Press, 2006.

———. *Liberty of Conscience: In Defense of America's Tradition of Religious Equality*. New York: Basic Books, 2008.

———. *The Monarchy of Fear: A Philosopher Looks at Our Political Crisis*. New York: Simon and Schuster, 2018.

———. *Political Emotions: Why Love Matters for Justice*. Cambridge, MA: Harvard University Press, 2013.

———. *Women and Human Development: The Capabilities Approach*. New York: Cambridge University Press, 2000.

O'Brien, David J., and Thomas A. Shannon, eds. *Catholic Social Thought: The Documentary Heritage*, expanded ed. Maryknoll, NY: Orbis Books, 2010.

———, eds. *Gaudium et spes*. In *Catholic Social Thought: The Documentary Heritage*, expanded ed. Maryknoll, NY: Orbis Books, 2010.

———, eds. *Populorum Progressio*. In *Catholic Social Thought: The Documentary Heritage*, expanded ed. Maryknoll, NY: Orbis Books, 2010.

O'Connell, Marvin Richard. *Critics on Trial: An Introduction to the Catholic Modernist Crisis*. Washington, DC: Catholic University of America Press, 1994.

Okey, Stephen. *A Theology of Conversation: An Introduction to David Tracy*. Collegeville, MN: Liturgical Press Academic, 2018.

O'Malley, John W. *What Happened at Vatican II*. Cambridge, MA: Belknap Press of Harvard University Press, 2008.

O'Neill, Kevin Lewis. *City of God: Christian Citizenship in Postwar Guatemala*. Berkeley: University of California Press, 2010.

Outka, Gene. "Christian Ethics." In *The Blackwell Companion to Religious Ethics*, edited by William Schweiker. Malden, MA: Blackwell 2005.

Pásara, Luis, and Carlos Indacochea. *Cipriani como actor político*. Lima: IEP, 2014.

Pérez Vela, Rolando. "Las apropiaciones religiosas de lo público: El caso de los evangélicos en el Perú." In *Diversidad religiosa en el Perú: Miradas múltiples*, edited by Catalina Romero. Lima: IBC, CEP, and PUCP, 2016.

Petrella, Ivan. *Beyond Liberation Theology: A Polemic*. London: SCM Press, 2008.

———. *The Future of Liberation Theology: An Argument and Manifesto*. Aldershot, UK: Ashgate, 2004.

Pinches, Charles Robert, and Jay B. McDaniel, eds. *Good News for Animals? Christian Approaches to Animal Well-Being*. Maryknoll, NY: Orbis Books, 1993.

Pixley, Jorge V., and Clodovis Boff. *The Bible, the Church and the Poor: Biblical, Theological and Pastoral Aspects of the Option for the Poor.* Tunbridge Wells, UK: Burns and Oates, 1989.

Pogge, Thomas. *Realizing Rawls.* Ithaca, NY: Cornell University Press, 1989.

————. *World Poverty and Human Rights: Cosmopolitan Responsibilities and Reforms*, 2nd ed. Cambridge, UK: Polity Press, 2008.

Pope, Stephen J. "Proper and Improper Partiality and the Preferential Option for the Poor." *Theological Studies* 54 (1993): 242–271.

Porter, Jean. *Nature as Reason: A Thomistic Theory of the Natural Law.* Grand Rapids, MI: Eerdmans, 2005.

Portocarrero, Gonzalo. *Profetas del odio: raíces culturales y líderes de Sendero Luminoso*, 2nd ed. Lima: PUCP, 2012.

Powers, Tom. *The Call of God: Women Doing Theology in Peru.* Albany: State University of New York Press, 2003.

Rabbia, Hugo H., Gustavo Morello, Néstor Da Costa, and Catalina Romero, eds. *La religión como experiencia cotidiana: Creencias, prácticas y narrativas espirituales en Sudamérica.* Lima: PUCP, EDUCC, and Universidad Católica del Uruguay, 2019.

Rawls, John. "The Idea of Public Reason Revisited." In *Political Liberalism*, expanded ed. New York: Columbia University Press, 2005.

————. *Political Liberalism*, expanded ed. New York: Columbia University Press, 2005.

————. *A Theory of Justice.* Cambridge, MA: Harvard University Press, 1971.

Ricœur, Paul. *The Course of Recognition.* Cambridge, MA: Harvard University Press, 2005.

————. "Experience and Language in Religious Discourse." In *Phenomenology and the "Theological Turn": The French Debate*, edited by Dominique Janicaud. New York: Fordham University Press, 2000.

————. *Freud and Philosophy: An Essay on Interpretation.* New Haven, CT: Yale University Press, 1970.

————. *Interpretation Theory: Discourse and the Surplus of Meaning.* Fort Worth: Texas Christian University Press, 1976.

————. "Manifestation and Proclamation." In *Figuring the Sacred: Religion, Narrative, and Imagination*, edited by Mark I. Wallace, translated by David Pellauer. Minneapolis: Fortress Press, 1995.

————. "Toward a Hermeneutic of the Idea of Revelation." In *Essays on Biblical Interpretation*, edited by Lewis Seymour Mudge. Philadelphia: Fortress Press, 1980.

Roberts, J. Deotis. *Liberation and Reconciliation: A Black Theology*, 2nd ed. Louisville, Kentucky: Westminster John Knox Press, 2005.

Romero, Catalina. "Católicos en Lima: Viviendo encuentros interreligiosos." In

La religión como experiencia cotidiana: Creencias, prácticas y narrativas espirituales en Sudamérica, edited by Hugo H. Rabbia, Gustavo Morello, Néstor Da Costa, and Catalina Romero. Lima: PUCP, EDUCC, and Universidad Católica del Uruguay, 2019.

——, ed. *Diversidad religiosa en el Perú: Miradas múltiples*. Lima: IBC, CEP, and PUCP, 2016.

——. "El Perú, país de diversidad religiosa." In *Diversidad religiosa en el Perú: Miradas múltiples*, edited by Catalina Romero. IBC, CEP, and PUCP, 2016.

——. "Religión y política en el Perú, 2000–2010." In *Cruces, intersecciones, conflictos: Relaciones político religiosas en Lationamérica*, edited by Aldo Rubén Ameigeiras. Buenos Aires: CLACSO, 2012.

——. Interview by Raúl E. Zegarra, January 8, 2020.

Rowland, Christopher, ed. *The Cambridge Companion to Liberation Theology*, 2nd ed. Cambridge, UK: Cambridge University Press, 2008.

Sánchez Paredes, José. "Cambios y modernización en el pentecostalismo peruano: El Centro Apostólico Misionero Ríos de Agua Viva de San Juan de Lurigancho." In *Diversidad religiosa en el Perú: Miradas múltiples*, edited by Catalina Romero. Lima: IBC, CEP, and PUCP, 2016.

Sandel, Michael J. *Liberalism and the Limits of Justice*, 2nd ed. Cambridge, UK: Cambridge University Press, 1998.

Sanders, E. P. *The Historical Figure of Jesus*. London: Allen Lane, 1993.

Sauvage, Pierre. "Genèse, évolution et actualité de la théologie de la libération." In *Dictionnaire historique de la théologie de la libération: les thèmes, les lieux, les acteurs*, edited by Pierre Sauvage, Luis Martínez Saavedra, and Maurice Cheza. Brussels: Lessius, 2017.

Schneiders, Sandra M. *The Revelatory Text: Interpreting the New Testament as Sacred Scripture*, 2nd ed. Collegeville, MN: Liturgical Press, 1999.

Schreiner, Susan E. *Are You Alone Wise? The Search for Certainty in the Early Modern Era*. Oxford Studies in Historical Theology. Oxford, UK: Oxford University Press, 2011.

Schüssler Fiorenza, Elisabeth. *In Memory of Her: A Feminist Theological Reconstruction of Christian Origins*, 10th anniversary ed. New York: Crossroad, 1994.

Schweiker, William. "Humanism and the Question of Fullness." In *Aspiring to Fullness in a Secular Age: Essays on Religion and Theology in the Work of Charles Taylor*, edited by Carlos D. Colorado and Justin D. Klassen. Notre Dame, IN: University of Notre Dame Press, 2014.

——. "On Religious Ethics." In *The Blackwell Companion to Religious Ethics*, edited by William Schweiker. Malden, MA: Blackwell, 2005.

——. *Responsibility and Christian Ethics*. Cambridge, UK: Cambridge University Press, 1995.

Segundo, Juan Luis. *Liberation of Theology*. Eugene, OR: Wipf and Stock, 2002.

Sen, Amartya. *Development as Freedom*. New York: Anchor Books, 2000.

Shiffrin, Steven H. *The Religious Left and Church-State Relations*. Princeton, NJ: Princeton University Press, 2009.

Shils, Edward. *Tradition*. Chicago: University of Chicago Press, 1981.

Smith, Christian. *The Emergence of Liberation Theology: Radical Religion and Social Movement Theory*. Chicago: University of Chicago Press, 1991.

Smith, John E. *The Analogy of Experience: An Approach to Understanding Religious Truth*. New York: Harper and Row, 1973.

Sobrino, Jon. *Jesus the Liberator: A Historical-Theological Reading of Jesus of Nazareth*. Maryknoll, NY: Orbis Books, 1993.

Stout, Jeffrey. *Democracy and Tradition*. Princeton, NJ: Princeton University Press, 2004.

———. "Public Reason and Dialectical Pragmatism." In *Pragmatism and Naturalism: Scientific and Social Inquiry After Representationalism*, edited by Matthew C. Bagger. New York: Columbia University Press, 2018.

Sullivan, Susan C. *Living Faith: Everyday Religion and Mothers in Poverty*. Chicago: niversity of Chicago Press, 2011.

Taylor, Charles. "A Catholic Modernity?" In *Dilemmas and Connections: Selected Essays*. Cambridge, MA: Harvard University Press, 2011.

———. *A Secular Age*. Cambridge, MA: Belknap Press of Harvard University Press, 2007.

———. *Sources of the Self: The Making of the Modern Identity*. Cambridge, MA: Harvard University Press, 1989.

———. "What Was the Axial Revolution?" In *The Axial Age and Its Consequences*, edited by Robert N Bellah and Hans Joas. Cambridge, MA: Harvard University Press, 2012.

Tilley, Terrence W. *Inventing Catholic Tradition*. Maryknoll, NY: Orbis Books, 2000.

Tovar, Cecilia, ed. *Ser Iglesia en tiempos de violencia*. Lima: CEP and IBC, 2006.

Tracy, David. *The Analogical Imagination: Christian Theology and the Culture of Pluralism*. New York: Crossroad, 1981.

———. *Blessed Rage for Order: The New Pluralism in Theology: With a New Preface*. Chicago: University of Chicago Press, 1996.

———. "The Christian Option for the Poor." In *The Option for the Poor in Christian Theology*, edited by Daniel G. Groody. Notre Dame, IN: University of Notre Dame Press, 2007.

———. *Dialogue with the Other: The Inter-Religious Dialogue*. Louvain, Belgium: Peeters Press, 1990.

———. "Gustavo Gutiérrez, teólogo." In *Memoria, presencia, y futuro de la teología de la liberacion: A los 50 años de Teología de la liberación*, edited by Andrés

Gallego, Carmen Lora, and Pedro De Guchteneere, translated by Raúl E. Zegarra. Lima: PUCP, IBC, and CEP, 2021.

———. "On Naming the Present." In *On Naming the Present: God, Hermeneutics, and Church*. Maryknoll, NY: Orbis Books, 1994.

———. *Plurality and Ambiguity: Hermeneutics, Religion, Hope*. San Francisco: Harper and Row, 1987.

Troeltsch, Ernst. "Historical and Dogmatic Method in Theology." In *Religion in History*. Fortress Texts in Modern Theology. Minneapolis: Fortress Press, 1991.

———. *The Social Teaching of the Christian Churches*, vol. 1, translated by Olive Wyon. New York: Harper Torchbooks, 1960.

———. *The Social Teaching of the Christian Churches*, vol. 2, translated by Olive Wyon. New York: Harper Torchbooks, 1960.

———. "What Does 'Essence of Christianity' Mean?" In *Writings on Theology and Religion*. Atlanta: John Knox Press, 1977.

Van Gerwen, Jef. "Origins of Christian Ethics." In *The Blackwell Companion to Religious Ethics*, edited by William Schweiker. Malden, MA: Blackwell, 2005.

Weber, Max. *The Protestant Ethic and the "Spirit" of Capitalism and Other Writings*, translated by P. R. Baehr and Gordon C. Wells. New York: Penguin Books, 2002.

West, Cornel. *Democracy Matters: Winning the Fight against Imperialism*. New York: Penguin Press, 2004.

Williams, Delores S. *Sisters in the Wilderness: The Challenge of Womanist God-Talk*. Maryknoll, NY: Orbis Books, 1993.

Wilmore, Gayraud S. *Black Religion and Black Radicalism: An Interpretation of the Religious History of African Americans*, 3rd ed. Maryknoll, NY: Orbis Books, 1998.

Wilson, Catherine E. *The Politics of Latino Faith: Religion, Identity, and Urban Community*. New York: New York University Press, 2008.

Wingeier-Rayo, Philip. *Where Are the Poor? A Comparison of the Ecclesial Base Communities and Pentecostalism, a Case Study in Cuernavaca, Mexico*. Eugene, OR: Pickwick, 2011.

Wolterstorff, Nicholas. *Justice in Love*. Grand Rapids, MI: Eerdmans, 2011.

———. *Justice: Rights and Wrongs*. Princeton, NJ: Princeton University Press, 2008.

———. "Why We Should Reject What Liberalism Tells Us About Speaking and Acting in Public for Religious Reasons." In *Religion and Contemporary Liberalism*, edited by Paul Weithman. Notre Dame, IN: University of Notre Dame Press, 1997.

Yoder, John Howard. *The Politics of Jesus: Vicit Agnus Noster*, 2nd ed. Grand Rapids, MI: Eerdmans, 1994.

Zegarra, Felipe. "Juan XXIII: Temas centrales de su teología y espiritualidad." *Páginas* 255 (March 2012).

Zegarra, Raúl E. *Dos lenguajes teológicos: un ensayo sobre el carácter público de nuestras creencias religiosas.* Bogotá: Editorial Bonaventuriana, 2015.

———. *La subversión de la esperanza: diálogo contemporáneo entre teología de la liberación, filosofía y opción por los pobres.* Lima: PUCP, IBC, and CEP, 2015.

———. "The Preferential Option of the Poor: Liberation Theology, Pentecostalism, and the New Forms of Sacralization." *European Journal of Sociology/ Archives Européennes de Sociologie*, forthcoming 2023.

———. "The Revolution of Tradition: Liberation Theology's Contribution to the Formulation of a Comprehensive Theory of Social Justice." PhD dissertation, University of Chicago, 2021.

———. "Una fenomenología (hermenéutica) de la revelación para una teología de la liberación." In *Jean-Luc Marion: límites y posibilidades de la filosofía y de la teología,* edited by Jorge Roggero. Buenos Aires: Editorial SB, 2017.

Index

abolitionism, 134, 145
abortion, 111, 137
agape, networks of. *See* love; Taylor,
  Charles
agency, 8, 19, 40, 70, 95, 105
ambiguity, 48, 52, 58–59, 61, 63, 68. *See
  also* plurality; Tracy, David; tradition
Ames, Rolando, 101–2, 107, 109, 119,
  190n50
analogical imagination. *See* Tracy,
  David
Aparecida, Brazil, 114–19
apocalyptic genre, 65–67, 77
appropriation. *See* distanciation
atheism, 18, 20, 29, 89, 102, 163n34,
  172n1, 191n58
authority, 11, 35, 58–61, 66, 89–90, 124,
  130. *See also* ambiguity; plurality
autonomy, 23–24, 26, 34, 118. *See also*
  liberty
Ayacucho, Perú, 83–84, 86, 90, 94

Barger, Lilian Calles, 24, 26–28, 104,
  159n8, 161n3; "The World Come of
  Age", 24, 27, 159n8, 161n6
Bartolomé de las Casas Institute, 95, 98
Bergoglio, Jorge. *See* Francis (Pope)
Bible, 11–12, 38, 40–42, 47, 65, 93, 122,
  170n105, 175n26, 180n89
blackness, 78, 169n102, 169n103,
  172n121, 184n126
Brackley, Dean, 19, 167n74
Brazil, 16, 115

Câmara, Helder, 13, 16
Capabilities Approach, 150, 152. *See also*
  Nussbaum, Martha
capitalism, 11, 16, 109, 159n8. *See also*
  free market
Casanova, José, 24–25, 27, 110, 125–26,
  153, 166n61, 195n3; *Public Religions
  in the Modern World*, 159n9, 166n64.
  See also secularization theory
Las Casas, Bartolomé de, 99, 106,
  159n11. *See also* Bartolomé de las
  Casas Institute
Catholic Action, 15–16, 22
Centro de Estudios y Publicaciones, 95,
  100
charity, 7, 9, 13, 35–36, 70–71, 151,
  206n99. *See also* poverty
Chenu, Marie-Dominique, 12, 14
Chile, 15–16, 86, 100, 113, 192n70
Christ-event, 56–57, 63–66, 72, 74–75,
  77–78, 80, 180n83, 183n121. *See also*
  Jesus
Christendom Mentality, 17, 31, 34
Chuschi, Ayacucho, Perú, 83, 86
Cipriani, Juan Luis, 90, 94–95, 103
civil rights, 23, 134–35, 145, 160n2,
  172n121
Coll, Pilar, 85–88, 92, 104
colonialism, 26, 159n11
Comision de la Verdad y
  Reconciliación, 83–84
communion, 19, 31–32, 34, 37–38, 76,
  79, 96, 143, 153

Cultural Memory | in the Present

Jill Bennett, *Empathic Vision: Affect, Trauma, and Contemporary Art*
Ban Wang, *Illuminations from the Past: Trauma, Memory, and History
    in Modern China*
James Phillips, *Heidegger's* Volk: *Between National Socialism and Poetry*
Frank Ankersmit, *Sublime Historical Experience*
István Rév, *Retroactive Justice: Prehistory of Post-Communism*
Paola Marrati, *Genesis and Trace: Derrida Reading Husserl and Heidegger*
Krzysztof Ziarek, *The Force of Art*
Marie-José Mondzain, *Image, Icon, Economy: The Byzantine Origins
    of the Contemporary Imaginary*
Cecilia Sjöholm, *The Antigone Complex: Ethics and the Invention
    of Feminine Desire*
Jacques Derrida and Elisabeth Roudinesco, *For What Tomorrow . . . :
    A Dialogue*
Elisabeth Weber, *Questioning Judaism: Interviews by Elisabeth Weber*
Jacques Derrida and Catherine Malabou, *Counterpath: Traveling
    with Jacques Derrida*
Martin Seel, *Aesthetics of Appearing*
Nanette Salomon, *Shifting Priorities: Gender and Genre in Seventeenth-Century
    Dutch Painting*
Jacob Taubes, *The Political Theology of Paul*
Jean-Luc Marion, *The Crossing of the Visible*
Eric Michaud, *The Cult of Art in Nazi Germany*
Anne Freadman, *The Machinery of Talk: Charles Peirce and the Sign Hypothesis*
Stanley Cavell, *Emerson's Transcendental Etudes*
Stuart McLean, *The Event and Its Terrors: Ireland, Famine, Modernity*
Beate Rössler, ed., *Privacies: Philosophical Evaluations*
Bernard Faure, *Double Exposure: Cutting Across Buddhist and Western Discourses*
Alessia Ricciardi, *The Ends of Mourning: Psychoanalysis, Literature, Film*
Alain Badiou, *Saint Paul: The Foundation of Universalism*
Gil Anidjar, *The Jew, the Arab: A History of the Enemy*
Jonathan Culler and Kevin Lamb, eds., *Just Being Difficult? Academic Writing
    in the Public Arena*
Jean-Luc Nancy, *A Finite Thinking*, edited by Simon Sparks
Theodor W. Adorno, *Can One Live after Auschwitz? A Philosophical Reader*,
    edited by Rolf Tiedemann
Patricia Pisters, *The Matrix of Visual Culture: Working with Deleuze
    in Film Theory*
Andreas Huyssen, *Present Pasts: Urban Palimpsests and the Politics of Memory*
Talal Asad, *Formations of the Secular: Christianity, Islam, Modernity*
Dorothea von Mücke, *The Rise of the Fantastic Tale*
Marc Redfield, *The Politics of Aesthetics: Nationalism, Gender, Romanticism*
Emmanuel Levinas, *On Escape*

Dan Zahavi, *Husserl's Phenomenology*

Rodolphe Gasché, *The Idea of Form: Rethinking Kant's Aesthetics*

Michael Naas, *Taking on the Tradition: Jacques Derrida and the Legacies of Deconstruction*

Herlinde Pauer-Studer, ed., *Constructions of Practical Reason: Interviews on Moral and Political Philosophy*

Jean-Luc Marion, *Being Given That: Toward a Phenomenology of Givenness*

Theodor W. Adorno and Max Horkheimer, *Dialectic of Enlightenment*

Ian Balfour, *The Rhetoric of Romantic Prophecy*

Martin Stokhof, *World and Life as One: Ethics and Ontology in Wittgenstein's Early Thought*

Gianni Vattimo, *Nietzsche: An Introduction*

Jacques Derrida, *Negotiations: Interventions and Interviews, 1971–1998*, edited by Elizabeth Rottenberg

Brett Levinson, *The Ends of Literature: The Latin American "Boom" in the Neoliberal Marketplace*

Timothy J. Reiss, *Against Autonomy: Cultural Instruments, Mutualities, and the Fictive Imagination*

Hent de Vries and Samuel Weber, eds., *Religion and Media*

Niklas Luhmann, *Theories of Distinction: Re-Describing the Descriptions of Modernity*, edited and introduced by William Rasch

Johannes Fabian, *Anthropology with an Attitude: Critical Essays*

Michel Henry, *I Am the Truth: Toward a Philosophy of Christianity*

Gil Anidjar, *"Our Place in Al-Andalus": Kabbalah, Philosophy, Literature in Arab-Jewish Letters*

Hélène Cixous and Jacques Derrida, *Veils*

F. R. Ankersmit, *Historical Representation*

F. R. Ankersmit, *Political Representation*

Elissa Marder, *Dead Time: Temporal Disorders in the Wake of Modernity (Baudelaire and Flaubert)*

Reinhart Koselleck, *The Practice of Conceptual History: Timing History, Spacing Concepts*

Niklas Luhmann, *The Reality of the Mass Media*

Hubert Damisch, *A Theory of /Cloud/: Toward a History of Painting*

Jean-Luc Nancy, *The Speculative Remark: (One of Hegel's bon mots)*

Jean-François Lyotard, *Soundproof Room: Malraux's Anti-Aesthetics*

Jan Patočka, *Plato and Europe*

Hubert Damisch, *Skyline: The Narcissistic City*

Isabel Hoving, *In Praise of New Travelers: Reading Caribbean Migrant Women Writers*

Richard Rand, ed., *Futures: Of Jacques Derrida*

William Rasch, *Niklas Luhmann's Modernity: The Paradoxes of Differentiation*

Jacques Derrida and Anne Dufourmantelle, *Of Hospitality*

9 781503 635586